INDEPENDENT
MONTHLY
LITERARY
MAGAZINE

Adelaide

REVISTA
LITERÁRIA
INDEPENDENTE
MENSAL

ADELAIDE

Independent Monthly Literary Magazine
Revista Literária Independente Mensal
Year IV, Number 27, August 2019
Ano IV, Número 27, agosto de 2019

ISBN-13: 978-1-951214-24-1
ISBN-10: 1-951214-24-2

Adelaide Literary Magazine is an independent international monthly publication, based in New York and Lisbon. Founded by Stevan V. Nikolic and Adelaide Franco Nikolic in 2015, the magazine's aim is to publish quality poetry, fiction, nonfiction, artwork, and photography, as well as interviews, articles, and book reviews, written in English and Portuguese. We seek to publish outstanding literary fiction, nonfiction, and poetry, and to promote the writers we publish, helping both new, emerging, and established authors reach a wider literary audience.

A Revista Literária Adelaide é uma publicação mensal internacional e independente, localizada em Nova Iorque e Lisboa. Fundada por Stevan V. Nikolic e Adelaide Franco Nikolic em 2015, o objectivo da revista é publicar poesia, ficção, não-ficção, arte e fotografia de qualidade assim como entrevistas, artigos e críticas literárias, escritas em inglês e português. Pretendemos publicar ficção, não-ficção e poesia excepcionais assim como promover os escritores que publicamos, ajudando os autores novos e emergentes a atingir uma audiência literária mais vasta.

(http://adelaidemagazine.org)

Published by: Adelaide Books LLC, New York
244 Fifth Avenue, Suite D27
New York NY, 10001
e-mail: info@adelaidemagazine.org
phone: (917) 477 8984
http://adelaidebooks.org

FOUNDERS / FUNDADORES
Stevan V. Nikolic & Adelaide Franco Nikolic

EDITOR IN CHIEF / EDITOR-CHEFE
Stevan V. Nikolic
editor@adelaidemagazine.org

MANAGING DIRECTOR / DIRECTORA EXECUTIVA
Adelaide Franco Nikolic

GRAPHIC & WEB DESIGN
Adelaide Books LLC, New York

CONTRIBUTING AUTHORS IN THIS ISSUE

Elie Axelroth, Mike Sharlow, Jeff Bakkensen,
David Rogers, Annabelle Baptista,
Victoria Harris, ML Paul, Jeffrey Hill,
Annette Freeman, Matt Chacko,
Thomas Heine, Paweł Markiewicz, Paul Lamb,
Keith Hoerner, Richard Bader, Ruth Deming,
Mark Massaro, Catherine Lin, Judson Blake,
Steve Slavin, Barbara Borst,
David Landsperger, Alex de Cruz,
Joseph Albanese, John L. Stanizzi,
Bettina Rotenberg, Edward Lee, Brenda Yates,
Roberto Loiederman, James Padgett,
O. Howard Winn, Robin Ray, R. S. Stewart,
Phil Kemp, Cameron Morse, Diane Webster,
Ezekiel Archibong, Edward Lee, Daniel King,
Stella Prince, Robert McCloy, Sarah Conklin,
Lynne D. Soulagnet, Gloria G. Murray,
Eileen Flaxman, Louis Gallo, Korkut Onaran
Roger Singer, John Grey, Jan Little,
Christopher Di-Filippo

CONTENTS / CONTEÚDOS

Editor's Notes
Stevan V. Nikolic

THE WORLD OF ANU

In the distant galaxy, many light years away from the planet Earth, exists a world quite similar to our own. It is believed to be somewhere in the constellation of Orion. There isn't a present name for this domain, but old Babylonians were calling it "the world of Anu," Anu being the main god of the heavenly realms.

Most people don't know that the world of Anu is very important for the inhabitants of Earth. This is a secret that very few know, but from the beginning of time this far away world was in a constant, unbroken connection with our world. The reason is simple: Earth and Anu are two parallel or twin worlds and the same people inhabit both of them simultaneously.

However, there is one major difference between these two domains of existence. On our planet we are born, live, and die in the material world, facing our realities regardless of circumstances, whether they are good or bad, or at least that is the life process we believe. In this other world people live forever in a world of dreams, or as we on Earth would say, in the "virtual world." We are convinced that our lives exist in a material reality, however people on Anu are conscious that they live in dreams. Of course, the world of Anu is not much different from ours except for the fact that everything is a dream.

Some may wonder how it is possible for living beings to be in two distant worlds at the same time. In the dream world there are two kinds of inhabitants: permanent residents and visitors. All of us go to Anu occasionally - that is all of us who dream, but whenever we visit Anu, we are unaware that we are in a world of dreams. A dreamer does not have to be asleep to visit Anu. There are many daydreamers who are able to be awake and at the same time, be in the distant world of dreams. The journey to Anu happens instantly; the moment we start dreaming we are already there.

When it comes to permanent residents of the world of dreams, the story is a bit different. The soul of every living being, including human, has a much longer life span than his carnal body. It usually takes few journeys through many bodies for a single soul to complete its lifetime in the material world. For some souls, unfortunately, it never happens, and they stay forever in the vicious circle of life and death. But those that succeed to complete their journeys continue to live eternal life in the world of dreams.

So, it is not a surprise that from the ancient times until the present, people gaze into night skies towards Orion, trying to find Anu. Every so often we look at the stars saying, "Somewhere there is my true home," without ever realizing why we have that feeling. Many legends were made, stories written, monuments built—all witnessing the efforts of men to secure the successful voyage of their souls into the world of eternal dreams.

(From the novel ***Weekend in Faro***)

THE RESCUE

by Elie Axelroth

The stranger who rescued him was a dark-skinned woman. He heard the swish of her silky dress, the clicking of high heels as she approached along the pedestrian walkway on the bridge. She must have seen him because he heard her gasp and then the sound of her high heels abruptly stopped, and all that was left was the moaning of bridge cables and cars on the overhead deck. Even without looking in her direction, he could feel her edging toward him, one cautious step at a time, so as not to startle him where he stood on the other side of the railing, leaning in the direction of the water, his feet tenuously planted on the steel footings.

It was a steamy, moonless night in early October, the kind of balmy night that cools off only reluctantly as dawn approaches. He'd spent the day alone in his brother's tiny Brooklyn apartment, smoking pot, playing video games all day long to fend off the boredom. He'd been crashing on the couch; Roy and his wife and their three-year-old slept in the bedroom. Earlier that day, they'd invited him to go to Coney Island with them, but the thought of all those screaming children made him cringe. Two years after coming back from Afghanistan, he couldn't bear to be around crowds or sudden movements or loud noises or flashes of light, all of which overwhelmed him, setting off spasms of prickly pain and searing headaches. It wasn't just the lights and crowds, either; he avoided blind spots like dark alleyways and stairwells, and he stepped cautiously whenever he walked across an open field. Every once in a while, everything went quiet. That was scary too.

Leo's hands were sweaty, but he didn't dare let go to wipe them off on his jeans.

"Come down from there," the woman said.

He reluctantly turned toward her voice. Only her silhouette was visible in the chalky light of the streetlamps.

For months he'd been thinking about the surest, cleanest way to end it all: his life that overflowed with desperation and offered so few moments of relief. He didn't want Roy to find him, much less his wife or three-year-old nephew, and he didn't want anyone to have to clean up the mess. The sticky puddles of blood and the lingering smell of explosives—he knew from experience what that was like. Online he'd researched about jumping from a bridge; the hard slap against the water would probably kill him, like being hit by a car at seventy-five miles an hour. The blunt force would shatter his ribs, his internal organs would be blown apart and his bones thrust upward. If all else failed, he'd drown, his last remaining breath bubbling to the surface with no one in sight.

The young woman stepped closer and reached her hand out to him. The pleading in her eyes made him question if he'd thought through all his options. Maybe there was someone out there who cared. After everything that had happened, he didn't want his life to end in regret.

"Whatever you're thinking, things can always get better." Her tone was tender but unambiguous. It reminded him of the time his own mother had spoken to Leo and Roy with the same certainty, reassuring them that they were strong enough and smart enough to weather whatever happened. She'd died a few weeks later.

He looked down into the murky water beneath the bridge and then across the river at a string of lights. Lively conversation floated toward him, young people casually hanging out at a waterside patio. It was Saturday night. He imagined them sipping fancy blue drinks and locally brewed beer. A barge chugged slowly toward the mouth of the harbor, letting out a cheerless blast. A frothy blanket of oil coated the water, and there were scraps of wood and a plastic bottle carried lifelessly along the ripple of tide, and what looked like an abandoned fishing rod, garbage caught in the tangle of line. The air reeked of decay and indifference.

"Come on, now," she said, taking one step closer—close enough so Leo could see that she was wearing a green dress with flowers and a matching sweater, delicate pearl buttons running down the front. She smelled exotic like rose petals.

Then sirens were approaching, and the red-and-blue lights of an emergency vehicle were flashing at the end of the bridge. Doors slammed. There was shouting, and then men in uniforms were running toward him, and for a moment he was back there, in Afghanistan, peering through heavy metal fencing and barbed wire. Then the woman was tunneling through the haze, motioning with her delicate painted fingernails for him to climb back over the railing. It was the simplest of gestures. Stern but loving. The kind of gesture he imagined his mother might have offered—if only she'd been alive.

The EMT's loaded Leo into the ambulance; he was admitted to the psych unit at the VA hospital on the Lower East Side. The night nurse, Sonny, was a roundish guy with no chin and a receding hairline, making him look clownish in his blue scrubs and white sneakers. Leo might have found it funny but for the harsh florescent lights, the locked doors and bars on the windows, and the anxious smell that permeated the ward. Sonny coaxed him into a small interview room adjacent to the nursing station. The air was heavy, and Leo could hear snoring and feverish groans coming from the patient rooms.

Sonny offered him a paper cup with sludgy coffee, a packet of sugar, and some powdered creamer. Leo didn't much like coffee, but he took the cup just to hold on to something. Without much of an introduction, Sonny fired away: Did he know where he was and how he'd ended up here? Who was the president? Could he count backward from one hundred by threes? Was he taking any medications or illegal drugs? Did he have nightmares? Flashbacks? Leo answered cautiously. He wanted to tell him: I'm not crazy. I just can't go on feeling so hopeless and inept.

"Why'd you walk out onto the bridge?" Sonny asked. "Were you trying to kill yourself?"

It seemed too obvious to answer, but Leo, who hadn't slept the previous three nights, was dying to go to bed. His only choice was to comply with the rules.

"Of course, he said.

But then Sonny wanted to know why, and Leo didn't have the energy to tell him: He couldn't figure out how to stop seeing Jerry D and Tommy Cutter and Brady with that stupid cowlick at the back of his head. On their last mission—the one that had sent Leo home—a kindly old Afghani had fed them hot chai and bread and told them about a stash of munitions in an abandoned building on the other side of the village. Twenty of them ran inside the building only to discover too late that it had been booby-trapped. Half his buddies died, including Jerry and Tommy, and another quarter lost limbs. Leo had suffered a concussion and temporarily lost his hearing in one ear. He was supposed to feel lucky, but mostly he felt guilty for having trusted the old man.

The next morning on the psych unit wasn't any better. After runny eggs and cold toast, a psych tech escorted him to the group room. A dozen or so ill-tempered guys were seated in a circle, hands trembling, their hair unkempt. It looked to Leo like the group was being run by two medical students, barely old enough to shave. They seemed uncomfortable in their white coats with their slicked-back hair and freshly polished leather loafers. Leo had been promised a shower, but for now he was dressed in scrubs and paper slippers. He took a seat on one of the metal folding chairs. It was hard and cold against his butt and the back of his legs, so he scooted forward. Being the new guy, it was expected he'd go first. He told them about walking out onto the bridge. Which bridge, they wanted to know. Were you really gonna jump?

They were making it into a schoolyard dare, like he'd lacked the courage to go ahead with it. Maybe that was true. Even at the time, leaning over the railing, Leo had hesitated, and now he wasn't sure about anything except the woman who'd rescued him. Who reminded him of his mother.

"I don't know," he said. There was no way he was going to leave himself open to ridicule in front of those guys.

Two days later, they released him with a checklist of appointments and his solemn promise to stay away from the bridge.

But he couldn't keep his promise, at least not in the way the doctors had meant for him to. He couldn't leave the woman behind and the memory of something unalterable that had happened. He was back on his brother's couch, waking up in the middle of the night to her whispering in his ear, her kind words that had given him hope, the sweet smell of her, the softness around her eyes, the warmth in her fingers, the way her dress had fluttered in the nighttime breeze. Leo couldn't remember ever having felt such longing, even during the couple of months when he'd been dating Cora from the veterans job center. She was a good listener, and she'd been nice to him in the beginning, before his neediness scared her away.

He fell into a routine, leaving work early to take a shower and scrub away the greasy garage smells oozing from his pores. Then he'd head out the door again. When his brother asked where he was going or if he'd be home in time for dinner, he was guarded, saying he was off to his support group at the vet center or an appointment with his shrink. It wasn't a complete lie because mostly he did go to his appointments. But on the nights he was free, he'd take the C train—early enough to beat the crowded press of rush-hour bodies—and barricade himself by the doors so he could be the first one off the train. Once above ground, he'd

search for open sky between the chasm of buildings, trying his best to tune out the acrid smell of smoke and diesel fumes, the noise of pigeons flapping and cooing, buses lurching away from the curb. On the way up the bridge stairs, he'd stop long enough to peer through the metal grid and cables at the pedestrians and bicyclists on the walkway above him. He'd remind himself not to get too close to the railing.

One afternoon, midway across the bridge, Leo paused to watch a construction site on the north side of the river. A crane operator was swinging long shafts of steel onto a towering high-rise. If he squinted, Leo could make out the vague outline of workers in hard hats coaxing the steel beams into place. The buzzing noise on the bridge faded with a lull in the traffic. Suddenly Leo could hear the clicking sound of high heels. Turning around, he saw the woman approaching, the woman who'd rescued him, her mint-green dress swishing back and forth as she sauntered in his direction. She was smoking a cigarette, her cheeks drawn in as she inhaled. Then she blew a thin spiral of smoke over her shoulder. Leo was surprised that the woman smoked: he'd imagined she was the kind of person who shunned unhealthy habits like drinking too much or overspending on her credit cards. His breathing quickened; it was the same jittery rush of adrenaline he'd felt on reconnaissance missions, crouched behind rocks, creeping through burned-out buildings. He took in a deep breath to try and calm himself—something he'd learned just last week in his support group.

The woman didn't see Leo until he stepped out into the middle of the walkway, blocking her path.

"Hello," he said. He smiled so she'd know he was being friendly.

The woman stopped, tossed her half-smoked cigarette off to the side then backed away.

He started to say, I guess you don't remember me, but then he realized she wasn't the same woman. The woman who'd rescued him had been taller, younger, prettier, carefully dressed with her hair straightened and tied back with a ribbon. This woman was wearing a waitress's apron, and she smelled not of rose petals but fried fish and grilled onions.

He stepped aside. "Sorry. I thought you were someone else. Don't mean to bother you."

The woman quickened her pace, turning around to look back at him when she was nearly out of sight.

The next day, Leo showed up at the shop an hour late. A rusted-out Chevy pickup was on the lift; Roy was standing underneath with an air wrench, taking off the tires.

"Where were you last night?"

Leo watched as his brother sprayed the lug nuts with WD-40, squeezed the trigger on the air wrench, and then tossed them one at a time into an overturned hubcap. He winced with the spinning and the harsh metallic sound each time the lug nut hit the hubcap.

"I can't keep from thinking about her," Leo said.

"Jesus. You been out on that bridge again?" Roy was rolling the tire around to the back of the car. He stopped to wipe his hands on a rag, waiting to see if Leo would deny the accusation. Roy was shorter than Leo, and he was slim and cautious; he'd never gotten into trouble at school, never argued with his father the way Leo had. Being the older brother, Leo had always felt protective of him, although now it was the other way around.

"It's not that easy," Leo said. He could see how his brother would be scared for what might happen, but Roy didn't understand that without that woman, he'd likely be dead.

Roy tossed the rag onto the workbench. "Just like before. You never learn, do you?"

Leo knew exactly what his brother was talking about. In high school, he'd almost gotten himself expelled for texting too many times to one of the girls in his biology class. His father had been called into a meeting with the vice principal. She claimed he'd been bothering her for months, that she already had a boyfriend.

Maybe it was true. In any case, he'd caught hell when they got home.

"That was different," Leo said. "Becky was leading me on."

Roy stared at him and wiped a bead of sweat with the back of his shirt sleeve, leaving a streak of grease on his forehead. "Just one thing I'm asking. Talk to that shrink of yours about it. Will you do that for me?"

That evening, Leo stayed home.

It wouldn't have surprised him if his brother had called Dr. Bender, told him about how he was trying to find the woman on the bridge, because at his next appointment Bender didn't start in with his usual questions about the medication. Instead, he wanted to know about work and how was he getting along with his brother, details that had previously seemed unimportant or irrelevant. The questions were benign, but it felt like a trap. It reminded him of the times when he was younger and his father, angry over nothing at all would cast around for some hapless victim—usually Leo— to blame for his foul mood.

Leo glanced at the clock; his time was almost up. That's when Bender came out with what he'd been leading up to all along. "Tell me about the woman on the bridge," he said.

"Tell you what?"

"For starters, what's important about finding her?"

"I just wanna say thank you."

"Let's suppose you find her. Tell her you're grateful. Then what?"

Bender's glasses had slid down the bridge of his nose, and he was staring at Leo over the rims. It made him feel pressured, Bender leaning forward on the other side of the coffee table, Leo having nowhere to hide.

"I was thinking she'd want to know," he said, "that she helped someone. That it made a difference."

"You must be hoping for some kind of reaction," Bender said, urging him on.

"Not really."

Leo could feel his chest tighten. He looked away, hoping Bender wouldn't notice how much the questions were getting on his nerves. He was afraid he might get angry or, worse yet, start sobbing. That was something that happened without warning from time to time, too.

"A smile? Her name? Where she lives?"

"I wouldn't ask her that."

"She was kind to you. It's understandable that you'd want to see her again."

Bender was expecting him to trip up, but Leo wasn't fooled.

"No, sir," he said. "I can see how that's not a good idea."

It occurred to Leo that the woman who'd rescued him might not work anywhere near the bridge. He found himself wandering the streets well beyond the bridge—to Battery Park, the Lower East Side, the old meat market near Chelsea. He sat on park benches, tossed the stale ends of his sandwiches to the pigeons, stared at the Statue of Liberty and the tourists lined up to take the ferry across to Ellis Island. From a pizza parlor on Old Fulton Street, he watched the business suits with their briefcases. Delivery men hurried by on bicycles with padded envelopes and express packages. He studied every dark-skinned woman in high heels. Was that her? The one in the tan raincoat? A couple of times he chased a woman down the street. But inevitably, she was too short. Or overweight. Her clothes were wrinkled. One woman had a mole on her cheek that Leo was sure he'd have noticed on the woman who'd rescued him.

Then he spotted her. At a coffee shop around the corner from City Hall. She was wearing the same green sweater with the pearl buttons, and her hair was tied back, not with a ribbon, but with hair clips. She was sitting in a booth by the window reading a paperback book, sipping coffee, eating a slice of pie one delicate forkful

at a time. Leo stared at her from behind a streetlamp. Yes, it was her. This time he was sure.

He walked into the restaurant and slid into the booth opposite her. His hands were sweaty, and he could feel the scar on his forehead pulsing—the scar from that last reconnaissance mission gone bad. Wanting to make a good impression, he sat up straight and looked across the table at her.

The woman's jaw tensed, and her eyes were darting between Leo and the restaurant patrons seated behind him.

"I guess you don't remember who I am," Leo said. Through the nervousness he forced himself to smile, as friendly a smile as he could manage. He understood why she was flustered but he was sure that in the end she'd be pleased that he'd taken the time to find her. He was hoping she'd see his confidence as a sign that he was doing better.

"No," she said. "I haven't a clue." The woman was gathering up her scarf and coat; she shoved the book into her purse.

"I'm Leo." He reached out to shake her hand, to reassure her that he meant no harm.

Instead, the woman motioned toward the waiter and mouthed, Check, please.

"Sorry," Leo said. "I can see you're in a hurry. I just wanted to say thank you for being so kind to me."

The woman nodded and offered him a jittery smile, but it was clear to Leo that she still wasn't making the connection.

"Don't you remember? The bridge? You kept me from jumping off."

The waiter brought her check. As she was sliding out of the booth, she pulled a twenty-dollar bill out of her purse and laid it on the table—way too much even with a sizable tip.

"I don't know what you're talking about. It must have been someone else," she said as she dashed out of the restaurant.

The next day at work, Leo was sweeping up; Roy was working on an engine rebuild. Belts and tools, nuts, bolts were laid out on the workbench. "I met her," he said.

Roy didn't say anything, making as if he was too focused on flipping through the manual, examining the engine specs, to be paying attention.

"She's real pretty," Leo said. "Like I remembered."

His brother put down the wrench and turned around. "So you got to say thank you," he said. "I hope that's the end of it. For your sake."

"Sure," Leo said. "Isn't that what I said all along? That I just wanted to say thank you?"

His brother worried too much. He'd imagine Leo doing something impulsive or stupid. Of course there was no way he was going to tell him about how she'd run out of the coffee shop, her scarf haphazardly wrapped around her neck, or that he'd followed her into the subway station at City Hall. Or that he'd ridden the subway in the next car over all the way to Brooklyn Heights and followed her down Tillary Street, where she keyed herself into a high-rise apartment building. He'd crossed the street to stand back and get a better view. There was nowhere to sit, so he just stared up at the apartment building, wondering which floor she lived on. It was nine o'clock before he'd retraced his steps and headed home. But now he knew where she lived.

In the end, it wasn't hard to find her name and phone number, even a college graduation photo. It was all a matter of patience and determination, a little snooping on the Internet, casually asking around. When Leo described her to the cashier at the fancy grocery store on the bottom floor of her apartment building, the man seemed hesitant to give out any information.

"I'm pretty sure her name is Nina," Leo said. "I was stationed in Afghanistan with her brother, Paul. Real nice guy." Leo knew from the Internet that she had a brother named Paul who taught history at a community college in the Bronx.

The cashier seemed relieved to have some kind of explanation for Leo's snooping. "Sure. She comes in here maybe once a week. Picks up a bottle of wine and a quart of ice cream—pralines 'n cream. Works some place in the City."

"I'm sure that's her," he said. Leo already knew she wasn't married, but he wondered if she had a boyfriend.

"I wouldn't know anything about that," the man said, ringing up a stick of beef jerky Leo had purchased.

Nina Hawkins. Leo discovered that she worked at the Whitney Museum in the development office. So he was right about her being smart. One Sunday afternoon, he saw her drive out of her underground garage in a late-model Honda Civic. He couldn't see what she was wearing, but she was alone. She didn't come back until late that night.

It wasn't lost on Leo that the woman reminded him of his mother, who'd died of ovarian cancer when Leo was ten. His mother had been kind and patient, and he sometimes wondered what his life would have been like if she hadn't died so young. Or if his father hadn't been abusive to her. All the drunken yelling, shattered beer bottles, Leo and Roy crouched in the corner.

Of course, his mother hadn't been black; she wasn't even that dark-skinned with her olive complexion and tight black curly hair. Her grandparents had been immigrants from southern Italy. As often as not she was mistaken for Puerto Rican or Haitian. The only photo of his mother Leo had was from a trip they'd taken to Montauk Point when he was a kid. He remembered the long drive out to the tip of Long Island, the sparse countryside, the fancy McMansions. Leo wondered what it was like to live like that. They'd stopped at a gas station to use the restroom; his father had bought them Corn Nuts and Popsicles, even let them eat in the car. In the photo, Leo and Roy and their mother were standing by the roadside. Just as his father snapped the photo, a convertible with the top down had whizzed by, a blur of red with white leather. Off in the distance, a sliver of ocean and the suggestion of sand.

What he remembered was having watched her walk up the subway steps and out into the wintry air on her way home. Then he'd stood on the other side of the street from her apartment, pacing to keep himself warm, watching buses and cars and motor scooters. A man on a Segway trundled by. Periodically he'd pull his hand out of his pocket and look at her phone number inked across his wrist. By eight o'clock, there wasn't anything to do but call.

When she answered, he heard music in the background. Or maybe it was the opening credits to a TV show.

"Nina. This is Leo," he said. When the line went dead, he immediately called back. "Please don't hang up."

A moment of silence, but this time she stayed on the line.

"Make it quick," she said.

"I just want to say thank you."

"You've already said enough. Besides, you've got the wrong person."

After she hung up, he must have wandered for hours down Tillary Street, through the park, past the carousel, and then back to the bridge, where he stood until the morning light inched across the river. He didn't understand why she denied having helped him. As much as he hated to admit it, his brother had been right. And Bender. All along, he'd wanted more than just to say thank you. And even that was too much for her to accept.

He stood against the railing. A ferry packed with morning commuters was chugging across the river. If he leaned over, he could see the Statue of Liberty and Staten Island. His brother would be wondering where he was. Probably he'd be relieved not to have to worry about him anymore. He looked over his shoulder. It was early enough that the bridge was mostly deserted. He counted to ten. There wasn't

anyone around to rescue him, so he counted to ten a second time. Still no one.

Leo was sorry the instant he let go. In the four seconds it took to hit the water, he pictured Roy and his little nephew, who squealed when Leo twirled him around the room. And the woman with the red hat and rusted-out Volvo who'd given him a gift card to Starbucks for making sure her car passed inspection. His mother the time she let him cut school and they spent the day at the movies.

The water was colder than he'd imagined, and the pain that wracked his entire body was unbearable. He'd been sure he wanted to die, but now all he wanted was to get to the surface of the water, to the light. This far down, it was hard to tell which way was up. Suddenly, he was bobbing up and down and choking on salty water. His whole body was shivering and he had the sense that his clothes had been wrenched off. There were sirens in the distance. And then he was underwater again and he could feel his arms foraging upward. Again, above the water he saw the foamy crest of a wave approaching; he tried to yell for help, but his lungs were burning and he couldn't force out anything resembling a sound. He went down again. Please don't let me drown. Then spotlights were blinding him; he was coughing. And breathing.

It was probably not more than ten minutes before the Coast Guard picked him up. They strapped him to a board, put on a neck brace, and wrapped him in blankets. He woke up the next night after the anesthesia from surgery had worn off.

That's when he saw the nurse hovering over him, adjusting the IV, checking his pulse. He had a collapsed lung, and most of his ribs and a couple of vertebrae were broken, his spleen ruptured. "You're mighty lucky," she said. "Not many survive jumping off that bridge."

He stared at the tag pinned to her scrubs. She had a kind face. Her name was Jessie.

About the Author:

As a clinical psychologist, Elie Axelroth, worked for many years in a university counseling center. She has published in Packingtown Review. Her first novel, "Thin Places," won a National Indie Excellence Award. When not traveling the seven continents, Elie lives in San Luis Obispo, California where she hikes and blogs about creativity. "The Rescue" is based on a character in her current novel-in-progress.

THE FIELD OF PLAY
by Mike Sharlow

Our world revolved around "the field." It was about fifty yards wide from the street to the block wall of St. Dominic's Convent and about two blocks long. In the spring and summer, we played baseball there, and in the fall, we played football. In the winter it hibernated under deep snow.

We had enough kids in our neighborhood to have five guys on a team, if everyone came out to play. Today, we had everybody: Matt, Tim, John, Larry, Joe, Joey, Paul, Eric, Todd, and me. Matt and John were usually captains. John was the best baseball player. My brother Matt wasn't even the second best, but he always bullied his way into being a captain. He wasn't the biggest, but he was the meanest. It could have been easily argued that Eric or Joe be a captain, but Eric didn't want to be a captain, if he couldn't be on John's team. Joe quietly deferred to Matt because he was presently best friends with him, and he didn't want to get beat up.

"Pick a number between one and ten," Larry called. He was the fat kid in the neighborhood. He always wore white t-shirts in the summer. By the end of the day his round belly looked like a globe of the world with stains, dirt, and grime representing countries and oceans. "I got the number." He pointed to head.

"Write it in the sand," Matt ordered. Larry plopped down in the sand and drew a 7 and covered it with his hands before anyone could see it. "I pick five." Matt blurted.

"Six," John said.

"It's seven!" Everyone called out as Larry lifted his hands.

Pissed off, Matt rubbed out the number with his feet.

"Eric," John picked first.

Larry had turned his back and was trying to hide behind the rest of us. He didn't want to be on Matt's team. Most of us didn't.

"Joe." Matt pointed. Joe was probably a little bit better than me, but also a year older. He was a better hitter, but I think I was a better fielder. Joe was the rich kid in the neighborhood. His house was the biggest and right across the street from the field. He also had the nicest newest Schwinn bicycle, a shiny blue five speed with handlebar brakes. The only thing wrong with him was that he had a bit of a lisp. Other than that, he was a nice-looking polite kid with thick brown hair and a fortunate smile. He had it good and he knew it.

"Mick." John picked me, and I could tell it bugged Matt. He hated to lose, but he hated to lose to his brothers even more. Not to say we were going to win, but things were looking pretty good at that point. I was thinner than Matt and, even at the age of nine, it was evident that I was going to be taller than him and a better athlete.

"Paul," Matt snapped. He looked like Moe from the Three Stooges when he scowled. He even had the haircut and hair color. My brother Tim and I had similar cuts, the Beatles bangs, but my hair was sandy blond, and Tim's was almost white.

Paul ran over to Matt's side. Paul's dad was a big, bald, muscular construction worker, and Paul was a smaller version of him except his head was a buzzcut. His dad was a prick to him, so Paul felt comfortable being on Matt's team.

John picked Larry. Matt should have picked Larry before Paul, but Matt didn't like Larry.

Then Matt picked Todd, Eric's brother. He struck out a lot, but if he connected, he usually laced a line drive into the outfield. Todd was imbued with a fearless and wild athleticism. He was constantly hurting himself, but he was stoic, and his body was built to take the punishment. At nine years old he was muscular and strong. By the time he hit high school it would all come together, and he would be hurling eighty-five mph fastballs.

John picked Joey. He was a sticky, wet, mess. His fingers were constantly in his mouth, as he voraciously gnawed on his fingernails. An intermittent stream of mucous drained from his nose, until he wiped it away with his hand onto his pants or shirt. When he took his fingers out of his mouth to talk, an overflow of saliva coated his tongue and lips until he spoke, and then his words were accompanied by a burst of spit. "Say it don't spray it!" everyone always said.

Joey was the better choice, as in it was better to get a cold than the flu. If the ball came at Joey, he either jumped out of the way, or held up his glove in a defensive posture to protect himself rather than catch the ball. If he happened to make a catch, it was a complete surprise to everyone including him. At bat, a skinny lid with weak arms, Joey rarely made contact, but if he did, he had a bad habit of throwing his bat about as far as he hit the ball, which was never very far. Everyone yelled at him for it, because it was hard to catch a ball when a bat came flying at your head. "That's an automatic out next time you do that!" Matt threatened, unless Joey was on his team.

Matt acted disappointed that he was stuck with Tim again. He struck out more than Joey, and he couldn't catch any better. The good thing was that he could make Tim pitch.

Joey would quit and go home before he would pitch. Pitching in our game was the least desired position. We played slow pitch underhand, which made our game a hitting game and high scoring. The salvo of line drives that came back to the pitcher's mound was terrifying.

Conventionally, we did play baseball. We played three outs with all the ways you could get out. We had bases, first, second, and third, each was about a three-foot patch of sand. The area around home was a large sandbox. We typically scratched the outline of a home plate over and over through the course of a game, as it wore away. The only significant rule changes were that there were no walks, no called strikes, and no stealing.

"You guys have a better team," Matt protested.

"You can have Joey." John gave Joey a little shove towards Matt.

"I want Mick." Matt pointed at me.

"No." I stepped away from Matt. I hated being on his team. It was bad enough playing against him, but it was worse being on his team.

Matt glared at me like he always did just before he was going to pound on me.

"Let's play!" John ran into the field, and the rest of us followed.

"I'll pitch," Larry shouted and grabbed the ball. He was slow, and he didn't like to run, so he wasn't a good outfielder, but he was a good pitcher. He could toss the ball across the plate from almost second base. The farther back a pitcher was from the batter, the less chance there was to take a line drive off the forehead.

Matt's team was up to bat first. The batting order was Joe, Matt, Paul, Todd, Joey, then Tim.

Joe chopped at the first pitch that came in at eye level. He drove a line drive into right center between Eric and me. I was playing right. Eric got to the ball before I did, which was a good thing because he had a better arm. He threw to John, who had run to third, but the ball flew over his head, and Joe raced around the bases and scored.

Matt hit a hard grounder to center at Eric. John ran in from left to cover third. I ran to second. Eric's throw to me cut off Matt at second. Matt kicked the ground in frustration, and a cloud of sandy dust rolled away. "C'mon Paul, hit me home!"

Paul struck out swinging for the fences. The field didn't have a fence, but it did have a block wall about six feet tall that ran parallel to our diamond along the first base side. The wall enclosed St. Dom's Convent, which owned the field we played on. As the wall extended, it became a left field wall, progressively getting deeper.

Joey's at bats frustrated and lulled us into complacency. He watched pitch after pitch go by. "C'mon, swing!" Matt yelled at him.

"Swing, batta, batta, swing!" The rest of us called from the field. Joey let so many pitches go by, the cacophony of our chant probably made us sound truly odd, as our voices bounced off the wall and echoed through the neighborhood, "Swing, batta, batta, swing!" over and over.

Joey finally swung and connected. The ball dribbled between second and third directly at Eric, and the bat, traveling farther than the ball, flew down the third baseline. We had shifted in the field because Joey rarely hit the ball out of the infield. I was playing near second, and John was at first. Eric fielded Joey's softly hit grounder, as Joey raced to first. Eric had a strong, but wild arm, and fired a rocket to John. The ball sailed over John's leap and outstretched glove, bounded into the street, and disappeared into the lilac bushes in John's yard. Everyone waited for John to retrieve the ball. Matt scored, and Joey got to second. After the game Joey would gloat about how he hit a double.

Tim was up next and struck out on three straight pitches.

Matt's team scored five runs the first inning, which wasn't nearly enough compared the onslaught our team perpetrated on them. We ran the bases for almost a half hour and

scored fourteen runs. By the end of three innings, we were ahead 34-18. This wasn't an insurmountable lead, but we had relaxed a bit, while Matt had worked himself into a fervor, as he berated his teammates. It wasn't completely unwarranted, but the skill level of his team had to be taken into consideration. A misjudged fly ball landed behind Paul. "Come on, Charlie Brown!" Matt yelled. Another fly ball hit Joey's outstretched little glove and bounced out. His glove was small, but the worst of it was that it wasn't broken in and locked in the closed position. "What? Did you close your eyes on that one?" Matt's sarcasm made John, Larry, and Eric roar. John laughed so hard he swung and whiffed on the next pitch. Larry had to sit down on second base for fear of pooping his pants. He tended to hold it rather than go home to go, even though his house was only about a block away. Sometimes he couldn't hold it any longer, like when he laughed too hard, so sitting down helped to hold it. Joey stared at the ground and pounded the pocket of his glove.

In the fifth inning we were up 48-23. We had no outs, and it was approaching supper time. Matt's team was ready to quit. Their body language showed they had grown weary of chasing balls all over the field and Matt's constant abuse. Joey would usually walk off the field first, followed by Joe. At that point the game would be over, even though Paul would never quit. Taking abuse from Matt made him feel loved. If Tim even whimpered that he wanted to quit, Matt would threaten to pound him.

At my fourth at bat in the fifth inning, Matt decided that he wanted to pitch to me. I had already gotten three hits and scored three times. There were two outs, and this was his best chance for his team to get up to bat again.

"That's not fair!" I stood back from the plate. I knew what Matt was up to.

"I can pitch if I want to. Get up to bat."

"It's okay, Mick. Just bat." John said. He knew what Matt was doing.

Matt pitched the ball fast. It was way too high. The next one almost hit me. The third was right down the middle, but I didn't swing.

"Why didn't you swing? Afraid of striking out?" Matt smiled.

He was right. I was.

"Mick, swing quick if it's another pitch like that," John coached.

The next pitch was across the plate but slightly lower. I swung and connected solidly sending a hot grounder back at Matt. He didn't get his glove down fast enough, and the ball ricocheted off his shin. He groaned then hobbled to the ball as quickly as he could while yelling at Paul to cover first. By this time, I had reached base. This didn't prevent Matt from firing the ball, even though Paul wasn't even close to covering. The ball hit the ground, and I had to hop to prevent it from hitting me. I knew he threw it at me on purpose. The ball bounded into the street and disappeared in John's lilac bushes again. I ran to second.

Tim was pitching again. His arm must have been getting tired, because he was having a hard time getting the ball across the plate. Matt told him to move up.

"I don't wanna pitch anymore," Tim whined. So far, things had gone well for her him, but the closer he got to the batter, John, the more precarious the situation became. He took one small step forward and pitched again, but the ball dropped ineptly short of the plate.

"Move up two steps!" Matt ran over and physically shoved Tim.

Tim began to whimper. He had been here before. "I don't wanna pitch anymore."

"Pitch or I'll kill you!" Matt threatened.

The first pitch dug in the sand two feet in front of the plate, like a golf ball in a sand pit.

"C'mon!" Matt screamed.

The next pitch came in low and fast but right down the middle. The crack of the bat was the first sound, and the next was not quite as sharp, more of a thwack! than a crack! as the line drive off John's bat struck Tim in the forehead. It knocked him to his hands and knees, and then he rolled onto his back. For a few scary seconds he didn't make a sound, and

everyone was silent and frozen. John didn't even run. Then Tim began to cry. Matt was the first one to his side. We stood around Tim like the handlers of a prizefighter recovering from getting knocked out. This wasn't the first time this happened to Tim. It happened to me once, and I refused to ever pitch again.

Tim stopped crying and stood up. "My head hurts. I'm goin home."

"You don't have to pitch," Matt said. Everything was about keeping Tim at the field now. He couldn't let him go home alone and tell his story before Matt got a chance to tell his.

Tim rubbed his head where a knot had already risen. When he took his hand away everyone could see the marks left in his forehead that would become as famous as the signs of the stigmata, at least in our neighborhood. The baseball had struck Tim in such a way that the stitches from the baseball had embedded perfect little wounds exactly like the stitches of the baseball in the middle of his forehead.

Everyone stared in amazement in a moment of silence admiring the miracle then burst into laughter. Tim laughed too, and he began dancing around and making weird faces. He loved the attention, but his concussive state might have had something to do with his silliness.

"That's three outs," Matt called. This was our own rule: if you hit a line drive back to the pitcher and hit him in the forehead (always Tim), it was an out.

The next inning would be our last. It was quickly approaching supper. The score was 62-28, a thorough ass-kicking, and I couldn't wait to announce it to Mom and Dad at supper time. Dad would add his own special humiliation to Matt and Tim, particularly stinging Matt, very possibly making him teary-eyed. I would feel bad for him, but anything up to that moment I would enjoy. It was how our family functioned.

It was 62-40 with two outs. The 12-run rally had Matt's team acting like they still had a chance. Our play in the field was lax at first, but when we picked our intensity we got the first two outs quickly.

Joe came up to bat, and he smashed the first pitch. The ball was hit deep down the third baseline. John raced to cut it off. The ball ricocheted off the wall about a foot from the top. John dove anticipating the angle. His long body stretched out parallel to the ground. His glove reached out and snagged the ball before it hit the ground. Rolling onto his back, he extended his glove to the sky, affirming the catch.

"Out!" Larry yelped.

Eric and I ran towards John, but he got to his feet before we reached him and trotted towards us. Eric leaped onto his back in celebration. I didn't say anything. I stared at John in awe, while the few seconds of his catch played over and over in my head. Willie Mays was my favorite player. I had a crush on Willie. In the Scholastic Books paperback biography, I ordered through school, I wrote on the inside cover, "I love Willie Mays." In my family no one ever told anyone that they loved them. John's catch was like the catches Willie Mays made.

"That's not an out!" Matt yelled. "Keep running!" He waved on Joe, who had stopped running once he rounded first. Confused, he walked towards second. "Run! Run! Run!" Matt urged.

John ran at Joe and tagged him. Even though he believed Joe was out, he knew Matt well enough to know that Matt wouldn't give it up. Now, there was no doubt. Joe was out.

"No fair!" Tim ran over to John and unsuccessfully tried to knock the ball out of John's glove.

"Do over," Matt contested.

"I have to go home for supper." Larry walked off field.

"Me too," John gathered up his bats. "What ya doin' after supper, Mick?"

"Come over?" I asked.

"Okay."

"Let's keep playing," Matt stood in the middle of the field. Almost everyone had run off towards home. Tim was the only one standing on the field with Matt. "Mick!" Matt yelled. I acted like I didn't hear him and raced home to

announce the score of the game and how our team beat Matt's team.

At the supper table Matt asked Dad if the ball caught off the wall was an out.

"What happened?" Dad looked at Matt first.

"Joe hit the ball, and John caught it when it bounced off the wall."

"On a fly. It didn't hit the ground," I added.

"I don't know. Sounds like an out to me. He caught it on a fly off the wall?" Dad was more interested in how John made the play.

"He made a diving catch just like Willie Mays." From my chair I did my best to mimic John's outstretched body, and I almost knocked over my milk.

"Mickey!" Mom shrieked.

"It wasn't an out!" Matt almost came out his chair at me.

"John tagged him anyway," I said smugly.

"John tagged him?" Dad took a bite of his crispy fried pork chop.

"Matt said it wasn't an out, so John tagged him out."

"It wasn't fair," Matt growled.

"Yeah, wasn't fair." No one was paying attention to Tim.

"It's never fair, when you lose, Matt," I said.

Dad laughed.

"Shut up, Mick!" Matt nearly came out of his chair at me again.

Dad smacked Matt alongside the head, and Matt fell back into his chair. The sting and the dizzying white flash from the crack on the head was blinding. Matt began to cry, and I did feel bad for him.

Everyone remained silent until Mom said, "We don't say shut up. We say, 'Be quiet.'"

She didn't mention anything about not giving your children a concussion at the supper table.

Tim's knot on his forehead wasn't noticed, until he took a bath and his wet bangs parted around the baseball stitched egg. "My God! What happened to you? Look at this?" She called for Dad. He knew exactly what happened and laughed.

Years later, long after the convent shut down, and the field was built up with a housing subdivision, I looked up the rule about a ball hit off a wall or fence but caught before it hit the ground, and I discovered that it wasn't an out. That's why outfielders let the ball careen off the wall and hit the ground. It's easier to play it.

Still, John tagged out Joe.

About the Author:

Mike Sharlow lives and works in La Crosse, Wisconsin, a small city on the banks of the Mississippi River. He has had many publications in various anthologies, journals, and magazines. The bibliography for his work can be found at www.mikesharlowwriter.com

THE DAY OF THE FIRE

by Jeff Bakkensen

There's a special smile when they see you walking a dog. Like, Yep, one of the tribe. Mei's said pregnant women get it too, earlier than you'd think. But the funny thing I noticed was that we wouldn't get the smile when all three of us were out together. As if people wanted us to pick a side. Have a child or get a dog; both at once was just selfish.

Lola wakes me when she jumps down from our bed and sticks her nose against the gap at the bottom of the door. Mei will sleep through the day while I work in the spare bedroom. Then she and I will walk Lola to the subway, and Mei will head back to the hospital. She used to work days, but nights pay more. She says nighttime is when she can think most clearly.

We have yogurt for breakfast/dinner, coffee and herbal tea. We brush our teeth. Then Lola and I leave for our walk.

If I could speak to Lola, I'd tell her that if life is a series of reinventions, I still get surprised at the version of ourselves we've landed on.

But our choice of words is limited. "Sit," means, Sit. "Wait," means, Keep sitting. A scratched door means, I would like to go out. A tugged leash means, I would like to go over there. We can only talk about the things we can talk about.

Our apartment is on the third floor of a three-story brick row house that hasn't quite hit its upswing towards being nice again. The carpeted staircase Lola bounds down, nearly falling forward in her excitement, is scuffed and threadbare. We pass through a tiled foyer, and then go down one more flight to the basement, where the back door leads to an alley. The two basement apartments sit at either end of a concrete hallway, the boiler room and a washer/dryer fitted between them. Lola walks ahead of me, nose to the mouse droppings lying along the baseboards. I'm always a little apprehensive of what she might find. A year ago, just after we moved here, she found a body.

We were on our way to the back door, just like today. Lola had gone down ahead of me, and when I reached the bottom of the staircase, she was standing over a man lying on his stomach in the middle of the hallway. He was wearing jeans and a light jacket. As I watched, she bent down to lick the area around his mouth. I made a sound like Hepp! which was the fastest sound I could make, and ran to pull her away.

But a funny thing happened. The man's eyes popped open, he rolled over and became a living thing and then my downstairs neighbor, Jonathan. I'd met him while we were moving in.

His eyes wandered the walls until he saw me. He sat up. Lola was beside herself with joy.

"I think I lost my keys," said Jonathan.

I helped him stand. He looked around the floor and patted his jacket and pants pockets. He tapped his apartment door, and the door swung open. His keys were on a table just inside.

"Oh," he said. "Fuck."

It takes time, in a new place, to settle your sense of what's normal and what's not. You find your neighbor sleeping on the basement floor, and you think, That's just the way things are here, because you have no context to know anything different. Wish the broker had told me about that. Then the next day you don't see him, and the next day you don't see him, and eventually a year goes by and you're still reminded of those first scattering days every time you pass through the basement, and you think how strange it was you ever didn't know the things you know now.

We continue through the back door and into the alley. It's a crisp late summer day. The windows in the building in front of us glare in checkerboard pattern.

There's no mystery to the interior lives of dogs. I can tell Lola's mood by her walk. There's the prance, the buck against the leash, the salamander scuttle when she spots a squirrel. I have one style of walking, so far as I can tell. But maybe everyone in the apartments abutting the alley is standing by their windows watching, taking notes as I step, as I stumble, as I stride.

We stop at a gravel parking space so Lola can pee, and then turn onto another alley that slopes up to a residential street leading to the park. On the sidewalk, we pass two men dressed for work. Lola sniffs them as they walk by.

The park is a green strip running from the train station at Back Bay to the one at Forest Hills. A bike path weaves a sine wave between tennis and basketball courts, community gardens filling the irregular slices left over. The house to the left of the entrance has a rainbow flag hanging from a window, and on the door is a poster that says Immigrants Welcome Here, with a picture of a mother holding a child. The train itself runs beneath us.

It's the type of place where you have a kid before moving to the suburbs. That's why it was so jarring last week when someone sprayed Trump eats babies in blue paint across the concrete wall at one end of the tennis court. We buzzed for a few days about who might have

done it: surely not the family with the Immigrants Welcome Here poster. Someone from outside the neighborhood trying to troll, trigger, or otherwise provoke a reaction from us libs. If that was the goal then it worked; the graffiti's still there, and it bothers me whenever I walk past.

At one point in the distant past, the train ran above ground and the city bulldozed a swath of buildings to put in a highway that was never finished. So they gave us a park instead. The neighborhood then was mostly poor and Black, which is probably why someone thought it was a good place for a highway, and as the neighborhood has Whitened, the park has too, acquiring first basketball courts and gardens, tennis courts, and finally a dog park, which is where Lola pulls me now.

We cross a street with traffic at a standstill in both directions, and pass more commuters and a few morning joggers. The dog park is a converted basketball court with a fence around the perimeter. The hoops still stand, nettles, at both ends.

The morning regulars are out in force: Tivoli, Max, Ruby and Rosie, along with their owners. They are, in order: German Shepherd, retriever, and mutt sisters with border collie bodies and reddish fur. Lola's a goldendoodle.

The breed is important because that's how we introduce ourselves. "I'm Jack and this is Russell, and he's a Jack Russell Terrier." Or if the new dog's some undetermined mix, the owner will scrunch up his face like a Harvard grad who's aware of the effect the Harvard name can have, and say, "We don't really know for sure. We haven't done any genetic testing."

Which is like, Alright buddy, keep on saving the world.

Lola and I go in through the double gate, and she runs to join the pack swirling around center court. Rosie, sniffing the wall, sees Lola and runs up to her and bows, then spins around and bows again. Lola takes the bait, chasing her around the edge of the park. They pass Ruby, who gets caught up in the chase and then turns on Lola, who has to slam on the brakes to avoid being caught, and almost runs into Rosie going the other way.

I give a wave to Ruby and Rosie's owner, Jay, and walk over to say hello.

Dog and owner pairs come and go at regular intervals. The gate opens and a man in a suit walks in behind a big St. Bernard. He has earbuds in and he's talking on the phone. He picks up a ball and waves it in front of the St. Bernard's face and throws it. The dog doesn't flinch.

"Any plans for the weekend?" asks Jay.

Mei and I are going out to the suburbs to celebrate her mom's birthday. Jay asks if they're pressuring us to have kids, and I feel my brows pinch. Did I tell him? But no, of course not. And he wouldn't recognize Mei if he saw her on the street. I'm the morning walker.

"Not yet," I say.

We're interrupted by the man in the suit yelling through his headset.

"Well why the hell isn't it on my calendar?" he says.

He leans down and guides his dog towards a potential playmate.

"Do you hear yourself? Why would I want to have that conversation?"

Jay and I look at each other like, Some people. I take out my phone to check the time. It's just before 8 a.m. It's too early to be yelled at, early enough that the person on the other end of the phone probably knew they were going to get yelled at when they woke up this morning. Hopefully it's not his wife. A secretary. Maybe she, assuming it's a she, gets yelled at every morning. Maybe she got yelled at on the first day of the job and thought, That's just the way things are here.

I'm reminded of a story, which I whisper to Jay as we watch the man in the suit pace through the swirl of dogs. Mei's med school had a cadaver lab, and at the end of the anatomy course, all of the donors' families were invited to come speak at a ceremony in the school auditorium. Most people used their time to say they were thankful something good came out of their loved one's death, maybe they told a quick story about a doctor who'd been helpful. One woman brought a stack of photographs

that she went through one by one, using each to illustrate another of her husband's qualities: here being generous, here empathic, etc. At first it was kind of heartwarming, even though we weren't close enough to really see the pictures. Then her tone shifted. She said her husband deserved better than his last years had given him. He'd suffered tremendously. But wasn't that the point? she asked us. Illness was profit. The goal was to treat, not cure. We rustled awkwardly as an administrator tried and failed to guide her offstage. Her husband was a brilliant man. We owed him this time. She gripped the podium like a bereaved Mussolini until the last deathbed picture was turned over. Then she smiled, waved, and walked calmly back to her seat.

"People have no self awareness," says Jay.

The man in the suit laps the park and comes to a stop a few feet from us. He looks at us and rolls his eyes as he points to his earbuds.

We both nod.

"I think that's my cue," says Jay.

Like, Don't involve us in your bullshit, man.

Jay calls Ruby and Rosie, and I call Lola, and we leave the park together and then go our separate ways.

Are they pressuring us to have kids?

Lola and I cross the street and pass the basketball court to our left, the house with the rainbow flag to our right. Beyond the basketball court, I see the defaced tennis court. Trump eats babies. As we turn onto the street next to ours, I dial city services and navigate to a live person.

"Hello," I say. "I'd like to report a graffiti."

At home, I check in on Mei to make sure she's fallen asleep. Then I pour Lola a bowl of food and head into the spare bedroom.

A boxed crib lies propped against one wall, a pollen-dusted post-it stuck on top reading, Build me. The crib needs to be moved to storage, but I haven't been able to find the time.

I journal now. That was our therapist's advice. If you can't say it, write it down. Today I write,

Mei got home around 6:30 and Lola and I woke up...

Then I begin to labor through the morning emails. I consult for small businesses, installing and testing network security software. It's self-directed work; I'm salesperson, technical support, and account services rolled into one. The only immediate item today is a suspicious email forwarded - stupidly - for me to decide whether it's an attempt at phishing.

I'm most productive when I take frequent breaks. Lola lies in a patch of sun below the open window while I walk around the apartment, or stretch and refill my water bottle, or sometimes just stand and look at my phone.

I'm doing just that when I realize the room has filled with smoke.

It's like when you're in the shower and the water turns from hot to scalding. I've been smelling smoke for a while without noticing, and suddenly it's too smoky not to notice.

I run to the kitchen and open the oven, open the apartment door and sniff the staircase. It's not in our building. I go back into the spare bedroom and look out onto the street. Lola puts her paws up on the window sill beside me. A woody skein is winding towards us over the park, but I can't see anything more specific. I walk around the apartment shutting windows and crack our bedroom door to make sure Mei's still asleep before heading up to the roof.

On my way upstairs, I search the Twitter feeds for the Boston fire and police departments, but there's nothing there. Nothing under local news. The air is thicker on the roof and Lola doesn't want to follow me, so I prop the door and walk to the edge on my own. Across the park, a building is one fire. Three spouts of charcoal smoke gush from the top row of windows, combine, and spread into the morning sky. I trace the smoke as it rises. It has an urgency almost, like it's escaping the fire, hurtling up and then, more slowly, out.

The park laid out beneath me is quiet. A mother pushes a stroller along the bike path. Two older women lob a ball back and forth across the tennis court. I wonder if they haven't smelled the smoke. For a moment it feels like

I'm the only one who's noticed something's wrong.

Finally there's a siren in the distance, getting louder as its pitch slowly rises and fall, and then stops. From this angle, I can't see down into the street across the park, but presumably the firemen have arrived. Lola whines behind me. I take her back down into the apartment and secure the roof door behind us.

There's no point in sitting back down to work. There is a fire in the neighborhood, and I have to go see it. I text Mei, Fire in the neighborhood!, and hear her phone ping in the other room.

I check Twitter again while Lola pees in the gravel parking space, and @bostonfire finally has an update about an apartment fire a few blocks away. We head that way, passing the tennis court, where the game of lob is still in progress. No one's been by yet to clean up the graffiti.

The fire is on a street that dead-ends against the far side of the park, nice old bow-fronted buildings with commanding entryways and a fenced strip of grass down the middle. Blue lights flash on the flowerbeds along the bike path, and Lola's strides get shorter and shorter as we approach. Then turn onto the street and suddenly we're up close to it, a different angle of the same three windows piping smoke and there, yes, a tongue of flame reaches out to scorch the brick.

Have you ever stopped to watch a fire? One Fourth of July when I was a kid, there was a fire in a house on the back side of the hill where we lived. A neighbor and I snuck away from our family barbeques and ran down to watch. We stayed until the firemen carried a woman out onto the crumbling porch and made us go home. We were told later on that she'd fallen asleep with a lit cigarette in her hand. Poof.

There's no one to carry out here, it seems. Two gawkers stand by a wooden barrier halfway down the street, a police officer leaning against its far side. Lola and I walk over and join them. The firemen in their helmets and black and yellow jackets walk slowly back and forth between the fire engines and the building. One of them has his jacket open. Everything seems utterly normal.

If there were a fire in our building, Lola would bark and scratch at the bedroom door to wake up Mei, and we would help her dress and gather our essentials. I would hold Mei's hand and carry Lola as we made our way outside, and everyone gathered to watch would break into applause when they saw us because we were so calm and so brave, and we finally would have suffered something public to match our private sense of tragedy.

Because you can talk about a fire. On those scattering aftermath days, people will want to know where you were, what you were doing. You'll wait until you have the whole room's attention, and then begin, On the day of the fire. You were barbequing. You were heating some water for tea, and you got a feeling in your gut that something just wasn't right, and then the phone rang. The first kernel of the microwavable popcorn that you'd just popped into the microwave had just popped when you heard...

Lola stands and sniffs, and I look up to see the man in the suit from this morning. His St. Bernard is pulling on the leash, and he's got his feet spread apart so he doesn't get pulled over.

I bet he's been walking around yelling at his phone this whole time.

He turns towards me, and I realize I've been staring. A light of cautious recognition comes over his face, and his hand comes up like he's not even sure what it's doing, and he gives me a little wave. Then my hand comes up, and I wave back.

About the Author:

Jeff Bakkensen lives in Boston. Recent work has appeared in A-Minor Magazine, Oblong Magazine, Smokelong Quarterly, and The Antigonish Review.

GHOSTS

by David Rogers

When the ghosts started to appear, I knew it was only a matter of time til Stephen would show up. Again.

#

"Laura, you're out of uniform," Jimmy Neutron said. Like Joe's Mexican Restaurant is the army or something. Jimmy used first names only when he was cranky. I think he read in some Idiot's Guide to Success in Business how using names is supposed to make people take you more seriously. He was standing behind the sink when I came in the back, through the kitchen. Probably waiting for me. He loved to catch people making some minor mistake so he could make a big deal about it.

Neutron was not his real name. It was Neville, but everybody called him Neutron because he was so not a genius. He could barely work his phone. That's why he was the assistant manager. An actual job that has to be done for the restaurant to function, like cooking, feeding customers, or clearing tables, cannot be given to

someone like Jimmy.

I tried to ignore him, so he repeated: "Laura, I said you're out of uniform. Black pants, white shirt. You know that."

"So dock my pay a nickel," I said, tying on my apron. "Jimmy," I added, and grabbed the big plastic bin the dirty dishes go in. "Better yet, give me a raise, so I can afford to do laundry."

#

I would ask to switch from busboy to waiter, because tips are better for waiters, but I have always sucked at pretending to like rude people who tempt me to dump food on their heads. At least busboys deal mainly with dishes. Lovely, silent, dirty dishes, whose problems can all be solved by a nice, hot trip through the dishwasher. However, busboys are still entitled to a fourth of the tips. Unless the customer leaves actual money on the table, in which case, a fourth is how much I say it is.

Jimmy claimed he was also supposed to get a fourth, but again, a fourth is what's left after the waiter and I take our cuts. Was then, still is now. Not that I would cheat. I'm not that kind of girl. And yes, I'm a busboy, even though I'm a girl. Busboy, occasional bartender, entrepreneur of the future. Deal with it.

Besides, I'm not going to be a busboy forever. As soon as I graduate, I'm getting a job that pays real money. Then I'll come back and buy the restaurant and watch Jimmy's replacement grovel. After what happened, I don't expect I'll see Jimmy again.

#

Stephen was not the worst boyfriend ever, when he was alive. But he was the worst ex ever. Worst for me, anyway. Even before he was a ghost, he was the sort who wouldn't give up and go away, the kind who didn't know when things were over. Kind of natural he would become a ghost.

Plus, he never had money. I'm no gold-digger, you understand, but a guy can be kind of dull, yet if his date-night budget is exciting enough, good times may be had by all. As the Bible says, charity forgives a multitude of sins, including boredom.

You wonder how he died. I'm coming to that, okay? Just give me a minute.

It wasn't any one thing that made me break up with him. Just a general lack of enthusiasm. On my part, that is. I could tell he was getting more attached to me all the time. I dreaded the moment he might profess undying love in sentimental terms that he would think were romantic. To me they would sound desperate and clingy.

And then there was the ketchup and mustard thing. I said it was not any one particular thing, but the ketchup and mustard did not help. He had a way of dipping his fries in ketchup, then mustard, and once more in ketchup. I mean, mustard on fries--who does that? And the triple dip--ketchup, mustard, and then ketchup again. Every time. To top it off, he didn't immediately eat the fry, but he would wave it around, gesture with it, like the old-timey male stand-up comedians with their cigars.

Condiments should never be a fashion statement.

Seems like a small thing, doesn't it? Well, truth be told, small things have made or broken many relationships. If Anne Boleyn, Henry the Eight's second wife, hadn't had a habit of delicately patting her lips with a napkin after each sip of wine, she and her head and Henry might have lived to a ripe old age together, male heir or no.

Well, okay, he probably still would have dumped her. He was just that kind of guy. But he might not have had her beheaded. And I made up the bit about the napkin. But you get the point. The butterfly effect--small events whose consequences magnify over time to cause disasters--it happens in relationships, too.

I am not heartless. It would hurt him worse the longer I waited. So I knew I had to end it, before that particular butterfly's wings flapped the fateful breeze that would lead to a hurricane.

"Stephen, we have to break up," I said, one evening, just after he took the fries out of the oven. He cooked me dinner at his place. He insisted, which was a bad sign, so I had to start fast.

"Hmmm?" he said, pausing and looking up from my plate, which he was mounding up with far too many fries.

"I said, we have to break up."

"Oh, right. No, you don't mean that. We'll be together forever." He put some more fries on my plate, the rest on his plate, and set the pan aside.

"Mustard?" he asked, holding out the squeeze bottle.

I shook my head. "No, thanks."

Two hours, later, I thought I had convinced him we were broken up. But the next afternoon, a dozen red roses arrived, with a card that said, "I'm sorry about that little fight we had yesterday. I know we'll be together forever."

I sighed, deposited the roses and card in the bin by the curb--it was trash pick-up day--and went inside, wondering why I always attracted the weird ones.

#

Every problem has a solution. I undid the top three buttons on my shirt and talked to Jimmy. He had to try so hard not to let his eyes drift downwards, he forgot to blink. Probably would have given me his car if I'd asked. All I wanted was a bartending shift. At least there, customers had to be 21. I figured I could deal with the average drunk better than someone's entitled juvenile delinquent.

Predictably, Stephen showed up, noticed I was tending bar, and came right over. He was almost broke, cards maxed out, as usual, but I kept serving him. Soon he was so bombed he could barely stay on his stool.

I poured him another, wiped down the bar, and waited. Stephen gulped his eighth whiskey in one drink, closed one eye so he could focus, stood unsteadily, and headed toward what he thought was the bathroom. It was really the emergency exit, but he never got there. He did, however, upchuck, hugely and gloriously, on Jimmy, just as he came around the corner.

This was going better than I planned. I had hoped only that he would pass out at the bar, be thrown out, and be too embarrassed to come back, at least for a while. Jimmy's outraged-indignation face was better than I could have imagined. He escorted Stephen to the door and promised that if he showed his face there again, the police would be called immediately.

Jimmy came back to the bar for a towel to wipe the second-hand whiskey off his pretty white shirt and blue paisley tie. "Why the hell did you keep serving that guy?" he demanded.

"I poured him only one drink, then cut him off" I said. "He must have been pretty bombed before he came in."

Outside, tires screeched. From right in front of the restaurant came a sound like a watermelon and a large bag of dry cat food being dropped from a tall building and hitting the pavement simultaneously. I stared in horror out the big plate glass windows. So did Jimmy. For the second time in five minutes, his tie was decorated with the former contents of someone's stomach, this time his own.

I had planned to put Stephen in a cab when the time came. How was I to know he would be thrown out of the bar and wander straight in front of a bus?

I would have felt a lot worse about it if he hadn't at least gotten to be a ghost.

#

The ghosts started to show up everywhere about a month after Stephen was hit by the bus. The timing was pure coincidence, as far as I know. Even as a ghost, he did not have the charisma to lead a supernatural revolt or an otherworldly revolution.

It's not like I sat around pining over Stephen or what had happened to him. I have a life, so I had to get on with it. I dated a couple of other guys, and then a girl. She was cute, and fun to

be around, but she had a disturbing fixation for really, really bloody slasher movies. No judgment here. That sort of thing just doesn't turn me on. I was planning to break up with her, but she saved me the trouble.

Her name was Chelsee. "With three es." She made a point of that extra e every time she introduced herself. It was one of the least pretentious things about her.

We were sitting on the sofa, the popcorn bowl still full. The movie had made me lose any appetite I might have had. The lurid red letters of the credits rolled on the gore-fest we'd just watched, at her insistence. She turned to me and said, "I think we should see other ghosts."

"You want to date a ghost?" I took a second to process. "Wait, 'other?' You think I'm a ghost?"

"Aren't you?"

"No. Of course not," I said. "Are you?"

"But--your skin is so pale, I never see you eat, and you love slasher flicks. All ghostly qualities."

"Just because I don't want to get fat or get skin cancer doesn't make me a ghost," I said. "And I hate these movies. I watch them only because you like them."

"But you picked it out."

"Because I knew you'd like it. I was trying to let you down easy. I want to break up."

"Okay, fine. We're broken up," she said. "I already said we should see other ghosts."

"Yeah, about that word. 'Other.' I'm not a ghost, so that means . . . ." I was still letting it sink it. Having your girlfriend come out as a ghost at the same time you're breaking up is very confusing. "I'm not a ghost, so that means --you're a ghost?

"Well, yeah. Again, pale skin, I don't eat. What did you think? And why do we always have popcorn?"

"I had sex with a ghost," I said.

"I had sex with a mortal," Chelsee said.

"Well, that's just icky," we both said. It was the last thing we did together.

That's the problem these days. You can't tell the living from the ghosts.

After that, things got really weird.

#

No one knows why the ghost population increased so much. Or why everyone could suddenly see them. The world woke up one day, and there were ghosts everywhere. People adapted. It's amazing what you can get used to.

I asked Stephen about it. He shook his head. Even after he was hit and killed by the bus, he kept coming to see me. Hard to believe, huh? But I talked to him. Might as well be civil. Even though it's not like I actually poured the drinks down his throat or pushed him under the bus, I felt kinda bad about what happened.

Anyway, he said, "It's a big mystery why there are so many ghosts now. People just find it harder to move on. There are different theories. Some say it's caused by population growth. More people born, more people die, more ghosts. Conspiracy nuts say it's something to do with the planet's magnetic field being off-kilter, the drift of the North Pole, or global warming. One theory says the ultimate destination, the space past the point of no return, is running out of room."

"You mean, heaven is full up? Or hell?" I said.

"Dunno. I haven't been there. I'm just a ghost, remember?"

"What do you think?"

"I think wild speculation is pointless. And remains pointless as long as beautiful

women remain beautiful. And occasionally take off their clothes."

"I see being dead hasn't made you any less of a perv," I said.

"Ghostly pleasures are severely restricted," he answered, defensively. "We don't eat, alcohol goes right through us, and has no effect anyway. We can't smoke, since we basically already are smoke, most of the time. Some carnal pleasures must remain."

"Being a ghost hasn't stopped you from being horny, either."

"I can materialize all the way, rock-solid, for long enough to make love," he said, and wiggled his eyebrows. He thought the look was sexy, but really it was just ridiculous.

I didn't ask about ghostly wanking. Some things are too horrible to imagine.

"The old-timers tell me the ghost gig used to be really tough," Stephen said. "A lot of spirits didn't have what it took, so they moved on."

"Moved on where?"

Stephen shrugged. "How should I know? Ghosts can't see anything more than mortals about The Great Beyond. Dying doesn't make you omniscient, or psychic. It doesn't even make you smarter. All it does is make you dead. Phony mortal psychics claim to be in touch with 'the other side.' They say they get messages about all sorts of things from ghosts. Fiddlesticks."

"So how did you find out where I moved?" I asked.

"Well, we ghosts don't know any more than you mortals do about the Great Beyond. But think what you could learn if you had the option to turn invisible and walk through walls. Which is entertaining for a while, then boring. Most people's secrets are sordid, and that's why they are kept secret, yet they are remarkably similar to other people's secrets. Sex and drugs, mostly. It's sad. You'd think being dead would come with a better severance package than getting to know stuff you suspected already and didn't care about."

"But at least you don't need health insurance or have to pay rent or worry about money anymore. That's something," I said.

He agreed.

#

Even after I moved, Stephen came to the restaurant. I didn't move just to get away from him--better apartment, cheaper rent, closer to school--but I did refuse to tell him where I moved. Not that it mattered, of course. If he came to my apartment, he knew I could put the chain on the door and ignore him until he went away. That was before he became a ghost. After, he somehow found my new apartment, and since he could dematerialize, I couldn't even be sure if he was there or not. At the restaurant, he could sit in my section, no way to avoid him and not get fired. Tables must be cleared, even if your almost-a-stalker ghost-ex is sitting right next to them. Cute customers must also be flirted with, especially if it means they might leave a big tip.

One day, I was clearing a table where a family with particularly messy four-year-old twins had dined, and Stephen materialized in the seat right behind me. Startled the heck out of me when I turned around. Which is about the scariest thing most ghosts do--turning up when or where you don't expect them.

"Stephen, why do you keep hanging around? We're done. We've been done for months. Find a nice ghost and settle down with her. Or him. Whichever. Just please leave me alone."

"I'm persistent," he said. "It's the secret of my success."

"No, it's just creepy," I said. "And you know who else is persistent? Stalkers. Now go away."

Which he did. But he always came back.

Something had to be done.

#

Many people had ghostly stalkers, and some were more than mere nuisances. The ghost economy made theft by spectral entities a relatively pointless exercise, at least, as ghosts had no use for money. Or most ghosts didn't. Some clung to the notion of cash as a status symbol. Probably the same kind who, when they were alive, became billionaires and still could think of nothing but how to make more money.

The vast majority of ghosts were harmless enough, however. They were considerate and minded their own business, and if they haunted any places, they were the houses they had lived in or the offices they worked in when they were alive. They remained invisible most of the time, so as not to disturb the living, who, as usual, soon found it easy enough to ignore what they didn't see or hear. Out of sight, out of mind.

Then some genius discovered that a certain kind of electromagnetic field is impervious to ghosts. Shield generators soon hit the market. Install one of these in your house, and ghosts could neither enter nor leave. Any ghost already in your house was trapped, but psychics could be hired to swear your house was ghost-free before you turned on the system. Like Stephen, I think most psychics are are fakes, maybe all of them. But I dated a ghost, so what do I know?

The shield generators were ridiculously expensive at first, of course, and bulky, but soon smaller units were developed, so cars could be ghost-proofed. Next, mobile ghost zappers the size of cellphones were developed, so you could project a fifteen or twenty-foot "clear-zone" wherever you went. This inevitably led to huge conflicts. Harmless ghosts who were minding their own business found themselves being randomly jolted by mobile zappers. The sensation was reportedly similar to what being stunned with a taser or electric-shock gun felt like for mortals. Not the highlight of anyone's day.

Shield generators, along with phones, microwave ovens, masturbation, and living too close to big electric power lines, were all supposed to cause brain cancer or blindness, or at least hairy palms, in mortals. Well, we all have to die of something. Meanwhile, the lawyers need jobs, like everybody else.

A whole new legal field, "spectral legislation and litigation" had to be invented. Did ghosts have rights? If so, didn't they also have responsibilities? If a ghost broke the law, what could you do? Jail, fines, and judgments in civil suits were pointless for beings that could walk through walls and had no actual need for money, nor any way to earn it. Or much of it, anyway, in most cases. Some ghosts could materialize for several hours per day, enough to hold down jobs. Naturally, unemployed mortals deeply resented this fact, and the Hire the Living movement commenced.

Many mortals didn't mind the proliferation of ghosts, or even welcomed it, hoping to become ghosts themselves when they shuffled off the mortal coil, but others became rabid anti-spectralists, arguing that ghosts had no place among the living. "They should have their own country" was the battle-cry of the ghost-haters. Some even wanted a ghost-zapper-dome to be generated over the entire continent. These ghost-haters avoided questions about how ghosts of people who died inside the dome would get out. "Send them back where they came from" was another popular slogan, despite the fact that many ghosts came from right here. People were irrational as ever.

#

"It has nothing to do with your being a ghost," I said to Stephen the last time I saw him. "We broke up before you died, remember?"

"No, you broke up," he said. "I didn't give up on us."

"For the hundredth time, there is no us!" I yelled in frustration. Stephen chose that moment to dematerialize. He was never good at real conflict. We were sitting on a park bench. People in the park moved away from the crazy girl who was screaming at no one.

#

So I saved my tips for a couple of weeks and bought a ghost zapper. Also borrowed all the funds from the tip jar and left an anonymous IOU. I'm not proud of it, okay? Not proud of what happened afterward, either. I just want to state that unequivocally.

But Stephen was driving me nuts. Always there. Even when I was trying to make friends, or more than friends, he would turn up. If you are an exhibitionist, you might not mind if your ex is probably watching you try to make love. I am not an exhibitionist. Not that kind, anyway.

By now, the portable zappers were the most economical, so that's what I got. The range was short, maybe fifteen feet, but at least it would keep him out of my bedroom. And I could clip it to my belt at work. Zappers were prohibited in the restaurant. A big sign on the door said "NO ZAPPERS" in bigger letters than the "No Smoking" sign. Jimmy had a curious fit of open-mindedness and declared them cruel and discriminatory, but I took it along anyway. As long as Stephen did not materialize, I could live with his possible lurking at the restaurant, but if he

did appear, I wanted the option. I wore a shirt long enough to cover the little bump it made.

#

Juliet showed up at the bar. I'd found I liked tending bar. Jimmy kept giving me shifts there, even after--or maybe because--Stephen up-chucked on him. Jimmy decided not to blame me too much for whatever role I might have played in my late boyfriend's transition to the ghostly realm. I guess Jimmy though it was justice, or something like that.

Juliet is not her real name, and yes, I do have nicknames for everyone who annoys me. (Stephen--Stevie Ray Gone. Go ahead, roll your eyes. I won't see.) Even though Juliet is twenty-two, at least according to her ID, she has that precious, entitled fourteen-year-old air about her, like every Romeo in the world must be dying to stand outside her window and pine for her affections.

That day, Juliet was wearing a white tee-shirt that said Hey, Ghosts! Get a Life! Clever, huh? Anyway, she had her ghost zapper prominently displayed, the power light flashing away, when she walked in. Jimmy spotted it instantly from the other end of the bar. He spoke loudly, "No, no, turn that thing off or get out. You can't use it in here."

Juliet ignored him, at first. Jimmy looked at me. I went over to Juliet and said, "No zappers in the restaurant. You'll have to turn it off."

"Says who?" she said, pouting her already pouty lips, as if she hadn't heard Jimmy. People out on the street heard Jimmy.

"The manager," I said, and inclined my head Jimmy's way. I turned to wash some beer mugs. Let him deal with her. That was why he got paid the big bucks.

Out of the corner of my eye I spotted Stephen, who had snuck in the back door. Or maybe he'd just walked through the wall and materialized. He was standing right behind Jimmy.

Juliet turned and walked toward Jimmy, who began backing away from her. I started toward the three of them. Jimmy stumbled over Stephen's feet. I turned my zapper on, intending to teach Stephen a little lesson.

Feeling the shock, Stephen turned rigid, arms and legs locked into position, a surprised look on his face, left hand reaching out, frozen, the way department store mannequins used to be posed. Unable to move, he toppled over like a scarecrow in a high wind.

I didn't even think about the stories I'd heard, tales about what happened to ghosts who got caught in a vortex caused by a double zapping, until I noticed the light still flashing on Juliet's belt. Normally, zappers are unpleasant but relatively harmless. However, it is said, there are limits to what even a ghost can tolerate.

"Stephen!" I said, and tried, too late, to catch him. But before I could reach that far, Jimmy began to convulse, then froze also, and followed Stephen to the floor. His face struck the freshly cleaned tile floor in what was sure to leave a blood stain.

Except there was no stain. From either of them. I didn't expect Stephen to bleed--he's a ghost, after all, materialized or not, so why does he need blood?

They faded away.

I tried to convince myself I was a little surprised that Jimmy got zapped into oblivion right along with Stephen. I wondered when he had become a ghost, what happened to him. But the truth was, he'd had that "I'm special, I'm a ghost, I can do whatever I want" attitude for a long time.

#

That was five weeks ago. Nobody has seen Jimmy or Stephen since then. I'm a little worried about the whole situation, but I refuse to lose sleep over it.

As a wise mortal once said, So it goes.

I mean, ghosts are already dead, so it's not murder if you kill one.

Is it?

About the Author:

David Rogers is the author of two novels: *Thor's Hammer,* and D.*B.Cooper is Dead: A Solomon Starr Adventure.* His fantasy novella is called *Return of the Exile*. All are available from Amazon. He also curates "David Watches Movies" on Facebook. More of his work can be read at https://davidrogersbooks.wordpress.com/.

PUNCH DRUNK

by Annabelle Baptista

I clutched my jaw as if I'd been sucker punched. Genevieve looked up from my case file, her piercing grey eyes like pressed pickle-loaf from some kindergartener's soggy lunch sack. Over the past year, she'd written adjectives like lazy, bored, depressed and demoralized in my file summing up my personality without ever using a highlighter. For five years, I'd had a social working advising me to pick myself up as if I had a third arm, I wasn't using folded behind my back. For myself, I had learned to read upside down. I was my own worst enemy she'd say like maybe I needed to get over myself. Okay, but how? We were attached, me myself and I.

"This time it's for real, Genevieve," I spat out. I had a known addiction to pain killers. I'd sat through five years in therapy talking about it to a Japanese psychiatrist who was married to a star of Kabuki theater. I knew when I was making up pain and when it was real. She looked up at me and began throttling her neck -of Italian descent, she was drawn to drama.

"Really, Rochelle?" She picked up her pen, five gold bracelets clinked in unison punctuating the alarm in her voice. She shook her head, causing pearly curls to fall in front of her eyes.

"I am in pain, and I should know; I've broken my femur, fractured my hip, broken my sesamoid bone, broken my nose twice and once had to rip off a toenail because of an embedded splinter. I'm not faking it." I adjusted the bra beneath my t-shirt.

She stared with piercing eyes. Her red lacquered nails tapped her silver pen, her name, Pyro, printed along the side caught the light.

She added the word dysfunctional in my file, fancifully drawing the "y" like a noose. I hissed and cursed her under my breath. She was passed seventy. She should have retired, but according to her, she had nothing to retire on; therefore, she kept working. Another American dreamer suffering from sleep disorder.

"I'm going to have to work until I'm eighty." She said in protest, her vocal chords raw.

"If you live that long," I said, trying to cheer her up.

"Yeah, thanks, if you don't start taking care of yourself, you won't live half as long as I have," Genevieve said her voice rattled.

"If I don't get this tooth fixed. I fucking won't want to either." I dug my tongue inside my impacted molar. My whole body throbbed down to my nether regions. I pulled a tight curl out to its full length from my fro. Pulling my hair out gave me brief relief.

Genevieve handed me the paperwork to apply for dentistry.

"Thanks, Genevieve. I know the drill." I said, winked and smiled.

"You're awful, Rocky," she'd said, using my nickname from the boxing ring.

I signed a dozen forms then, finally I was finished. I felt like I'd just given blood.

"I could kiss you, Genevieve."

"Don't." She said sweeping floppy gray curls out of her eyes.

I laid the forms and her pen face up on her desk.

I was one of her oldest clients. I could tell because my file, the size of the Guttenberg bible, wasn't computerized. The office definitely was not state-of-the-art social services. I walked past bamboo cubicles fit like a maze made by a mad basket weaver. When I got to the door, I yelled, down the dimly lit corridor.

"Ok all you fruitcakes, get back in your baskets." Everyone on the floor remained silent.

"Rochelle Banks!" Genevieve yelled. I ran as fast as I could down five flights of stairs and out the municipality door into sunshine. Full of myself, I grinned.

II

The dentist, who was doing this piece of charity work, held office in a pristine building in midtown Chicago. When I stepped off the elevator on the 20th floor, the air rushed the hall like a vacuum left by a speeding train. This floor held several offices without doors. I was surprised to see the building was still under construction. "Do not Cross This Line" yellow hornet tape, stretched across the hall blocking passage to the polyurethane covered floor to ceiling window at the end of the corridor. Conference tables sat, stacked against the wall, unused price tags intact. I pulled up my black sweats and tied my trainers.

In waves, depression would come, and I would recount the black hole I'd been thrown into. I had coveted a belt, the UFC flyweight title belt, but I'd lost and been forced through poverty to take up residence on public assistance when it was offered by Genevieve Pyro and the Department of welfare. Still, on my knees, I looked down the long hall, the windows gaping hole covered only by a thin diaphragm of plastic which whistled, catching the air as if the building were breathing. I wondered how far I'd fall before I'd lose consciousness. I was in my trainer, which meant I could get a great running start, but I felt underdressed for the occasion. I felt someone behind me. I turned and nearly jumped out of my skin. Wearing a white jumper and air sole shoes, the dentist's assistant stood at the opened door. "Coming?" she asked.

I studied her shocking white skin, pink plastic lips, thick with wet gloss and big blue eyes. Those weird big-wet eyes you see on bobbing dog dashboard ornaments. Her hair burst from a rubber band into a strawberry cotton candy puff. Her name shield said, Toffy.

"Come with me." She beckoned.

I followed like a lapdog suddenly with renewed focus. Toffy led me into a state-of-the-art operating room and left. We'd chatted on the way, and she told me she was Transylvanian as was Dr. Malselvicbourn. He sauntered into the arena on six-inch steel-heel stilettoes. He may have been three feet tall, the size of a bar stool, without the extension shoes. He wore a black hair helmet that came over his forehead into a widow's peak. He rolled a ladder towards the chair. His syrupy brown eyes fixed on me as his angular nose twitched. He looked like an angry black bird.

I squirmed in the chair. Leaving came to mind. Unfortunately, my options were limited due to pain. The next dentist appointment for sure wouldn't be tomorrow, as Genevieve would see me as having a diminished need if I could ditch a doctor.

His slight Romanian accent was matter-of-fact as he eulogized his grandfather, who had been born in Transylvania.

"My grandfather did all the dentistry on his animals as well as the family. When we moved to America, he opened a practice here. My mother was his nurse." As he jabbered on, I rolled my eyes and grabbed my jaw, the universal sign for tooth pain.

He accepted my passive reproach, elevated the dental chair, and switched on a monitor. I moaned and rolled my eyes, dreading I'd be forced to watch his home movies. Instead, the screen showed a saliva stream that ran beneath a worn tooth, a cracked filling, a hole filled with detritus.

"Thanks to fluoride in the water, or you'dth have no teeth at all." He laughed.

I grunted considering the joke was not funny at all.

"Today, you will be fitted for a crown." He snapped a powdered latex glove above his

Rolex and the other against his pale right wrist. His bushy eyebrows travelled like centipedes across his face while he gazed into my gaping mouth using a jeweler's loupe. Looking through it from the opposite end, I could make out the spidery veins in his skin. Then, he pulled my jaw wide and stabbed a hypodermic filled with Novocain between my back molars.

Fifteen years in the flyweight ring - teeth were a luxury. I was a punch-drunk forty-something with twenty knockdowns and seven knockouts. I got up more times than I got knocked down, not bad.

His assistant stuffed gauze between the neck of my t-shirt and damp skin. It took all my strength not to smear my ashy thumb in her lip-gloss. She bent over me and attached a metal cape; the smell of sunflowers overwhelmed my senses.

"It'd protect you from radiation. In case you vant children," She spoke with a thick Transylvanian accent that I could tell she put on or took off at will. The lead cape hung to the floor, pinning me to the chair.

"Children, I thought they were a myth you heard about when you started your period."

She smiled, and I felt my lips slip around my numbed gums.

Lying motionless, my afro matted, and chin up- the tooth no longer screamed with pain. From my vantage point in the chair, Toffy refilled my water cup and provided suction to my flowing saliva. I snatched glances of the tan stretch marks between her breasts.

When the dentist began, again, I winced, and he pauses, holding the drill mid-air to let me catch my breath. I spit metallic blood, from the cracked filling into a porcelain bowl. Toffy smiled, patted my hand, raking my skin a little with her three-inch pink nails. I started having heart palpitations when I caught a glimpse of her out of the corner of my eye. After the procedure, Toffy gave me my next appointment, placing a folded piece of paper in my palm after Dr. Malselvicbourn shook my hand. I had tried to make eye contact even though I was looking at the top of his sonic hair helmet.

Back on the street, I waited for the next bus. I would get a crown. I had another date with Toffy, okay an appointment. I closed my eyes and constructed a vision of the future. The first time I had seen a future with myself in it without the title belt. It was a future where I would be flossing.

About the Author:

Annabelle Baptista is a poet and short story writer born in Indianapolis, Indiana. She currently teaches English as a second language and lives near Heidelberg, Germany with her husband. She has been published in *Coloring Book: An Eclectic Collection of Fiction and Poetry, Andwerve magazine* and *Families: The Front Line of Pluralism.*

SHOP

by ML Paul

Like a photo plucked from developer too soon, she appeared underdeveloped to herself as she looked in the mirror of the third floor bathroom. To correct this problem, she opened her laptop, selected a self-portrait, cut out her head, and digitally replaced it with a pineapple, avocado, full moon, or antique five-franc coin: "Viva la France." A painter friend said it reminded him of the work of Alexander Rodchenko, the Russian photographer: images in eyeglasses, eyes on open hands. Kiara would look into his work; she needed a destination.

Living illegally in a small artist studio within an old downtown Providence building, Kiara had to hide her stovetop, microwave, and other signs of daily living. Also she had to forage for showers, but here she could do her photography and make rent with occasional work on a catering wait staff. With the help of her many artist friends in the building, she organized street-level photo shots of her Westminster Street window in various time of day and light, sometimes including herself in the shots. These were inspired from a book of historical Providence photos, which included images of female workers in workplace windows from the 1920's and 30's. She took and scanned photos of the women and shopped them into her window. She sought out existing windows in the photos, shot them, and shopped the women's faces into the same window, only eighty years later. She said she felt reverential. As she looked through the book, Kiara searched for her window.

Unable to find it, she searched the Special Collections Department of the Providence Public Library. There she found pictures of parades, crime scenes, political rallies, and celebrity sightings, and often there would be workers starring out the windows. She captured the pictures with women in the windows with her phone. Finally, she found her window: "Dolores Hat Shop" was stenciled on the four windows of her floor. It was Columbus Day, 1930. At home she enlarged and studied it.

In the séance of sleep, these women talked to her about their lives, as she became a worker, too. On this late January night, they watched the sun set through groups of buildings, watching colors change, having no vocabulary to capture it. When she woke, she remembered the sky, and poured over her Dolores Hat Shop collection without even making coffee. No one spoke now, but in their eyes was recognition. Then she remembered something one of the women said, "Don't forget this." Or maybe it was "Don't forget us." As the shadow world was slipping into the light, she repeated both lines.

She studied more now: payroll records, census tracts, and city event notices: the events when the women would lean out the windows to watch. At the Special Collections Office, she found a diary and letters from early 20th Century women, event posters, and other "ephemera." It became her favorite place to go.

Back on the studios, everyone was buzzing about a rent increase. Some feared that this was an attempt to make way for condos. OK, she needed a real job.

That night in another hypnagogic hallucination at the hat shop, the women were all calling her

Helen. There was nothing special about her, just one of women who hailed from Italy, Ireland, and Sweden. The women wore hats adorned with silk flowers and ribbons, while they created new ones.

She thought about asking her artist friends to call her Helen, but she knew that they would think her eccentric. Already some had given her the moniker, "etc. etc. eccentric." But they were sympathetic about a job. One knew someone, an operative in Democratic Party politics, who could help her.

On her fourth visit to the Dolores Hat Shop, Kiara/ Helen was making hats, repeatedly pricking her fingers with the needle. She cried out, and Aline, an Irish immigrant, showed her the technique of pushing the needle bit by bit instead of all at once. Then she held Helen's hand and kissed her fingers, wrapping the injured one in gauze. Aline jerked her head over to the group of six Italian women: "To hell with Enrico Caruso; those girls are giving me a headache." The Italians entertained the women singing opera along with Caruso records at the top of their lungs.

Helen said, "I rather like it. It makes the day go by faster."

Aline said, "We all love Nona, but the old hag has a terrible voice."

"Don't call her a hag."

"I say that with reverence. Nona is the wisest one here. May she pass that knowledge down to us." Aline walked over to her bench, and pulled out a book from her bag. She came back and handed the open book to Helen. It was open to a poem called "Witch –Women." Helen flipped to the book cover and saw that it was Edna St. Vincent Millay. "She's one of yours, an American," said Aline. "Only the old hags can save us; they know everything."

Kiara awoke to throbbing fingers. It was her first day as a Special Project Assistant to the Deputy Superintendent in the city school department, where she used pieces of old grants to rough out new proposals. While she didn't know the field of education, she did have a college education (RI School of Design, 2011) and she could figure a lot of it out. And she could type well and move electrons around with alacrity.

At night in dream-suggestopedia, she worked in the hat shop with needles, thread, glue, felt, silk, ribbon and bird feathers, while the Italian women sang opera. The women laughed a lot, cried sometimes, and always worried about money and children. But all the women agreed: work was better than stuck behind four walls. Once Helen asked, "Do you work because of the money?" Someone answered, "No, it's because we have each other, women-time."

One of the shop opera singers, Mamie of Genoa, explained that in these bad economic times, they were lucky to be in the hat business. "Every woman needs hats, one for summer and one for winter at least. Everybody is equal in this country, they say, but if you don't wear stylish hat, ladies, you find that a lie."

Nona spoke to Kiara: "What's you name, dearie?" Nona was big everywhere, and fearless. She was the only one who would speak up to Albert or "Albertino" as she called him. "If he tries any of that hanky-panky, you let me know. He maybe the owner, but I am the boss!" She said, yelling out the last part. "He's lucky to have hard-workers and beauties, too."

"It's Helen, Nona."

"Really? Did the girls put you that name? That's a movie star name. That name is a trick to make war, send sons to die. You have 'nother name?"

"Yes, Kiara?"

"Like the thing girls put on their heads?" She gestured her hands placing something on her head.

"No, Nona, that's a tiara. It's Kiara."

"OK, I like that better. You listen to those girls they make you crazy. When we do the good thing, we helping, helping everyone." Nona spread her hands to show how much capacity we have to help.

One day on her lunch break, Kiara was working on a new art project: sunset in the city. She was shopping sunsets into sewer drains, windows and tree trunks, and taking over whole houses and busses. The back of a garbage trunk was her favorite. She was thinking of submitting them to a local gallery. Then the Deputy Superintendent walked by, stopped and looked. He flashed a smile and asked her to explain what she was doing. She was proud that he showed interest in her work. "Maybe you can help us on another project." He said.

Later he explained that he needed "readily consumable media platforms" that could be used in a labor dispute. He wanted her to shop in some differently worded signs carried by teachers at a rally. "Blogs are the new battlefield, " he said. She was asked to shop in Longchamps bags and expensive-looking coats on teachers leaving work. What did she think?

Shocked, she didn't know what to say, but she was able to come up with, "why are you doing this?"

"I guess you could call it "slew-footing"?

"What's that?" She asked.

"It's hockey, tripping an opponent with your feet. Just a two-minute minor penalty, so no big deal. You know, we want to authenticate some of the discordant members of the teacher's union."

She was intrigued with the work, something for which she was highly-skilled, but said, "I'll think about it."

"Did I mention that there is some extra money for this?"

After work Kiara was walking home on Westminster Street. She looked up to the window that once held the Dolores Hat Shop, and was blinded by the reflection of the sun. Nature, maybe the grand mentor of their artist community, doing her own art. If she was in dreamland last night she couldn't remember. She was thinking slew-footing workers wasn't minor. With the helping, helping of others, Kiara had it figured out: she remembered the shop that mattered.

About the Author:

ML Paul's work has appeared in *Pure Slush, Postcard Poems and Prose, Black Heart Magazine, Lockjaw, Right Hand Pointing, and KYSO Flash,* and is a member of Hi-Fi, a historical fiction writers group.

MEETING JOHN AND THERESA
by Jeffrey Hill

The people file out of the subway car. The people file into the subway car. It is cramped. Some sit. Some stand. The man, woman, and child choose to stand.

"When are we meeting John and Theresa?" the woman asks.

"Around six-thirty," the man replies. "Which is thirty minutes from now."

"But when are we actually meeting them?" the woman asks, exasperated before the man can even begin one of their seemingly endless arguments.

He doesn't reply, so she changes the subject. "How was work today?" the woman asks.

"Work," the man scoffs.

"Never mind him," the child interjects.

"He's had a rough go these last few days," the woman reassures, to no one in particular.

People are watching them now. Restless. Curious. Not quite scared, but on edge.

"Haven't we all," mutters the man, checking his watch and seeing that they will no doubt be late. It is already six o'clock and they have eight more stops and a ten-minute walk ahead of them. It's always best not to make John and Theresa wait.

The man, the woman, and the child ride in silence, returning the stares, the glares, and the glances at each stranger who deems them interesting, confusing, or downright threatening.

They are united in one thing: their hatred of on-lookers.

In every other sense, they are unique. Different. And, the woman would argue, special.

Eight stops and twenty-eight minutes later, they have reached their destination. It is time to walk now. The doors open.

The people file out of subway car. The people file into the subway car. It is cramped. Some walk. Some run. The man, woman, and child choose to run.

"Are we going to be late?" the child asks.

"Of course we are," says the man, dodging a subway musician and getting a strange stare from the onlookers as he begins to pick up his pace.

"Don't worry," says the woman. "He's always worrying," she fades, speaking to no one in particular.

They arrive at their destination at six-forty-three and John and Theresa are there to greet them in the back room.

"There's a problem," John says, taking the man's coat.

"I can see that," the woman replies, admiring Theresa's new earrings.

There are only three chairs.

John sits. Theresa sits. The man sits. The woman and the child are standing there, awkwardly, trying to stay out of the way until they can flag down a waiter.

A server walks past them. A bartender acts like they aren't even there. But it isn't until Theresa starts to cry and John holds her hand and begins to whisper to the man that it's not his fault that the woman and child start to panic.

"Do we have to go?" the child asks.

"I think we might," the woman begins, but she is cut short by John's authoritative tone.

"Your mother and I," he begins, clutching Theresa's hands tighter and tighter as he chokes back his own tears, "We need to talk about this."

The man is quiet, for once. The woman embraces the child.

"It's not healthy."

The man looks at the woman. The child. And sees them. Really sees them.

And then he doesn't.

Theresa lays out a series of options. Funeral arrangements. Casket colors. All tasteful.

"You need closure," John tells the man.

"Honey," Theresa whispers. "They're gone."

And when the man looks behind him, they are.

About the Author:

Jeff Hill is a moderately reformed frat boy turned writer/teacher splitting his time between Nebraska and New York. His work has appeared in dozens of publications and his mom has a binder full of printed copies for any doubters. He is the Chief Creative Officer of ComicBooked.com and is currently pitching two novels. Jeff is a regular participant of the Sarah Lawrence College Summer Seminar for Writers and has served as a faculty member of the Writer's Hotel since 2017. Follow him on twitter at jeffhillwriter.

A POCKET OF AIR
by Annette Freeman

Denny gave the cast of the play one round of perfunctory applause, a quick slap together of his palms, then he was heading for the door. He pushed out of the theatre as if he had an emergency to attend. When he hit the night air he pulled his phone from his pocket immediately. No messages, no updates.

He shoved the phone back in his jacket and headed for the carpark, on legs long enough to leap down the shallow steps two at a time. It loosened him up after a couple of hours sitting in the theatre. Kids wearing sparkly clothes were coming out of the concert hall, blonde mothers fussing. Elderly opera-goers shuffled arm-in-arm. Damn, he thought, there's at least three shows finishing at once tonight.

He hurried through the bars and restaurants along the concourse, where the din of drunk people vied with the bad amplification of a crummy band. He hunched his shoulders and shoved his hands into his pockets, pushed through the crowd, cursed the waiters who tried to cross his path. "Piss off," one of them said, as Denny knocked against a tray of beers. The bouncers at the corner raised their chins over folded arms and looked towards them. Denny ducked and hunched and hurried past, into the maw of the carpark.

He gripped the steering wheel and took a deep breath to calm his irritation. First he'd had to sit through a mediocre play, the third this week; now gridlock in the carpark. He grabbed a plastic bottle from the passenger seat and took a swig of water. It was hot down here.

Denny was in his beloved retro car, a powder-blue Datsun 120Y, stuck on the third level, inner spiral, blue/yellow, of the Sydney Opera House carpark. He'd give the play 2.5 stars at best. Theatre-reviewing wasn't an easy life, despite what some people thought, his wife for example. Hundreds of patrons of culture were trying to leave the carpark simultaneously now. The sparkly kids, fussy mothers and elderly opera lovers were spreading through the underground, beeping open Toyotas and Nissans and ancient Mercedes up and down the ramps. Denny was a veteran of these SOH carpark gridlocks. He turned off his engine and sat back in his seat.

The lugubrious SUVs that hulked around him grumbled on, belching exhaust, until they too figured out they'd be here for a while and shut off their engines. Huh, at last, thought Denny.

He flicked through his phone but there was no signal. The cars were spiralled deep underground in what had been, in its day, cutting-edge carpark design. It wound down six levels to a cross-over tunnel linking the red/green levels with the blue/yellow levels. The whole thing was constructed like a demonic underground double-helix, a spiral within a spiral. Traffic coming in spiralled down, and traffic going out spiralled up, with a couple of cross-tunnels linking them. Tonight Denny had parked on the fourth level, red/green, and to get to the exit he'd had to drive down and around and through the lowest cross-tunnel and now he was back up as far as level three, blue/yellow, and he was stuck. He felt like a constipated turd in a concrete intestine. That could be a metaphor for his life at the moment.

This was going to be at least a twenty-minute wait, maybe longer. Miranda was expecting him home by eleven. Normally she didn't care when he got in. She was used to his job and the way it sucked up so many of his evenings. But tonight she'd specifically asked him when he'd be back. One of their kids, the youngest, was in some kind of shit at school. Denny wasn't clear on the details. Miranda said she needed to talk about it. He'd told her he'd be back by eleven, give or take ten minutes for the carpark. Now, waiting in the Datsun, he wrote a text to her on his phone and pressed send, but it wasn't going anywhere.

There was movement ahead. Engines started. Cars rumbled and belched like a row of race-horses at a starting gate. They all inched forward, gained about one car length, then stopped again. Denny switched off his engine right away; he recognized a false alarm. Cars around him grumbled on hopefully for a few more minutes. He looked for the control on his retro dash to make sure that the air was turned to interior circulation. It was cancer-inducing territory out there in the carpark.

Denny and Miranda had three kids, which he'd always thought was one too many. Not that he didn't love all his kids. If anything, he loved them too much. Every time one of them was sick, or bawled because their best friend moved away, his heart couldn't cope with it. He left that stuff to Miranda. He did the morning school run, she took on the bedtime routine. She had to be at the office early; it was like that in law firms. The two of them didn't overlap much during the week.

Denny fretted. It'd been at least ten minutes, maybe fifteen, since he'd been able to check his phone. This was such a waste of time. He could be updating his Twitter feed. And he wanted to check the retweets on the review he'd posted yesterday. You had to be on top of social media in his job.

There was no radio reception down here either and his veteran car didn't have a working music system. There was a slot for cassette tapes. Denny was too young to even remember cassette tapes. He was stuck with only his thoughts for company. He did love the Datsun. It was his baby, his hobby, the thing that kept him sane. It took up a lot of his weekends, working on it, going to rallies, getting together with his enthusiast mates. Miranda drove a nice little Toyota Corolla that he'd picked up for her second-hand. It was a couple of years old but well-looked-after. It only just fitted the three kids across the back seat, but Miranda managed.

Denny drummed his fingers on the steering wheel and pressed his lips together. He gazed out at the low concrete roof above the line of cars. It was claustrophobic down here, if you thought about it. Some of these SUVs, these urban trucks, barely fitted under the structural beams. The carpark must be over twenty years old by now, maybe more, bored into the ground years after the Opera House was completed.

Denny imagined a bunch of engineers sitting around drinking beers and coming up with the bright idea of building it like a double-helix. He imagined light bulbs going off over their heads, them getting all excited about how many more cars they could fit into the space. He'd read something explaining how it was such a great design because the last cars in would be the first cars out, in some kind of Biblical carpark parable. In reality, the first cars in took the spaces closest to the exit, leaving the deepest, unpopular places for the later comers. People weren't that stupid, not even SUV drivers.

Miranda wanted to get an SUV. When she'd brought it up, he'd said maybe, when they could afford it. The kids were out-growing the Corolla, he could see that. He promised to do some research, check prices for pre-owned. She'd said that he didn't get what she meant. That she was going to buy an SUV, a Toyota Rav 4, new. Her salary would cover it; there was a deal through her firm. He recalled his shock at that pronouncement. If he was no longer the automotive expert in the marriage, what exactly was his role? He should have said that to Miranda at the time but he didn't think of it. He thumped the steering wheel again and remembered the bile that had risen in his throat. He shifted his butt in the Datsun car seat.

The traffic took another of feeble shuffle forward, hopeful revving followed again by resigned switching off of engines. Another metaphor for Denny's life. He leaned his head back and closed his eyes for a minute. When he opened them the concrete roof was still looming over the windshield. This carpark was designed to have a fifty-year life span. Or was it thirty? He'd read about it somewhere. Concrete didn't last forever. Wasn't there concrete cancer? All kinds of shoddy work went on these days. Those crumbling apartment towers you saw in the news, shocking stuff. Thirty years wasn't long for concrete.

Denny tried to work out which year the carpark had opened. He thought backwards over his life, the plays he'd reviewed, when his kids were born, when he'd still been acting, when he and Miranda were students and went to the theatre on dates. Bloody hell, he thought, this car park is close to twenty-five years old. How far underground was he?

He imagined then that the concrete roof, only a couple of metres above his car, might collapse on him, and on all the others stuck here. The whole double-helix spiral might settle down upon them like layers of pasta added to a lasagna. If the thing collapsed, if it was too old, or if the tunnelling for one of those new motorways made the rock unstable, then all the layers of the double-helix would settle down on top of each other and they'd all be bolognese sauce.

It could happen, Denny thought, peering through the windscreen of the Datsun. The glass needed a wash; there were dead insects stuck to it. It could happen. Structures you assumed were safe sometimes weren't. Things that had stood there all your life could easily be torn down and something new and unfamiliar replace them. That kind of thing happened all the time in Sydney. And these days, the city was sitting on a network of tunnels, sandstone bored through with hollow tubes. It had to be unstable.

If this concrete lasagna came down, what would he do? He probably wouldn't survive such a cataclysm but he thought he should have a plan, give himself the best chance. He could throw himself sideways across the front seats, get down as low as possible. The Datsun had bucket seats, with the gear stick between them. He pulled his jacket from the back where he'd thrown it and spread over the gear stick. It would give him some padding if he was trapped in that position, lying across the car, under tonnes of concrete. The Datsun was pretty strong, and much lower to the ground than the SUVs around him. Maybe the fall of the concrete would be arrested a bit by the higher cars and he'd be left uncrushed, with a pocket of air. Unlike the SUV occupants, though of course he wished them luck if the worst happened. A pocket of air, yes, that was it. Didn't people survive earthquakes in crumpled buildings if they had a pocket of air? They could tap out messages and call feebly to rescuers. He looked at the plastic water bottle he'd tossed on the passenger seat and was sorry he'd drunk half of it. He'd conserve it now. The cars remained at a standstill, engines switched off. He'd been there half an hour.

When Denny finished drama school there were great roles around for newcomers. They paid peanuts but he worked with some big-name directors. He was tall, and lean back then too. He'd often score the 'lanky, iconic Australian man' roles. Summer of the Seventeenth Doll had been his peak. The theatre gave him a buzz, he loved it, though like everyone he hoped for television, for the money. He remembered emerging from stage doors late at night, the black roads shiny with rain, his face shiny with make-up remover, and Miranda waiting for him. She'd looked childlike, bundled in her winter coat. She was still at law school then.

Of course if the carpark collapsed, they'd all be buried deep in this cavern or hole or whatever they were in. He thought about where the entrance to the carpark was and figured out they must be under the Botanic Gardens, in a monstrous pit, with the fig trees and lawns somewhere above. There'd be an enormous sinkhole in the Gardens if this whole structure gave way.

He wondered if his marriage might give way, disappear into a sink-hole. He couldn't remember the last time he and Miranda had done something together, the two of them. She hadn't been to the theatre in years, though she used to come to all his opening nights when he still had acting gigs. And what was up with the little guy, their youngest? Denny should have listened properly when Miranda had started to tell him. It was something about getting into fights at school. That little guy? He was way too young for fights at school. Wasn't he only seven? Or eight? Instead of listening to her (and now he thought about it, she'd sounded really worried), he'd grabbed his jacket and car keys and said he'd be back at eleven, give or take ten minutes. Now, in the Datsun, he looked at his watch. It was eleven-thirty. The jam had lasted forty-five minutes already and it would be a half-hour drive home when he did finally get out.

Would the kids want to be actors? When they were small he'd done some terrific characterisations, reading stories to them. Where The Wild Things Are was great material. He could still recite that whole thing. He tried repeating it now to kill time in this infernal carpark. He made it to about halfway through, then lost the thread. "...called him the most wild thing of all and made him king of all wild things." He got that far. His two girls, the older kids, had loved that stuff. But was it irresponsible to encourage his kids to be actors? It didn't pay. Let's be honest, if it weren't for Miranda's job, they'd be poor. He wasn't worried about his two girls, they'd rule the world. If they did go into theatre they'd probably be stars. But what about the little guy? Maybe he should keep an eye on him. What did the kid like doing, anyway? What presents did he ask for at birthdays and Christmas? Denny left all that stuff to Miranda.

If he really wanted out of here, he had options. He could get out of the car and go upstairs to the fresh air and call Miranda. He could gulp in some clean breaths, take a look around at the Quay and the Opera House and the city and assure himself that the world was still standing solidly where it should be. But to do that he'd have to pull out of the line of cars and park; he'd have to give up his place in the queue. If he pulled out of line, if he parked and came back five or ten minutes later, they wouldn't let him back into the queue. He knew that. Even now, there was a poor bastard blocked into a parking space just up ahead. Earlier, Denny had seen his red tail-lights glow as he tried to reverse into the line, but no-one let him in. That's the way it went down here.

Eventually the guy had given up, switched off, and now he was just sitting there. No, Denny didn't want to leave his place in the queue.

A shudder of movement ahead animated the cars. Everyone started their engines and this time they made some progress. Denny advanced maybe half a turn of the spiral. At one of the cross-tunnels he let one car into the line, but only one. That was the etiquette down here in this carpark, when it was full like this. If you were stuck in a cross-tunnel you had to wait your turn. Denny beeped his horn at a Jag that tried to cut in. One at a time, that was the unwritten rule. He was now on the second level, blue/yellow. The exit wasn't far away. The Datsun hummed.

Then the cars stopped again. With the exit so close, no-one switched off their engines this time. The cars waited, growling like big cats defending their turf. Denny checked his phone but there was still no signal. He thought about the carpark collapsing, about surviving in a pocket of air. He might have a better chance if it happened here, on the second level, closer to the exit. Rescuers might be able to reach him.

He imagined himself lying sideways in the Datsun, maybe with his legs trapped, taking only a mouthful of his water at a time, trying to get his phone to work. Maybe the phone would pick up a random signal and ring, only to go dead before he could answer it. Or maybe he would answer it and hear Miranda crying and saying I love you! before it went dead. Surely she'd say that? If she thought it might be the last thing he'd ever hear?

The line of cars was still going nowhere. Denny had been without his phone for over an hour now. He sensed, like someone drowning, that his whole life was passing before his eyes. A shudder went through his shoulders; his legs were stiff. He had to move. He opened the door of the Datsun and stepped out. Pale-faced drivers in the other cars watched him. He stretched to his full height, threw his arms wide, tossed his long hair. What kind of husband did he want to be? What kind of father? I want to be the most wild thing of all! he yelled, throwing his head back and giving it all he'd got. The other drivers stared, stayed in their cars, checked the door locks.

About the Author:

Annette Freeman lives in Sydney, Australia. Her short stories have appeared in a number of Australian and international journals including *BrainDrip, South Broadway Ghost Society, The Writing Disorder and Typehouse Magazine.* She has a Master of Creative Writing and the support of a terrific writing group.

A RARE THING

by Matthew Chacko

When Joel opened with, "Oh my god, do I have the craziest thing to tell you," Ellie expected to hear of his roommates' latest transgression, a topic they frequented on their dates. Last month, Joel found his roommates having sex in the living room, and two months ago, he found a line of cocaine on the kitchen counter. A voyeuristic indulgence. That's what Ellie once called their rendezvous. They were eating oysters at a bistro that overlooked the East River, which was ridiculous because she didn't like oysters. Even more ridiculous was that she knew the conversations to be bullshit, senseless fluff. But the rose helped. It made her laugh, as it always did. So when Joel announced that Mark and Jeff had split, Ellie was taken aback. Yet she wasn't surprised.

"I don't think Jeff wanted kids," said Joel. "Mark did, but not Jeff." Ellie nodded and sipped her sangria, a summer's drink for a cool spring day. Dark clouds, pregnant with rain, were amassing in the sky. Joel looked at her quizzically, and she realized she hadn't removed her windbreaker. Joel, impeccably dressed in a blue oxford and white chinos, as handsome and poised as always. She, in her dowdy gray fleece and waterproof chelseas, very practical but not beautiful. Perhaps she should have done something with her hair. She threw it in a wet ponytail as she raced out the door ten minutes late, almost barreling into one of her neighbors. She glanced at the menu, remembering why she hadn't returned in several years. It was expensive, the portions conservative, and she was underdressed.

"I can't blame them for ending it," she said. "It takes a certain person to have kids. I was shocked that they were together for eight years, that they managed to last so long."

"I could never do children. I don't have the patience," said Joel while eating a slice of baguette. "Thank god my sister has two so my parents have grandkids. My mom told me to consider surrogacy or even adopt, but that's never happening."

"My parents gave up on the idea that I'll ever have any. I'm 36 and single, and in their minds, I should have a fifteen-year-old. Now, I don't know if I want them at all," Ellie said. But she had, at one time, envisioned motherhood. She was engaged at 24, back when the City felt fresh, before her youthful hopefulness matured into a lingering cynicism that now muted what was once a vibrant and colorful New York. On their first date at an Italian restaurant that was now long closed, she thought here was a man with whom she could have children. Even now, wisened after a dozen years, she knew it was a very good first date. He was handsome and successful—a fledgling hedge funder with a flat on the Upper East Side—and said exactly the right things. They both, for example, shared a mutual hatred of the Red Sox and preferred the Stones to the Beatles. And as the months passed by and the relationship grew more serious, Ellie began dreaming of a future in Connecticut near his parents, where there would be ample room and familial support for their children. She was disappointed when, two years later, the relationship dissolved.

"I just feel like we're on different wave-lengths," he said during the breakup. "We don't really know how to talk to each other." Three months later, he found someone on his wavelength—a girl as different from Ellie as possible—with straight, blonde hair, dressed in haute couture (or some cheap knockoff, more realistically), beautiful. Everything Ellie was not, with her ambitions, her curly hair that couldn't decide whether it was brunette or blonde, and her waist that stored the faintest of love handles that she would periodically touch out of insecurity. But Ellie moved on, and her priorities and expectations slowly shifted. She now felt fairly content with her life. She had a good career, one that blossomed after the breakup, and friends that stayed with her through the messiness of her twenties. And for her, that seemed to be enough.

Just then, a couple walked by, gay, she assumed, and trailing them a girl of five or so. The family greeted their party, another gay couple, who were already seated. The couples kissed each other on the cheeks then crouched to admire the girl's attire—a white dress decorated with roses and finished with a pink sash around her waist. A white bow framed her black curls, and her nails were painted turquoise. The fathers were the picture of polish and class; the girl, exquisite.

"I never really liked Jeff," said Joel. "I always thought he was pretentious. He's gorgeous, but still. Mark is such a sweetheart, too. He's just so caring and—," but his unfinished sentence hung midair as their food was served. A tuna nicoise salad for Joel, and a salmon and avocado tartine for Ellie. Joel looked at Ellie's plate and said, "Your sandwich looks good, but I'm trying to stay away from carbs." Ellie was mildly put out, sensing one of his usual covert criticisms. He continued, "Next weekend is my first at Fire Island for the year. You have to be ready for the beach, you know what I mean?"

"I get that," she said but didn't really. She looked at her plate with regret and, perhaps, resentment. But she knew how spartan Joel was when it came to food. She considered a piece of cake at their friend's birthday party a celebratory indulgence. He, a mortal sin. But while she cared about her diet, she wouldn't forego a slice of bread to attract stares at the beach. Nonetheless, she wondered if she should have ordered another dish, one that comprised less of flour and more of iceberg lettuce.

"Are you going on any more summer trips?" asked Ellie.

"I'm going to France for two weeks in August. One week at a villa outside Nice and another week in Paris. Mark and Jeff were going on the trip as well, but now, obviously, they're not." The waiter filled Ellie's glass with water, and she asked for another sangria. It was Sunday, and she had a long week ahead of her. Joel spoke of his itinerary—of jaunts through Provençal lavender fields and excursions to Avignon and Versailles. He always depicted his trips artfully and lavishly, and Ellie was always enchanted by his vision of the world. He was compelling, someone to whom she felt an irresistible attraction for reasons she hadn't yet known.

As he spoke, the little girl walked through the dining room, her hand enveloped in that of her father's. As she passed, women craned their necks and halted their conversations, bewitched by this site of uncommon loveliness. They then turned to their dates in hushed excitement, urging them to look, or rather, to behold. They would then talk of their futures—of the girls they would have and the clothes they would wear and how beautiful they would be. Amidst the tinkling of cutlery and china, Ellie heard their admiring chatter bounce off the white subway tiles—a quiet, joyful din.

Just then, Ellie had the sinking feeling that she had, after all these years, done something wrong. It was a subtle, nagging suspicion, one she felt every day, that was now palpable and strong. She felt she had somehow missed the mark. She wanted to say this, but only managed, "So you think that Mark and Jeff split because they had different ideas about kids?"

"There could always be other reasons, but maybe they just needed to move on. They'd been together for eight years. Sometimes people just grow apart," said Joel.

"That's true," replied Ellie and watched her avocado spread assume a brown patina. It began to rain, forcing people caught unawares to use whatever they had available—newspapers or jackets or backpacks—as protection.

"Yeah, they were unhappy with each other," said Joel, breaking their silence. "And sometimes you don't even know why you're unhappy. But that feeling is always there, always lingering in the back of your mind, and you often don't recognize it. You know something's not right, that something's off kilter. After you've lived with it for a long time, you do something. It's often not intentional, but you fuck up. It comes out of the blue to everyone, including yourself. All those years suddenly in smoke."

Jessica's older sister, Lydia, divorced her husband after an eleven-year marriage—a protracted and painful affair for everyone involved. Lydia called Ellie in hysterics on three occasions, uncertain and scared. She doubted that the children would cope well with the custody arrangement and was lost as to what their lives would be when the dust finally settled. Lydia lived with her parents for several months, unable to afford a place of her own. She had been a stay-at-home mom, out of the workforce so long she no longer had any employable skills. She and her children took over their parents' basement in Columbus, Ohio, sleeping on the sofa and a collection of air mattresses— an arrangement as chaotic as the rest of their lives. When Ellie finally asked her sister about the reason behind the divorce, Lydia's response was, "A marriage can't last if you're not really saying anything to each other." After pressing the issue further, she found out that Lydia had cheated.

For the first time in her three years of knowing Joel, Ellie understood what he said. His was one of those rare kernels of revelation, a deep mutual feeling you share with someone whom you least expect. It's the accrual of small griefs that amass over many years, calcifying into something too solid and too impacted to be dislodged. It happened to Lydia, and her marriage collapsed. And Ellie believed this was happening to Joel and her.

"Oh my god!" he said, interrupting her thought, "I have to get to spin. I promised Ben I'd be there."

"Oh," she said, blinking, "I hope you have a good workout." He failed to tell her he had another commitment.

"Ben is going to kill me if I'm late! And yes, I'll try to have a good workout. We'll talk soon." He blew her a kiss and left. She was disappointed that he hadn't blocked more of his afternoon for her like she had done for him. She then remembered that he had done this the last time they were together. Perhaps it was a trend. By now the rain had stopped. Alone at the table, she drank her sangria, now tipsy. She watched the passersby—some rushed to an appointment for which they were late. Others meandered, looking at their phones while their dogs pissed on piles of cardboard. The handsome family rose from the table and said goodbye to their lunch dates. The girl, not wanting to leave, showed her friends something on an iPhone while her parents gently coaxed her to put on her coat, a navy mackintosh with white vertical stripes. She stomped her foot petulantly but was eventually persuaded. The family was soon out the door, as lovely in departure as in entrance.

Ellie finished her drink and checked the to-do list on her phone, which was more exhaustive than she remembered. She felt a budding headache, the effect of too much wine on a body that was now closer to 40 than 30. Perhaps, instead of chores, she would read one of the long-neglected books on her nightstand, carefully selected though seldom opened. Yes, that was how she would spend her afternoon. It was Sunday after all, and her week was going to be a long one. She would buy a few groceries first and then she would read—a good compromise between productivity and pleasure. She felt a buzz in her pocket, a text from Lydia. Ellie settled the bill and walked out the door, feeling not quite good but also not quite bad. She rounded the corner and approached the subway. Another vibration, another text from Lydia. Instead of descending down the steps to a train that would whisk her to the Upper West Side, she kept walking. Surprising herself, she took out her phone and called Lydia.

About the Author:

A native of the Midwest, **Matthew Chacko** now lives in New York City. Matt earned his BA from Andrews University in Berrien Springs, MI and his MA from Syracuse University where he studied early modern literature. Inspired by his literary studies to help effect social change and render the world a more equitable place, he now works for an education nonprofit in the City while working on a collection of short stories.

NOT QUITE SO BLIND

by Thomas Heine

I have never experienced the sensation of sight, but I know a lot about it. I have an understanding of words such as bright, shades, black and white and colors, near sightedness and double vision. I know that sunrises and sunsets can be beautiful in their subtle hues and that staring at the sun can makes one's eyes burn. But I do not know sight itself, the way I know sound and touch, and I never will. Therefore I do not miss it as some might imagine.

I must have been about four before I realized that my ways of perceiving things were different from other people. One childhood incident remains vivid: I was "watching" television with cousins when they all began to laugh at something they had seen but I couldn't. When I got up to feel the television set they all shouted at me to get out of their way. I ran to my mother, tripping and falling down steps and landing on a wooden floor. I can remember the smell of the wood.

While being blind is not difficult if it is all you know, raising a blind child must be difficult for sighted parents. In retrospect I can see that my parents were not severe but merely overprotective. They worried that I would get lost in the world or fall victim to unseen forces. They thought I lived in darkness (I know what darkness is even though I have never experienced it). They kept me from playing with neighborhood children. I can remember longing to escape the prison of my house to be closer to their sweet tinkling voices. Whenever relatives or friends with families came to visit,

however, my parents never forgot to organize the Blindfold Game. At the time I did not realize that they had devised the game for my sake. All the players began in the living room. Then one was chosen to leave the room and return blindfolded. Meanwhile one or two of the others would retreat to the kitchen. The blindfolded one had to guess who had remained in the living room. Like everyone else I wore a blindfold, but unlike them I could always say immediately who was still in the room and where they were sitting. I remember the sound of their amazement. Of course at the time I couldn't explain how I did it.

My parents sent me to a school for the blind for several years. The teachers there determined that I had perfect pitch but also a serious learning disability for someone in my condition. I have problems with space. Most people without sight become very sensitive to the proximity of walls, large objects and furniture. They become adept at negotiating their surroundings after a short orientation. I marveled at the kids in my school who were able to race down hallways and up steps and who found their desks with ease. Sometimes I had to wander in the aisles looking for my place long after everyone else was seated.

I have found that the best way to live with my learning disability is to simply yield to it. While I instinctively try to remember my path through every new space (five steps, then two steps, then two more), I know that once I leave a room, its shape becomes vague to me and my mental picture of it unreliable. It is better for me to assume that I don't know where the next turn is or the next wall. I let people guide me explicitly or subtly.

When I moved into my apartment, I shared it first for several months with my half-sister Cheryl. She helped me learn my way in the rooms until I could get around without a stick. Then she moved out. I wanted to be on my own and I could sense that Cheryl was growing impatient with the burden of me. I am no burden to myself. I earn a living as a piano tuner and am good at what I do. It brings me in daily contact with new people and space is not a problem. I can easily find my way out the front door when the taxi arrives. I let my customers lead me to the piano and lead me to the door. I am not expected to get around in a stranger's home or remember the height of a table. I can relax.

During adolescence I began to notice that when I was with some people I felt strange things. A sensation different from hearing or touch that I thought was originating in me. I experienced different sensations depending on who I was with.

I had a boyfriend in high school. Todd was sighted and had a car and was very funny. I liked the feel of his hands, but sometimes with him I sensed emotions that seemed out of place, like giddiness at a tender moment or sorrow in the middle of laughter. And when he took me home to meet his family I distinctly felt something odd whenever his mother was in the room. Like bits of sand under my fingernails, her presence confirmed that I was perceiving these things in other people. Later when Todd was telling a joke on our drive home I sensed something I would call sadness, a soft depression in an otherwise hard flat surface. I asked Todd if something was wrong. "What are you talking about?" He answered sharply and although I could not see his eyes, I imagined them expressing surprise and discomfort. Soon after that he broke up with me, assuring me more than once that it had nothing to do with my blindness.

I made an attempt to talk to my parents about my confusing perceptions. I must have made it sound like a problem they couldn't solve because they insisted that I go to a support group

for the blind. I didn't need support. I needed an explanation or guidance. I found neither in the group.

I did not resist going to the group. On the contrary, at least initially, I enjoyed getting to know a new circle of friends. After several meetings, however, I grew restless. Although they talked about important things like careers and relationships, nothing they said gave me the impression that they had ever experienced other people as I had. Finally I asked if any of them had a sense beyond the standard five minus one. They had lots to say about sensing objects and feeling a person's presence, but I could tell that none of them really understood me. "It's like pressing against something you can't touch or hearing something that doesn't make a sound, like wood or metal..." The more I tried to explain, the more acute the sensations I felt became. Distracted by wave over wave passing through me, I stammered and then fell silent. I suddenly felt very blind indeed and very separate from them. I did not talk to anyone about my special sense for a long time after that. I concluded that people, sighted or not, did not understand me or did not believe me, especially since I am so clumsy, bumping into furniture and knocking over glasses.

I never felt the need for a man in my life any more than I long for sight. I can live by myself and with myself. But my attraction to Ed and his to me developed on our first ride together. Ed drove a taxi and aspired to be a songwriter. After my second ride with him he asked to take me out. I accepted. His voice was soothing and I perceived kindness in him, like a gentle stroke on my neck, and hope. We soon were spending all our free time at his place or mine. Although my apartment was the smaller of the two, I refused to move out. I could not bear the thought of being a stranger in someone else's space. And so Ed moved in with me.

Ed was the first person I felt at ease with when talking about my special sense. I made him promise not to divulge my secret for I had learned from experience that some people don't like to find out that I can know what they keep hidden from the sighted world. Ed was intrigued by my ability. Whenever we met people while we were out, he would always ask me afterwards what I had noticed in them. I tried to describe the sensations. "Like metal grinding in my hands...a balloon rising inside me...a tinkling bell I don't hear. I just feel the longing...something like a warm cloud." I don't think Ed always understood, but he never said stupid things like, "How can you know what a cloud is?"

Ed came to me with a song he said I had inspired. I was flattered, and when he played it for me I was touched. Even more than the song itself, the feelings I perceived in Ed as he played the song made me happy. He admitted that it still needed polish and some of the notes strained his range, but as he played I sensed in him an inner concordance, like bringing a string to the right pitch.

The first time Ed made plans to visit his brother in North Carolina, a six-hour trip over the mountains, I had a bad feeling. Every time he mentioned the drive, there was something like an unpleasant tightness in the back of my head. Finally I asked him not to go. "Are you sure?" he asked. I was only sure that I did not want him to go. "Perhaps I'm afraid to be alone." Ed called his brother and made up a story why he had to cancel the visit. From across the room he seemed to be holding my hand. Then on the day he would have left for the drive he ran into the room and said, "It just was it on the news. There was a rock slide. Took out a quarter mile of the highway. That would have been me."

After that Ed made jokes, like asking me first thing in the morning, "Do you have any advice for me today?"

I played along. "Yes. Get back in time to take me to the store."

"No predictions?"

"I predict that we both will be hungry tonight if you don't take me to the store." Ed laughed but I sensed disappointment, a soft grinding.

Whenever I enter a stranger's home I sense things about them. If the impression is strong, I make small talk to get to know them better. For example, if I feel something unpleasant, I try to cheer them up. If I perceive a smile in them, I let them tell me why. It gives me a

feeling of intimacy. If the sensation is too strong, it can distract me from my work and I have to ask to be left alone in the room. At one job I was nearly overwhelmed with despair. Reaching into an empty jar again and again, and having to feel the emptiness. The woman who met me at the door and guided me to the piano hardly spoke. She was not the source of the despair but it touched her as well. She deflected my attempts at conversation and went out of the room until I finished. The sensation persisted like a muffled moan behind a wall.

"I've got to go back there," I said that evening and asked Ed to drive me.

"Right now?"

"Yes."

"Call a taxi."

"I will if you don't take me."

My insistence convinced Ed, a curved line straightened.

"What are you feeling?"

"Intense anguish. I want it to be over."

"What are you going to do when we get there?"

"I have no idea."

Ed drove fast until we approached the house. Then I heard cars and a crowd. Ed left me in the car and returned a few minutes later.

"There was a murder. A murder suicide" He didn't know any details but I didn't want any. My sense of urgency had passed. There was nothing to be done.

"You should go talk to the police."

"Why?"

"Because you knew about it."

"I didn't. I don't know anything about it. Take me home"

Ed was affected by the incident more than I was. His initial sense of wonder at my feelings gave way to something else and he wouldn't let the incident rest. Didn't I care about the woman who was murdered? She was a stranger to me, just a name in the paper. I didn't even know for sure if the woman I met was the victim. She didn't let me near. Didn't I feel somehow responsible with the fore-knowledge? "No." I am an antenna that receives random impressions.

"Then why did you have to go back?"

"I needed to feel the relief."

"Relief?" Wood cracked. No gentle stroke on my neck. I know he stared at me and thought I was heartless. I felt the chill.

Just as every face is unique, so too is every person I encounter with my special sense. Most leave no lasting impression, but I know that at least ever since the Blindfold Game I can recognize individuals and distinguish them from one another. In a large group of strangers, however, I can only perceive the collective presence. I go to church sometimes to feel the serenity of hope and the purity of contrition. For that same reason I used to enjoy going with Ed to the writers nights at local clubs. Especially if the crowd was large, I experienced the intense swirling and crackling of ambition. Unfortunately Ed's inquiries into my perceptions became increasingly insistent, like needles.

"What did he think of my song?"

"I can't read minds."

"But what did he feel?"

"Nothing in particular."

Although my lack of sensation meant nothing, it added to Ed's growing self-doubts. And then there was the incident with Bret. When Ed introduced us and Bret shook my hand I felt a sudden – and exhilarating – spark in my spine. I foolishly asked Ed about Bret when we got home, and he became suspicious. Reacting to the grinding and scraping I assured Ed that he had no need to be jealous. Several weeks later news came that Bret had signed a record deal.

"You helped him, didn't you?"

"Ridiculous."

"You told him Roundtree was a good place to start."

"I was only repeating what I've heard you say."

Ed did not answer but I felt the chill in his silence. He thought I had given to Bret what I withheld from him.

When Ed made plans again to visit his brother I did not try to stop him.

"Don't you love me anymore?" Ed laughed out loud but not inside. I had to be careful how I answered him because whatever I said could be a prediction, adding more fuel to his fantasy.

"I'll see you when you get back," was the emptiest phrase I could think of.

"Yeah, in your special way." It was the first time he had said something so stupid. Dishes rattled in a distant cupboard. And there was something else I sensed, but I didn't know what it was.

Of the friends Ed brought home I like Kenny least. Something slimy and elusive. One evening Kenny stayed for dinner, and as soon as the table was cleared he and Ed began with the racing forms.

"When I told Kenny about you, he wanted to try this. It was his idea."

"His idea."

"Yes, but I agree. There's nothing wrong with putting your talent to good use."

"I can't help you."

"Should I bet on Breezeway?"

"No."

"Should I bet on Carumba?"

"No. You shouldn't bet on anything. Kenny, think of your kids. You can't afford to throw money away." I was a fool to think I could dissuade a compulsive gambler with words. Kenny went to the track and lost on every race.

"It didn't matter which horses he picked. He was going to lose."

"And you knew that all along?" Scratching, pointing.

"Now I know that I knew. I didn't realize that I knew at the time. It's not like that."

I could feel Ed's ignorance and disgust like the

pressure of overcoats under my skin. Increasingly he returned from jam sessions drunk and with bones rubbing against themselves. Sometimes he was too hung over for work the next day. One night he came home and said, "This is my latest." He played with clumsy drunken fingers and he sang off-key. The chorus was memorable. "She's a girl that watches them die. She watches them sink and won't say why." I know Ed meant to hurt me with that song but I only heard his frustration and sensed something else, slipping.

The next time I heard Ed drive away for the evening I went into a sudden frenzy. Without a plan or forethought I began pushing furniture in every direction until I had turned every room into chaos. Then I felt my way through the rooms. Again and again I went through the rooms. I tried to memorize the arrangements but of course I couldn't. Once I stepped out of a room, I couldn't pass through it again without groping. If I didn't move slowly, carefully, I would get hurt and suddenly the purpose of my frenzy became clear to me: the rooms now mirrored my relationship with Ed. Now he could see what he was doing to me. Concrete so that he could understand.

I fell asleep on the sofa, waiting for Ed to come home. I awoke to strong pulsing. The sensation was so strong that I thought it was coming from me. I heard Ed moving from room to room and the pulsing grew. When he reached me he shouted. The voice was angry and fearful and confused.

"What's going on? What's wrong with you?"

I tried to explain. "That is what you are doing to me."

"You've gone crazy."

"I can't move without bumping into something."

"Because you're blind, you fool!"

"But you can see." Every time I said that the pulsing intensified. But I could not keep the words back. "Look. What you see, that is what you're doing to me. Don't you see? Are you blind?"

Ed took me by the shoulders and shook me. I remained calm because all at once I knew that everything would soon be all right. Ed slapped me two, three, four times and with each I sensed ever more clearly that he was slipping into a pit from which he would never emerge. I wasn't afraid. As he slipped, I felt relief.

In the morning Ed was apologetic and offered to put the furniture back right. His voice sounded far away as if it were already receding into the past. I told him to leave everything the way it was.

"We can't live in a place looking like this."

"I can." I felt his confusion again, the same as last night, a gusting wind that kept shifting direction. What a mistake it would have been to move in with Ed. I would have been bound to him for the sake of a familiar space. I now knew I would rather move cautiously through rooms than have to be cautious inside. I told Ed he had to move out. He didn't argue. He apologized again but I felt him relax, not unlike the way Cheryl relaxed when we had our talk and agreed that she should leave. Like grass in the wind.

After Ed left I felt the absence intensely. Never again would I wake up in the morning and feel his glow. Never again would I recognize his touch from across the room. In moments of self-doubt I longed to hear his voice again. When I finally went to call him I tripped over a low table and crashed with it onto the floor. I remembered the overcoats and the pressure and the caution, and realized how relaxed I had become since Ed's departure. I got up from the floor knowing that I could survive alone and that it was time to return the rooms to some order. As I rearranged the furniture – something I had never been trusted to do – I made an unexpected discovery. I imagined I was merely bringing a terribly neglected piano back into tune. Each chair, each table or shelf was nothing more than a note. The final arrangement became a song. To be sure, it was a song that only I could perceive but afterwards I was able to learn my way around easily and on my own. For the first time in my life I had made progress with space. I thought that Ed would have understood my song of space but he was gone. He disappeared from my life.

To avoid the long evenings alone when the rooms were still and the human voices in the distance made me feel disabled and isolated, I began to invite friends over. It wasn't something I had done much. If they asked about the break up with Ed I told them he had left me at home alone more and more and we kept bickering. I never mentioned the occasion of violence. It had been so unlike Ed, and also I felt slightly responsible with the foreknowledge and with my subsequent sense of freedom. Apparently Ed had told stories about my special sense, the prediction of the rock slide, of a murder and of someone else's good fortune. Some of my friends had heard those stories, and while they agreed that I was better off without Ed, they also agreed with Ed that I had a gift. Eventually some returned to ask questions about themselves and their futures. The ground beneath some was shifting and threatened to crack. Even as I assured them that Ed had exaggerated my abilities, I could sense a balloon rising.

Some offer money but I don't take it. I cannot see their futures any more than I can see their faces. And I don't know anything except what I can't explain. When I think back on the incidents with Ed there are many good explanations. Coincidences. Misunderstandings. The unpredictable mystery of life. But people come to me now and I can not turn them away. I sit across from them sensing their hope and their expectancy and their fear, and I feel a stranger knocking on a door noiselessly somewhere inside me asking for intimacy. I open the door.

About the Author:

Thomas Heine wrote and staged plays in Nashville Tennessee from the 1980's until 2010. Recipient of the Tennessee Arts Commission Fellowship in Theatre in 2002, Heine teaches German at Middle Tennessee State University.

MY FIRST SOLE LITTLE LETTER

by Paweł Markiewicz

My first sole little letter Calling all ringing so beauteously-muse-like and winged like eternally gentle pinion of a melancholic harp

Dear valued mellow quaint readers-dreamers!

At 5.30 pm the meek time has come with the dream-full inception, so that a new flimsy Sturm and Drang period has begun (the second Sturm and Drang, to wit: the turquoise time). And I am spellbound therefrom simply. Such an one fulfilled miracle with a starry charm of a magic-full summer night has enforced in some fantasy. Any best poem from me and any glimmer of the philosophy from me haven't achieved that, but rather the most marvelous eyes of my cat such ghosts, in which the primeval ontologies of the antiquity slumbered in the lyrically Edenic way. The cat has looked at my dog plainly dulcet, what kindled a magical stark of time-philosophy and unveils spirit-like. These sparks aren't able to be blazing fiercely like a handful of Luther's flames, but they are glowing: tenderly as well as lovingly, in fine: muses-like as enchanted Apollonian moments, that touch deeply everybody's souls and that cherish a daydreams-wizardry everlasting zeus-like. And this cat is such a dainty dreamy herder of the infinite angelic philosophy and those cats from time immemorial have harbored primeval weird from Egypt.

From cat's eyes an eternity comes, which came along on my account at that early date At the moment i second era of Sturm and Drang is sparked, a primeval wild dream is freed and ready for the fantasy of the moon in the wonderful night.

Thee turquoise time – is sore contemporary created and alway internet-oriented. This melancholy-period comprises all poem in English from contemporary authors, who will write theirs most gorgeous poems from 1. July to 31. December 2019 and will publish them on sundry internet-pages.

Let this most gorgeous magic dream come true!

About the Author:

Paweł Markiewicz was born in 1983 in Poland (Siemiatycze). He published his English haikus as well as short poems in literary magazines, including Ginyu (Tokyo), Atlas Poetica (U.S.), and The Cherita (U.K.). Recently, he has published some poems in Taj Mahal Review (India) and Better Than Starbucks (U.S.). He has also published poems and and prose at Blog Nostics, to wit: short prose entitled The Druid. Paweł has published more than fifty German-language poems in Germany and Austria and three Polish-language chapbooks in Poland.

THREE SMALL WORDS

by Paul Lamb

Three small words. Just three syllables.

"Don't tell Mom."

What brother might say to brother, but less likely from father to son. Words calling for trust and, in the same breath, betrayal.

"Don't tell Mom," David had said, though cautiously, leaning toward Curt, his confidence barely above a whisper. Odd, too, since they were outside at a noisy intersection, rounding the corner where the old DX station once stood across from the hospital, where no one would hear their words and fewer would care. At first Curt wasn't sure what his father had said, but his next words clarified. "Not a word. It's just, I've been having this pain in the right side of my chest sometimes. When I run. Then it goes away. It's probably nothing. I'm seeing the doctor next month to get it checked. So don't worry."

Curt had been needling him earlier, urging David to join him on a run around the old neighborhood to see how things had changed since he'd moved away. But David had declined, suggesting their walk instead, then adding genially, "Though I guess running with a doctor is about the safest way I could do it."

"Does it hurt now?"

David paused their steps and took a deep breath of the cold air. "No, not now."

Curt, whose work often called for him to read between the lines, decided not to parse his father's murmurs, but he didn't forget them either.

His father, who had always been an elemental man, who for years had loaded trucks for a living, who had the physique of a man twenty years younger, who was, in short, invincible, had chest pains. Angina. What the doctor in Curt might reasonably expect, the son in him didn't want to believe. When had Dad become mortal?

It's easy to believe that your parents are unchanging, he knew. That they're static. But the better part of him knew that as long as they were alive, they were changing. It's only when they're gone that they truly become fixed.

"It's not right, keeping this from Mom."

"I know. But it's probably nothing. I'll talk to her after I see the doctor."

Curt had learned the toxic consequences of secrets, of unspoken truths, coming out to his father much later than he should have, or could have when he found, to his great relief, not a moment's hesitation in his father's love. But too many years of guarded silence by the son and gnawing doubt in the father had left their legacy, a chasm that remained difficult to span despite their love, and so the many gentle intimacies that father and son ought to be able to share were still too often strained and hesitant. That his father had shared even this much had surprised Curt, after the shock of it had subsided and he could reflect during their frosty walk around the old neighborhood. Was he scared; was that why he told him? Was it more than "probably nothing" but he didn't know how to say it? Was he trying in his measured, cautious way to open the door a little wider to his son? Or might he have said nothing at all had he not been chiding him?

As was often the case between them, opening that door did lead to a spilling of more words during their walk. Guarded and indirect, but potent with a meaning Curt knew he had to divine.

"I don't feel old," David had continued. "I don't know what that even means, really. I feel like I'm the same person living in my skin that I was yesterday, and last year, and even fifty years ago. The face in the mirror doesn't change much from day to day." A few strides of reflective silence that Curt didn't want to interrupt so his father would continue, which he did.

"But I have noticed something lately. My memories are old, if that makes sense. I was thinking about a conversation I had with my buddy Jon and it wasn't last month or even last year. It was more than twenty years ago. I can't be sure if what I remember about my life is true or if I'm just remembering it the way I want it to be. There are a lot more years behind me than in front of me, and I won't be able to do all of the things I've always imagined I could. Not because I physically can't so much, but because there isn't enough time. I probably won't ever go back to Italy with Mom, though we talk about it as if we could any time. I won't get a 5K PR anymore. I won't read all of those books Kelly is so eager to talk about. I mean, that old beater could be the last truck I ever own. Does that make any sense?"

"Sure," Curt conceded, focused as he was on people at the beginnings of their lives, pausing not only at such unexpected musings about this other end of life but that such musings had come from his father, a man Curt sometimes had to remind himself was more complex than he seemed behind the simple mask he never fully shed before his son. Yet such aging concerns weren't unique to David, Curt knew as he unwittingly did his best to banish them. He considered offering some confident, clinical dismissal, but he was interrupted before he could speak.

Not far ahead the bells of St. Luke's tolled the late afternoon hour. When they had first moved to Richmond Heights, Kathy had dragged younger Curt there, and even David on rare Sundays, but only enough to persuade her far-away mother that she was still "practicing." David waited for the bells to finish, their resonance to fade before speaking again.

"There's going to be a last trip to the cabin. I'll come home one time, put away the gear, wash off the grit, scratch the chigger bites, and it will be the last time; I won't make it back. I won't know it when it happens, but I know now that it will happen. I never used to think this way. I guess that's hard for a young person to understand." He was silent for a few steps, giving Curt the chance to speak, but no words came, so David continued. "I have to make choices now. I see that. I can't do all of the things that before always seemed out there, available. I'm not getting frail. That's not it. It's more that there just isn't enough time left to do everything. I need to start being selective." Another few steps, their gloved hands shoved deep in their coat pockets.

Their feet had taken them as far as the bridge over the interstate, a demarcation in Curt's youth that his bike rarely took him across — though he had once gravely announced to his parents that there was another Sunset Avenue across the highway, that the street where their home sat had been cut in half — and it was a demarcation neither man felt inclined to cross that Christmas afternoon.

But something uneasy stirred inside Curt now, something visceral that predated his medical training and existed well before the protective sarcasm he had cultivated for as long as he could remember. Why had his father mentioned the cabin? Or rather, the unpleasant concept — yes, the reality — of a final visit, of an unthinkable time when David Clark would never again return to his cabin? If there was anything holy in Curt's universe, it was the cabin and his father's immense presence there.

He had no words. Nothing glib. Nor anything clinical or comforting to offer his father. Curt suddenly found that it was he who needed soothing as they took turns kicking the same stone down a sidewalk in the neighborhood where he had grown up.

"Not soon, certainly," Curt mustered.

David let the words lie between them, unclear what his boy's reference was.

"You're going to wear those new chainsaw chaps Santa brought a bunch of times when you cut firewood at the cabin, Dad."

On task now, David said, "And these fancy new gloves Sprout gave me." He held his hands before him. "That sure is a bright orange!" Accustomed to leather gloves that he'd wear until the fingertips wore through, and would then toss in the fire, the fancy work gloves his grandson had selected for him would need to prove their worth around the cabin. He gave a muffled clap. "Didn't get the new chainsaw I was hoping for though."

"Mom said you have to pick that out for yourself."

"Still my birthday coming up in March."

So, back to the warmth of the house on Sunset, where Kathy had been indulging Clarkson – all day in his pajamas – with treats and unstinting attention and had extracted from her grandson the promise of at least one postcard from his upcoming trip to the Bahamas with his dads. And where Kelly still savored his wistful astonishment at a family that lived and loved so unlike what he had known. And where Curt could retreat for a time from the unwelcome, discomfiting thoughts of his father's mortality.

David had spoken no more of his mild complaint or his reluctance to run, having steered their conversation to an upcoming trip to Kansas City to see Kathy's mother and his own plan to skip out and spend the weekend at the cabin after dropping her off. "They'll be more relaxed without me around," he'd said and by which he meant – and Curt knew – that Kathy's mother had never fully accepted him as her daughter's husband.

That alone, Curt thought, could be enough to cause heartache in a hale, stoic man. His clinical side was already hectoring him, urging him to discover what ailment his father had that made his chest hurt sometimes on a run, because if he knew, he could make it right. Maybe his dad had mentioned it because he really wanted medical advice. Why else share such a personal concern with his son, which too rarely happened, when he hadn't even told his wife? Better to tell a doctor about something that might be nothing than to alarm the woman who loved him more than anything? Except that the doctor also loved him.

And because of this, what was Curt's next move? He wasn't a gerontologist; he was a pediatrician. What did he really know of his father's physical life? He didn't even know the name of his dad's doctor. If he dared to speak to his mother, would he be violating a patient's trust? He didn't think he had any HIPAA constraint in this, and perhaps there were some obligations even greater. But how could he begin to make a diagnosis – if that was what he was being called to give – based on a few whispered and then dismissed words?

Because it was asked of him, Curt didn't speak of it again during his visit. Christmas gifts were marveled at, including the bag of marbles Clarkson treasured most, and Curt saw with new and startled eyes the stethoscope David had given the boy, urging him to have a listen to the family heartbeats. Old stories were laughingly shared with Clarkson. Cheer was enjoyed in moderation, Curt noted with watchfulness, but then his dad had never done anything in excess. Curt witnessed no shortness of breath. No hand to chest or sudden grimace. No lapses in conversation, beyond the reticence Curt had always known in his father. There were no cryptic glances between David and Kathy, but then, she didn't know.

When their long Christmas day came to an end and it was time to leave, Curt made himself say "I love you," but only at the last moment and only into David's shoulder as they hugged briefly at the door, Sprout and Kelly already waiting in the running car with their holiday loot. It was the best he could summon and he felt a failure.

Then he was gone.

But the three small words remained. And what felt now like a duty nagged at him.

Curt did, however, have a place to begin whatever it was he felt he had to do: an old photograph of his father as an infant. Scribbled on the back were the words "Our Davey. Healthy again!" Some affliction in his infancy, at a time when he couldn't remember and those who could were long gone, might be playing its hand now. It was not much, but it was a start that a pediatrician could work with.

It could have been anything, of course. Or nothing. He'd seen plenty of children present with ailments both common and surprising, but mostly common. Most were treatable – most were not even all that serious – and most children would fully recover. Have healthy lives with no memory of their little bout, just as his father had no memory. So what might a long-shot, long-term affliction be that could creep up on his father more than half a century later? Myocarditis from a lung infection? Pneumonia? Whooping cough? A host of other, more exotic assaults on the infant's body in the darker days of medicine? Think horses, Curt, not zebras. Surely they had vaccinated the boy. Nonetheless, he wanted to find some moment, some event, some thing in the past that could be blamed and attacked and conquered rather than admit that his father had been mortal all along, was now simply getting old, and had a finite number of days as all men do. That he wouldn't be around for Curt forever.

And how could he find this thing? No formal medical records were kept for that long. The state didn't require it and the files of some family doctor's office from decades past – not that he could ever hope to learn who that might have been – would have long since been shredded or burned or simply carted off to the dump.

And, no, Curt would not allow himself to assure himself that, had his father's sickness been severe enough, his parents would surely have explained it to him when he reached an age able to understand. Unlike, say, a peanut allergy or a limb foreshortened by a bad break and thus always in mind, his affliction might have been, once defeated, gladly left in the past. His grandparents might not have even known how severe it was, just as Curt couldn't know that it wasn't.

He was without further resources, except perhaps one more. In David's tidy basement, with whitewashed walls and a floor kept swept whether it was needed or not, stood an entire wall of metal shelves filled with neatly labeled storage boxes, just as a man who managed a warehouse would be expected to have. Was it possible that in there, amidst what little had been salvaged from his grandfather's lifetime accumulations and from all of Curt's own fun and folly, was a thin, brittle envelope containing little Davey's medical records?

But if what he sought was there, would it be any of Curt's business to see it? Did he have any right? Or should he just push past such inconvenient ethical concerns and push ahead, impelled by his love? For too long he had been an aloof, inadequate son; was this his karma then? That when he and his father truly needed to bridge the gap between them, his father might not be around much longer?

Yet here he was again, with a new secret he had to keep, one only grudgingly shared with him, and one that he knew could easily fester as an infected wound might, which, perhaps, is what it truly was. Whatever else Curt may have been doing all of those years keeping his big secret, he was also giving his father an example of how it was done.

By the time the three got to their condo, Curt had dismissed his doubts about both the illegitimacy of his interference and the very real fact that occasional chest pains might not be diagnostic of anything serious at all. What he felt instead, all that he could feel, was urgency. Little time, less information, a reluctant patient, a doctor outside of his field, and a son desperately wanting back into his father's life while there was still time.

The car wasn't even fully unloaded before Curt had his plan worked out. He would return to his father's basement, on a day and an hour when he knew no one would be home, and search the boxes for what he wasn't certain even existed or that would tell him anything worth knowing if it did. Such were the wages of his love.

And if he were asked, if his father, so meticulous in this thing, noticed a slight shifting of his boxes, how would Curt explain his trespass? That he was looking for his race medals to show Clarkson? Or that he needed an old textbook? Or his own medical records? But would he lie to his father? Would he do that?

He needed to enact his plan soon. How could he revel on a beach, indulge his son and his husband and himself in mild hedonism, with such a question nagging at him? More importantly, how could he allow his life to go on without first doing everything he could to ensure that his father's own life would go on? Whether his obligation was to himself or to his father, Curt didn't know and didn't pause to analyze.

His opportunity came soon enough. Only days after Christmas, Curt found his chance to visit the silent basement of his childhood home one afternoon when no one was around. He'd even taken a cab so his car wouldn't be parked out front for the duration. He ignored the evidence that what he was doing must be wrong if he needed to do it with such stealth and walked silently through the house, not turning on any lights or touching anything, descending the basement steps carefully so they didn't creak and be heard by people who weren't even there.

And it was only here, in the farthest, deepest corner of the little house, that Curt finally pulled the chain for the bare-bulbed ceiling light before the wall of boxes. The mechanical click seemed to echo throughout the house.

Were there a hundred boxes before him? More? Was his mission too massive, too daunting to accomplish? Where in all of this might a single fact be, a single fact that could explain everything or explain nothing, or that might not be there at all? Worse, what else might be waiting for him in the boxes? What other things might he not want to know? One visit would not be enough he saw, and the starting gun had fired.

Curt studied the boxes, labeled with neat, hand-written notes and organized, he soon found, in sensible groupings. Three boxes marked TAXES with successive years bulleted beneath. INSURANCE PAPERS. HOUSE REPAIRS. MOM'S ART SUPPLIES, which gave him a pang, understanding that she'd never really had the chance to pursue her talent. A box labeled SWITCHES AND SOCKETS AND STUFF. One that read simply ITALY, which he guessed held his parents' keepsakes from the trip he and Kelly had sent them on. Then came a series of boxes about

him. CURT'S SCHOOL PAPERS. CURT'S TEXTBOOKS. CURT'S AWARDS. CURT'S TOYS. Even several boxes labeled CURT'S BABY CLOTHES. He touched these labels lightly as though to absorb some essence from them. Anyone could take it as evidence that this child Curt was truly loved, but this was something he had already known. He felt tempted to abandon his search and delve into Curt's life instead.

He didn't, but a part of him soon wished he had as his search grew more perilous. What could three boxes opaquely labeled CABIN possibly contain? What was there to know about the stolid, old family cabin, which had always been there and always would be, that he didn't already know? Were there secrets even there? Did he want to find out? But that too, he reminded himself, would have to wait for another time.

Soon he was among boxes simply labeled DAD, and while this seemed more likely territory, the number of them gave him pause. His search of just these couldn't be completed in a single visit, not unless he stumbled upon whatever it was he sought — and he wouldn't even know what it was until his eyes fell upon it — in the first box.

And quickly he saw his misconception. This DAD in the first box was not his father, David, but his grandfather, Joe. Curt thought that all of this, or at least much of this, had been lost in the move, when they had yanked his grandfather from his tiny but familiar house and put him in an even tinier, less familiar apartment, which hastened his decline, though none of them was ever willing to acknowledge this. It had been during this culling that Curt had come upon the photo of his infant father. "Our Davey. Healthy Again!" The haunting photo that, he realized, had steered him into medical school then and taunted him now as a problem he might never be able to fix.

He made a quick survey of the dozens of remaining boxes. "C'mon. Give me one that says DAVID'S COMPREHENSIVE MEDICAL HISTORY — FROM BIRTH TO PRESENT. ALL IN PROPER ORDER AND EASILY SEARCHED." No such box awaited him. But nor were there any that suggested they were close to what he was after.

Nothing labeled DAVID or MEDICAL PAPERS or even DAVID'S STUFF.

Where to begin? How to begin? He struggled with the immensity of his idea. The futility of it. That he might never find what he wanted or worse that he might not want what he found. And that he had discovered a deep well of sneakiness within himself to attempt such a thing. Why couldn't he just discuss this with his father, outright, the way two adults should be able to? The way a father and a son who really did love each other should be able to?

"It's not there."

Curt froze. The wall of his father's boxes was before him and his father's voice was behind him, but he didn't dare turn. He was caught with his hand in a box and he felt five years old.

"Are you sure?"

"Yes, I am."

Time to come clean. Curt turned to face his father.

"Then tell me."

"Tell you what, Curt? That the medical records from my childhood are gone or that I have no idea what it was that nearly killed me as a baby?"

"I'm that transparent?"

"You're my son. I guess I can understand a few things about you."

So it was not to be had. That thing in the past he wanted to throttle and defeat. There was to be no simple solution to an ageless problem. It was out of his reach. Out of both of their reaches. As clear and as final as that.

"I don't want you to die, Dad."

"I know, Curt." He smiled. "I don't either."

And with those three words, the man who was never good with words, spoke exactly the right ones. Curt threw himself on his father and cried, "I love you," then dissolved in his embrace until the two of them felt like only one person.

About the Author:

Paul Lamb lives near Kansas City but escapes to his Ozark cabin whenever he gets the chance. His stories have appeared in Aethlon, Foliate Oak, Magnolia Review (nominated for a Pushcart Prize), Halfway Down the Stairs, Little Patuxent Review, and others. He rarely strays far from his laptop.

THREE

by Keith Hoerner

To Clara: Regarding Your Critique

You shared your writing with me. An extension of friendship, like a handshake. More like the reaching out of hands with the chance to be held – or swatted – open palmed. Sharing… emptying pockets to reveal hidden things among the embarrassment of collected lint, is a dangerous proposition. Your shadows merged with mine, achieving the density of darkness that brings on the dawn. How can I thank you? For selflessly taking my hands and guiding me to an unknown resting place within the pages of you. I spoke in an attempt to reciprocate. My words: sandpaper to your beach of memory.

One of the Seven Deadly

She holds two swords of societal success. Her career of achievement, her marriage of love realized. Nice house, nicer car. The look men look at – even her husband. Meditative dreams on summer days under a comforter of cool breezes. Still, one regret reflects the swords' sharp edges. Cut her caesarean style – deep as you like; take out the child she cannot carry… his son. The single thing she cannot give him. Justice, she feels, is not in the cards for her. She seeks to be satiated through gluttonous eyes. Where are her maternity clothes, the infant boy she must steal?

Black and White Aren't Colors

I paint you by numbers, capture your features one by one… from the fair Irish skin; to the coal -black hair; to the rich, ruby lips; and the fiery-, emerald-green eyes. I reach for the palette of paint and thrust my brush like a mop into a bucket and swish it around. The color washes your face with only shades of grey. The numbers on the canvas do not add up. I am left only with a monotone portrait of shadow and sadness. Betrayed, my grip clenches. I see, I know your colors. I see, I know your lack of them.

About the Author:

Keith Hoerner, lives, teaches, and pushes words around in Southern Illinois.

ELIZABETH PETTIGREW

by Richard Bader

She opened the door before we could knock, in a long silver dress and hair the same color, scarlet lips framing too-white teeth. "How awfully kind of you to come!" she said. That's how I felt, awfully kind.

"Mrs. Pettigrew?" Andy said.

"Used to be," she said, laughing, a smoker's laugh. "I've reverted to Chandler. But yes—I am Elizabeth's mother. Call me Cassandra. Come, follow. Elizabeth will be thrilled to see you."

She led us down a hallway into a cavernous room of stone and dark wood, a glittering chandelier hanging over a rectangle of couches and chairs where people her age sat, the women in dresses that were variations of hers, the men in blazers and khaki, like it was a Gatsby-themed costume party. We had come straight from work, exchanging lifeguard swimsuits for shorts, T-shirts, and flip-flops. My ancient Jeep sat in the circle driveway behind two shiny black BMWs and a silver Audi, and Andy's motorcycle, which he and Tara rode up on.

"Everyone," Cassandra Chandler said, "Let me introduce Elizabeth's friends from the pool." We hand-shook our way around the room while Cassandra handled names and connections. "My sister Helen Merrick and her husband, Richard. Elizabeth's father Stephen Pettigrew and his new wife, Angela. And Rachel." She raised an upturned palm in the direction of a woman standing by herself looking at pictures on a fireplace mantel.

"The wiccan," Angela whispered to Stephen, but loud enough so everyone could hear. Helen Merrick giggled. Her husband rolled his eyes, but grinned. Rachel was younger than the others, somewhere between their age and ours.

"And of course you know Elizabeth."

She materialized in a doorway, her white dress stark against the dark of the space behind her. It's weird seeing someone all dressed up you're used to seeing in a bikini. She tucked a dark brown curl behind her ear with one hand, smoothed the front of her dress with the other, and stood there, slightly hunched, like she was waiting for permission. "Hey," she said. She waved an apologetic little wave. We did know her, but not all that well. Her invitation had surprised us.

"What's everyone drinking?" Stephen said.

***

He made us gin and tonics and the four of us took them out onto a porch overlooking the hillside, the city skyline in the distance, dark clouds building over it. No one said anything for an uncomfortably long time.

"So this is where you grew up?" Tara said, because somebody had to say something. The house was huge and made of stone. It sat like a castle on top of the hill.

"The Pettigrews built it," Elizabeth said, in a way that made it sound like the Pettigrews were somebody else's family. "I'm mostly at my mother's now. My father is about to develop it. Houses on the hillside. Turn the mansion into condos." I'd noticed a backhoe off the side of the road on the ride up.

"You have brothers and sisters?" Tara asked, meaning, to fill up such a huge house.

"An older sister. She died when I was five."

"Oh!" Tara said. "I'm so sorry. I didn't…"

Elizabeth said it was okay, and no one knew what to say after that. From the other end of the porch came the sound of a match being struck. Rachel, out for a smoke, silhouetted against a purpling sky.

"I feel like a slob," Tara said after a while. "We didn't know everyone would be so dressed up."

"It's for me," Elizabeth said, badly faking a southern accent. She spun ballerina-style in front of us, coming to a stop with one hand on her hip and the other, holding her drink, raised high. "It's because I am a debutante. Ready to come out into the world. And so, world, here I am." She spun again, stopping with her arms flung wide, then curtsied, spilling some of her drink as she did so. We all laughed. It was so unlike her. At the pool she mostly sat by herself and read a book, and maybe swam a few laps when she got hot.

"Are we early?" Andy said, meaning, where's everyone else?

"No," Elizabeth said, a forced lightness in her voice, but the word gathered weight as it hung there in the humid air of the porch. There would be no one else. The three of us, who worked at the pool where she spent her days, who barely knew her, were her best friends in the world.

Her father appeared in the doorway. "Anybody hungry?" he said.

Tara took Andy's hand. Elizabeth came up beside me and hooked her arm around mine. We followed her father inside.

Steamed crabs lay in piles on a long table covered in butcher paper. Plastic tubs held ice and expensive beer. Richard Merrick made a show of demonstrating how to eat a crab.

"Good lord, Richard, stop," his wife said. "It's Baltimore. The children know what to do with a crab."

They asked us about schools. Tara and I had just graduated from high school. "From Cathedral," she told them. I said from public school, then felt like an idiot for saying it that way. Andy said he would be a sophomore at Goucher. The Merricks told us about their sons at Princeton, one who played lacrosse and the other who rowed crew. The men offered advice on majors, wiped their hands with paper towels, and gave business cards to Andy and me. Tara took Andy's from him and pretended to study it, covering it in crab spice and eliciting a smirk from Rachel. Tara had been accepted to M.I.T. for the fall.

"What do you think about the meteor?" Cassandra said, changing the subject.

"Oh, for Christ's sake," Stephen said.

"Meteor?" Andy said.

"It's been all over the news. They say it will come the closest to Earth of any in a thousand years. And if their calculations are off by just a few degrees…" Cassandra raised her eyebrows, implying apocalypse.

"Maybe it'll dig my foundations for me," Stephen said, and he and Richard laughed.

"I think we should prepare for it."

"How, exactly, Cassandra?"

"By saying what needs to be said, though for the sake of our guests, Stephen, I shall refrain from that this evening. By doing things you would regret not doing."

"Like trying to be a lesbian?" Stephen said. There was silence, then the sound of Rachel's chair pushing back. She got up and left the room.

"Let's see," Angela said, quietly, but loud enough, "witch. Rhymes with…?"

Elizabeth took a wooden mallet and smashed a crab claw on the table, sending pieces of shell flying. She got up and left. The three of us sat there for a few seconds, not sure what to do, then excused ourselves and followed. We found her outside on the stone steps of the porch. She wiped tears off her cheek with the back of her hand as we approached. At the far end of the porch I could see the red tip of a cigarette where Rachel stood smoking. Lightning flickered in the distance, trailed by the low rumble of thunder.

"It's all my fault," Elizabeth said.

"Elizabeth…" Tara said.

"We used to have a playhouse, back in the woods behind the house. We could spend whole days there."

"We…?" I said.

"Me and Katie, my sister. One day we're in the playhouse and Katie says she's going to take a nap. We did this all the time—sometimes pretending to take naps, and sometimes actually falling asleep. There was a small bed we mostly used for our dolls, but if you cleared them off and curled up, you could fit on it. Anyway, she falls asleep. I stay there for a while, and then go back to the house because I have to go to the bathroom. When I come back, the playhouse is on fire. It's a big fire, all around the base, with flames taller than I am. I yell for Katie but she doesn't answer. I want to go in and get her, but when I get close the fire's too big. So I run back to the house to get my father. My mother is out somewhere. It takes forever. I'm going through the house calling for him and screaming and crying the whole time. Finally he comes out of an upstairs room we never use. By the time we get back to the playhouse it's engulfed. He hooks up a long hose from the house and starts spraying. Eventually a fire engine comes. But it was all too late."

"Jesus," Andy said.

Tara moved next to Elizabeth on the step and put an arm around her shoulders. "Elizabeth. You were five years old. It's not your fault."

"For my birthday that year my mother gave me this crystal or prism thing that would catch the sun's rays and turn them into rainbows. I hung it on a tree branch outside the playhouse. It made all these beautiful colors. It was a sunny day. They think what happened is that the sun's rays got magnified when they went through the prism and set some straw on fire near the base of the playhouse. Katie and I put

it there. We made a little stable for our toy horses. Anyway…"

"It's not your fault."

"When the fire engine came there was this woman standing around I didn't recognize. I didn't know who she was or what she was doing there. It was years before I understood that she had been in that room with my father." Elizabeth stared out at the driveway, as if living it all over again. "And now here we are," she said.

At the far end of the porch Rachel's cigarette carved a glowing arc as she flicked it into some shrubbery. She went into the house and came back out seconds later with her purse. "I'm sorry, Elizabeth, but I've had it with your horrible family," she said. She passed us on the steps, went to the Audi, and drove off.

"I'll bet she put a curse on them," Andy said as we watched her drive away. This was Andy being Andy, trying to be funny, to lighten the mood.

"Rachel's okay," Elizabeth said, meaning, enough with the witch jokes.

The storm hit, and we watched it from the porch, cat-scratch lightning and cannon-fire thunder, the rain coming in diagonal sheets. When it passed the skies were clear, and we were far enough from the city that the stars managed to put on a modestly impressive show.

"We should go before the next one," Andy said to Tara. We all walked over to Andy's motorcycle. He ran a hand across the seat to wipe off of some of the water.

"I can get a towel," Elizabeth said.

"We're good," Andy said, meaning he didn't want her to do anything that involved going back into that house.

"I'm glad you came," Elizabeth said. She hugged Tara and then Andy. She didn't try to apologize for anything. She and I stood there and watched Andy's taillight disappear down the hillside.

"Come with me," Elizabeth said. She took my hand and led me around the side of the house.

We passed a woodpile covered with a tarp, which she grabbed and headed off along a path into the woods. We came to a small clearing, a meadow maybe twenty yards across. I wondered if this was where the playhouse had been, but I didn't ask. I could imagine Elizabeth and her sister coming here when they were little, doing whatever little girls did. She spread out the tarp, dry side up in the wet grass, and we lay there on our backs, holding hands and looking up at the sky.

"We have to lie here until we see a shooting star," she said. Through the tarp the ground felt cool against our backs.

"There!" I said. It hadn't taken long. I squeezed her hand and she squeezed mine in return, and we stayed there, lying on our backs, looking up at the sky.

***

It was late when I said I should go. We walked to my Jeep, which was the only car left in the driveway. The house was silent. We hugged, and then I kissed her. I thought about what her mother had said, about saying things that needed to be said, but I couldn't for the life of me think of what I needed to say.

"See you at the pool," she said, and I said, "Sure," and I wondered if everything would just go back the way it had been.

Andy and Tara didn't show up for work the next day. I was a little pissed, because that meant I would have to do everything—the chemicals, the trash, and guard the pool the whole day, and the forecast was for hot and steamy.

Elizabeth came in the afternoon, and walked over to where I sat in the guard chair. She had big sunglasses on, but I could tell she'd been crying. "What?" I said.

Andy's motorcycle had slid on a wet patch going down the hill from the house, throwing him and Tara off the roadway and into some large piece of machinery, and that was where they found their bodies in the morning.

About the Author:

Richard Bader makes his living helping non-profit organizations tell their stories. At other times he likes to make up stories of his own. His fiction has been published by the Piltdown Review, the Burningword Literary Journal, Rkvry Quarterly, and National Public Radio, among others. He lives and writes in Towson, Maryland.

FINDING KRAMER
by Ruth Deming

Five or six years ago, in a private message on Facebook, Joyce told me that Kramer was a bag lady in Boston. It seemed improbable but two other people from our hometown in Shaker Heights, Ohio, validated the message. For a while, there were sightings of Kramer in Boston, but then she disappeared.

Now, at last, I had the opportunity to find her.

Are you familiar with Shaker Heights, Ohio? It was and still is an affluent integrated community on the outskirts of Cleveland, which had many nice well-built brick homes built after "The Good War," as the Second World War was called.

The principal was Mrs. Alice van Duesen, a pioneer in education. She would visit every single classroom at Mercer Elementary and encourage each and every student to do their best. Years later, our annual alumni report boasted the usual – doctors, lawyers, real estate developers, rabbis, business owners such as the Bobbi Brooks Apparel Company and the famous Ratner Brothers, great philanthropists.

What's that Jewish saying? "Help one person and you save the world."

Kramer was in my homeroom. She and I called each other by our last names. We were rivals on the outdoor hockey team – ground sticks, ground sticks, ground sticks – hit! And every other sport we played together.

Black men who had served their country with distinction came home but there were no jobs for them, unlike their white counterparts. Many of them took their own lives. They were familiar with weapons, so it was easy for them to use. Others turned to one of the easiest ways for American blacks to make money: selling drugs.

My late father, Harold J. Greenberg, had a large apparel operation downtown on Euclid Avenue, and the word was, "If you're a hard worker, go interview with Mr. Greenberg."

I worked for Dad for a few years. We would drive through terrible neighborhoods, rife with ramshackle homes, crack houses, abandoned houses crushed to the ground like sardine cans.

"In our family," said Dad, "we believe in equality." Many survivors of concentration camps worked at Majestic Specialties. He told me to watch for the little blue numbers tattooed on their arms.

I'll never forget the smell – even forty years later- of walking into The Arts Craft Building on Superior Avenue. It was a combination of old wood, lubrication from conveyor belts, and an old lumbering elevator for freight – boxes upon boxes of blouses and sweaters. Dad let me choose a lovely white shirtwaist monogrammed with LLG, Leah Lynn Greenberg.

He was proud of me when I married a Jewish man, Herb Weisberg, and we had two fine children, Elisa and James. Herb, who worked very hard at his insurance agency, died of a massive heart attack after the children were grown and had kids of their own.

Finally, there was no excuse. I must find Susan Kramer.

I was no longer young and had retired from my job as a librarian. I'd moved into a small condo, with only two bedrooms. In my study, light poured in during the day. A small bed with a lavender coverlet was ready for me when I took one of my frequent naps.

Specially built blond shelving contained books of every kind. Two shelves were devoted to history books, including the book I had written, "Apparel Companies in Cleveland, Ohio." People still ordered the book on Amazon. I was inordinately proud of getting a few hundred dollars a year of royalties. Yes, Alice Van Duesen would have been proud.

I asked no one's opinion of traveling to Boston to find Kramer. I didn't want to get into an argument about the perceived dangers of finding her.

From my book shelves, I took down an atlas of the United States, then turned to Massachusetts, and finally the city of Boston. With a yellow marker, I highlighted several pages around Boston. My destination.

Slipping on my purple back pack — purple is my favorite color — I waited outside the condo for Uber.

"Good morning," I said, as he came out to greet me. He gave a little bow and said, "Abdul is my name." He paused a moment and as if to answer my unasked question, said, "Originally from Iraq."

Immediately I wanted to apologize for ruining their beautiful and historic country, but I said nothing.

"May I sit up front?" I asked.

"Of course," he said, with his sibilant S's.

After sitting on the comfortable seat of his gray Kia, I said, "In my retirement years I am free to go anywhere I please. Are there communities of Iraqis in America?"

"The Windy City, so unlike our home country, has a "Little Iraq," at least that's what I call it. My cousin and his family live there. They are not rich, like they were in Erbil, but they are grateful for their new home."

I pictured a small townhouse with a lovely red Persian rug and a bronze-colored coffee urn.

As we drove Abdul regaled me of the wonders of his country.

"Before the soldiers and that bad man, Mr. Bush, destroyed my country, many thousands of years before him, we had famous monuments that were destroyed by armies, what for, I do not know."

I looked at his face, his profile. This is the face his wife saw. Her photo was on the dashboard, wearing a colorful head scarf.

He enumerated the treasures of his country, as if he were reciting the alphabet.

"The Colossus of Rhodes, the Lighthouse at Alexandria, the Hanging Gardens of Babylonia."

"And I, Mr. Abdul, am hanging my head in sadness. God makes and we destroy."

I am what they call "A Jew of the Heart," which means a nonbeliever. I must confess I am proud

of not needing a god to use as a crutch, to make things right for the terrible inhumanities since

humankind roamed around in caves.

At a rest stop, we got out to stretch our legs. I opened a thermos of Dunkin Donuts coffee and

drank a couple of sips, and ate half of my egg salad sandwich on rye.

Back in the car, I mentioned his beautiful wife — "Yes, Sarina, is a beautiful woman" — and then I told him about my friend Susan Kramer, who had disappeared.

"Such problems, the whole world over," he said.

"Have you any idea where she might be?" I asked, almost in a whisper.

"You must find out where the homeless people are," he said.

"Ah, yes," I said. "Their encampments."

He dropped me off and my credit card automatically paid Mr. Abdul.

I waved goodbye as I nervously looked around what must be "the encampment." Susan Kramer,

I thought. I will find you. I will save you.

It was a fine April day with a few clouds moving slow as an old woman in the sky.

Settling my back pack over my shoulders, I forced a weak smile as I walked among men and women sprawled over a vast acreage, as if they were at a picnic. Focusing on one woman, I saw she had missing teeth like a Jack-o-lantern, and her long dark hair was filthy. How do you get used to this, I wondered? Well, you can get used to anything, even Auschwitz.

I wanted to see if I could find Kramer myself, before asking a single soul.

"Herb, my darling," I prayed to my late husband. "Help me find Kramer." Often when I drove my white Toyota Corolla, I would ask his help in letting me merge onto the interstates in Philadelphia, and in one daunting case, "Please, Herb, don't let that cop car be for me," as the siren screamed to wake the dead.

Too bad I didn't have a cane to steady myself as I walked through what seemed to be dozens of people. These were God's people, made in his own image. After half an hour, I was tired. I looked down and saw a young man, handsome with mounds of black hair.

"Sir," I said. "May I sit down?"

"Do whatever floats your boat, Ma'am. I sure don't care." His head rocked back and forth. Stoned, I figured.

A woman sitting next to him offered me a joint. Yes, a stick of marijuana. I looked at her, thought a moment, and then inhaled, coughing afterward. I remembered how to do it from my college years at Drexel University,

where I got my master's in library science. Prudes we are not!

Was it giving me insight, as I inhaled and exhaled? I hoped so.

Standing up shakily, I traveled along in my pilgrimage.

"Susan Kramer. Susan Kramer," I called through the throng of noise that you find at a rock concert.

A couple of people heard me.

"Oh, you want Dr. Kramer?"

I couldn't answer I was so surprised.

"She's up there in that little shack."

Hoisting my backpack on my shoulders, I walked up a slight hill and came to a small tumbledown wooden shack.

My knock on the door was greeted with "Come in!" spoken in a midwestern drawl like my own.

When I entered, I saw a woman all in white. Her thick white ringlets fell over her shoulders. She

was wearing a white nurse's uniform and cushy white nurse's shoes.

I blinked my eyes.

"Kramer?" I asked. "Is that you?"

A broad smile played over her lips.

"Greenberg!" she said, laughing and grabbing both my hands. "I'd know you anywhere. Ready for some tennis?"

We laughed together and I collapsed on her soft green sofa.

About the Author:

Ruth Z. Deming is a poet and short story writer who lives in Willow Grove, PA, a suburb of Philadelphia. Her works have been published in Mad Swirl, Literary Yard, ShortStory,net and other writing venues. She runs New Directions, a support group for people with depression, bipolar disorder and their loved ones. "Yes I Can: My Bipolar Journey" details her triumph over bipolar disorder. A mental health advocate, she educates the public about this treatable illness.

DOWNTOWN WALDOS

by Mark Massaro

Riley, my pot-dealers girlfriend, arched her body over the enormous yoga ball in front of me while I sat on their couch as he weighed out quarter bags on a digital scale. A small tattoo of a Gemini symbol peaked out from her hip and a live Rusted Root album shook the walls while Riley's yoga DVD played on mute. She breathed in slowly, and out slowly. Piles of unfolded laundry sat in most chairs, one with an ashtray on top, and the smell of wet dog soaked the air. They left me alone earlier and I grabbed a nugget from the table and let it fall into my cargo short; it wouldn't be noticed missing. My eyelids were quite heavy, but my eyes remained solely focused on Riley.

Riley and Cambridge, "like the city," he'd say, had been together for two years. Upon their first meeting, she invited him to live with her because he had just gotten out of re-hab and didn't want to move back in with his father and step-mother. They were decent people, I assumed, but it was clear that they were in that weird phrase that fifty-year-olds go through: suddenly dancing at clubs, drinking, and relentlessly flirting. Apparently, years ago, Cambridge got deep into painkillers, and not in the fun way. He got arrested and made a deal to go to a rebab facility in Florida, coming back with long-hair and a Buddhist. He preferred to wear his bathrobe and used a carved walking stick. I met him through a mutual friend, Rabbit, who I went to high school with. His real name is Rahib, but everyone called him Rabbit. I asked Rabbit if he knew anyone to get pot from, because my guy was out of town,

and within an hour, Cambridge showed up at my work, with Riley peering from behind him.

"You Jack?" he asked.

"Yup, you Rabbit's buddy?"

"Yup."

"Good to meet you," I said. His long brown curls were tucked behind his ears and he had a Dr. Phil t-shirt on. I worked at a restaurant chain, that I prefer not to name at this time, as a server. The manager was a drunk and would come and go as she pleased so we took full advantage of the lack of attention on us. Most of us stole from the register by ringing up the order and hitting "No Sale." Then we'd give the change and the customer would leave. It was a group effort and we'd share the nights earnings. We'd drink and smoke bowls in the walk-in, even have sex, depending on who you were working with that shift. It was a common rule to not date someone that you worked with, but we seemed to operate on the exception to that rule all of the time. And that led to a lot of workplace drama.

Riley sat in an empty booth and Cambridge met me at the jukebox, asking, "How much you need?"

"A quarter?"

"Ninety. It's usually a hundo but Rabbit said you're old friends."

I gave him a hundred anyway as a goodwill gesture and he told me to keep him in mind for future needs. "Absolutely," I said. I gave him an empty to-go cup with a lid and he went into the bathroom, coming back a minute later. He handed me the cup and I put it in my locker, glancing quickly at the full plastic bag inside. It stank, so I spilled some bleach down the nearby sink to mask the smell.

Riley caught my eye, waiting patiently in the booth. She had a smirk like she knew an important secret that no one else was privy to. Her dark messy hair fell across her shoulders and her bright blue eyes were striking, even from feet away. A shimmer from a small stud on her nostril flashed as she stood, she didn't have on a bra, and I began to wonder what her story was. Why was she dating a dealer? Does she accompany him on all of his runs? Or did I interrupt their date night? And why was she so content with herself?

I got his number and Cambridge and we shook hands. On their way out, Riley turned to me and said, "Hi," and waved.

"Hi," I said, and then she was gone.

The moment of attention was nice. I had recently broken up with by one of my coworkers, Becky, who I still had to work with. We made a deal that whomever broke up with who had to quit but I had been working there first, so I figured that working opposite schedules would be acceptable. I had been trying to get out of that relationship for a while, but she wouldn't let it happen. There were threats of suicide, desperate phone calls, and some mild stalking. She finally slapped me in public because I was five minutes late, so I walked out of the bar. She followed me into the parking lot, flailing her arms and screaming. I got in my car and locked the doors. She started kicking the side. She got behind it, blocking me in, so I drove straight over the parking slab and straight home. She showed up a few minutes later, beating the doors, screaming my name.

The next morning, my car was completely covered in deep key marks. I'm talking the roof, sides, hubcaps...everything. I was numb with anger.

I couldn't prove it to the police because I didn't have a photo of her doing it, while holding up an I.D. and the day's newspaper. I called her but her lack of surprise made it clear that she was expecting the call. She denied it.

The next day at work, I left my pillow and pajamas in clear view in my backseat when I parked in the employee section to make it look like I spent the night out. I watched her look into my car and proceed with an emotional breakdown right there. She sat in her car for ten minutes, crying, her head down in her hands. The only reason that I felt bad was that I didn't feel bad. I wasn't used to feeling nothing for someone, especially after dating them, but she pushed, and pushed, to the point that I just didn't care about her anymore. I was relieved to get some distance.

She was fired a few days later because of bringing drama into the workplace. The cops needed more proof, but my boss knew better. She'd been a ticking time bomb for a while.

Months passed, and I failed out of college again. I'd sign up for the courses, with full intention of attending, but the Hawthorne Pub was on the way, and they had an early bird, two-for-one domestics. I began hanging out with Cambridge and Riley more. At first, it was just for the connection and pool parties, but I slowly found myself going over just to see Riley. They had a small house on a cul-de-sac, and his backyard had a large pool house with a stocked bar. A rope-swing hung from a tree that we use when jumped from the roof into the pool. Rabbit would be there most of the time and I started going over more and more. It became normal for people to head over once they were out of work, usually showing up in uniforms complete with nametags. It wasn't too long until Riley and I would start sitting alone together while Cambridge smoked cigarettes outside or went on 'drives.' I've never pursued a girl in a relationship, but most of the times that I went over, Cambridge sat in front of video games for hours. It was only natural that Riley and I would sit together, the neglected children of the dealer.

She was a reiki instructor at the Yoga Nook on Buckingham. Her parents were divorced. She said that her father would sit in his car in the driveway when he got home from work for hours, talking with his mistress on the phone. She and her sister would sit in their bedroom window and watch. Finally, the father left the family and moved in with his girlfriend, leaving the mother an emotional mess and the daughters with the classic absent father syndrome. Her sister was a few years younger than her but, Riley told me, she slept with over fifty men by the time she was eighteen. Two of them ended up in jail: one was a minister and the other was her high school gym teacher. "Yikes," I said.

"I know," she said, "Right?"

Riley went in the other direction. She immediately moved in with her friends and became the responsible one, trying to better her situation. She worked as a receptionist in lawyers offices and put herself through college and reiki certification. Her mother ended up committing fraud and stealing her identity, putting Riley in an insane amount of legal issues that won't go away. Her mom ended up in prison somewhere in Georgia, last she heard.

Riley and I started hanging out more and more. I went with her to buy shoes. I cooked supper for her and Cambridge. I dog-sat for them when they attended a three-day festival. I waited with her at the DMV when she needed to renew her license. Sometimes, we'd get stoned and sit on the floor, opposite each other, with a CD of Tibetan monks chanting Ohm. Our knees would touch, and she'd run her hands over my chest and head, never actually touching but close enough for me to feel her warmth.

My days were split between working and seeing her. I made it a point to buy a quarter twice a week from Came, as to be a good customer and welcomed visitor. I always brought a twelve-pack of beer, in an attempt to always-welcomed. It was an awkward situation to be in; I was courting a girl with her boyfriend directly beside her. If Came was aware, he didn't show it. His focus was on dealing and video games.

One day, Cambridge was playing a live shooter game. He was threatening someone through his headset. I sat on the couch, stoned as ever, watching him and waiting for more people to show. He began to tell me about how he was getting pot and edibles from California through the mail from his old rehab buddy.

"Dude," I said, "you're going to get caught. That's ridiculous."

"No, no," he said, "no. My guy makes the shipments look like a care package from a mom to a son at college. He packs socks and DVD's, random shit. He scoops out the center of a peanut butter jar and packs it up," he said, making the scooping motions with a cigarette between his fingers," and covers the top back up. Reseals it. Dogs don't pick up on anything through that peanut butter, bro. Believe that."

"Be careful, man."

"I will," he said, adding, "Don't tell Riley."

Riley walked into the room, holding a basket of laundry, asking, "Wanna help?"

"Sure," I said.

We went to their bedroom, the walls covered in rippling tapestries and nag-champa burning in a mushroom incense holder. Ani DiFranco played on a CD player and a Bob Marley poster was duct taped to the wall next to framed black and white photographs of Riley doing ballet. "When was this?"

"High school. I did it professionally since I was young."

"You look great," I said.

"Thanks," she said. "I was so wild back then."

"Me too. It's a miracle I'm not arrested by this point."

"Too bad we didn't know each other in high school," she said, "I probably would have fucked you three times a day."

"Jesus Christ," I said. "Don't tell me that."

She shrugged and laughed. I wanted her, and she knew it. After she said it, I knew that I'd replay those words in my head over and over again.

She started separate piles on the bed. I folded the towels. Her bras and throngs were tangled together and I worked my way around them as she smirked.

"I wish Came helped me with laundry. He's always playing those stupid games."

"Yeah, I noticed. After we smoke, I end up just watching him until I snap out of it and find you."

"I wish he was more like you sometimes."

"I'm like me," I said, smiling.

"That song "Don't Go Away," by Oasis always reminds me of you. I hate when you leave. It gets so boring here." I broke away from our shared gaze and tried to hide my excitement, but she knew what she was doing. "I love that song, "I said. "The end riff always reminds me of the end of some movie when someone's running through an airport to stop someone from getting on a plane."

"I know, right?"

I've never tried to steal a girlfriend from anyone, but it was becoming more difficult to remain passive in the situation. The more I couldn't have her, the more I wanted her. The more time I spent with her, the more inappropriate it got.

That night, more people came over, carrying cases of beer over their head, joints tucked behind their ears. Cambridge called his pool the "liquid crystal abode," and we walked around in his robe with his walking stick. Their front yard looked like a parking lot most nights. The backyard had plenty to do: beer-pong, frisbee, cornhole, and the rope swing. People started to assume that I lived there too, and I tried my best to avoid telling people how badly I wanted Riley. Rabbit showed up and I drunkenly put my arm around him and said, "Dude. I can't take it. I want her so bad. She's driving me crazy."

"Dude..." he said, "Stay clear of that shit. That's nothing but trouble."

"No, no. There's, like, something between us. You don't know what she says when we're alone." I knew how the words sounded as they left my mouth, but it was the truth.

"Dude," he said, "I've known her a while. A lot of guys fall for her." But I wasn't hearing it. I explained the situation in more detail. He listened patiently, caressing his dark beard occasionally and mumbled in agreement. "Just like Sadie Greene, dude."

"Bullshit," I said, "that was 6th grade."

I grabbed another beer from the cooler, and jumped off the roof into the pool, trying to get Riley's attention. She swam over to me, holding a drink above the water, and climbed on my back. Cambridge saw but he just smiled and continued to dance around. I didn't know what to make of it. If she was my girlfriend, I'd have a problem with me, but maybe I'm just considered family? Maybe I'm no threat to their relationship at all?

She started kissing my neck as I held her against me. Riley smiled, wrapping her arms around me, and began to drop slowly down my front, staring up to me, before disappearing underwater and swimming away. What...the...hell?

Rabbit and I walked down the road to the Mexican-themed bar to continue our debate.

The next week was Halloween and I picked Came and Riley up to grab costumes at the Party City. He sat in the back, texting, while Riley and I danced. The three of us decided to go as Where's Waldo? since it was the only decent costumes left and, as Came said, "Three Waldos are better than one."

Riley's sister, Jessica, showed up as Catwoman. I was surprised that they didn't look anything alike and Jessica seemed to not be interested in me at all. Every time I looked at her, I couldn't get the knowledge of her sexual history out of my head. Riley and Jessica disappeared into the backroom to change, but before they left, Riley whispered into her ear and Jess looked immediately at me. I smiled. Rabbit appeared, dressed in a sexy cop outfit, and he, Came, and I sat on his front porch and drank some beers, watching the holiday traffic pass. Came said, "You should try to hook up with Jess. She's a fun chick."

"I don't know," I said. "My last girlfriend was intense. I'm taking a break."

No one said anything until Rabbit finally broken the silence, talking about his baby that he never gets to see. Came told us that a new shipment from California arrived and he'll roll up some blunts when we got back later. Apparently, it was a super-rare strain of bud that tastes like Christmas.

"You gotta be careful using the mail, dude," Rabbit said.

"I am, I am, but I've been thinking about another avenue for more cash-ish, and I want you two involved," he said, lighting up another cigarette, his hair falling in this face. He leaned in closer, adding, "Trains."

"Trains?" I asked.

"Yup," he said. "And baby food jars."

"Baby food?"

"We see the country. Go from here to New York. My guy out there is well-connected. We can charge double down here, and the college kids will pay anything." He waved his hands through the air, as if adding a wonderment to his proposal.

Rabbit scratched his head and said, "I don't know, bro. I'm pretty busy."

"I'm down," I said, without hesitation.

The five of us got a taxi to the downtown area for the parade and to barhop around. There were costume contests and a zombie-walk. Music was everywhere. White flashes from strobe lights pulsated over crowds. As our taxi rounded the corner to drop us off, drunken partygoers yelled, "Waldo! I found him!" I didn't consider the added attention we'd receive because of our costumes. Rednecks dressed as Captain America and jocks dressed as Superman would bearhug me, yelling triumphantly, "I found him!" I stood at a urinal, noticing that I'm a Waldo, standing between Darth Vader and a zombie biker, all facing the wall, peeing together. Darth looked at me and said, "Found ya."

"Yup," I responded, giving him a thumb up with my free hand."

The five of us would lose each other randomly throughout the night, but Riley and

Came would be easy to spot. The eye can naturally find red and white caps and shirts within a mess of grey ghouls, bloody zombies, and slutty scientists. I saw some work friends and drank with them. Becky, the ex, was a sexy flapper-girl and she had her arm around a guy dressed as a 1920's gangster. We saw each other and I pretended like I didn't know her. It reminded me of a few times when we'd see her ex'es in public and they'd walk in the other direction. I thought it was weird at the time, but I ended up becoming one of them too.

I found Riley dancing to "The Monster Mash," on top of a stage at an Irish bar. She made small cuts around her shirt, revealing small windows of flesh. Smoke machines poured white mist throughout the crowd and the floor was sticky with spilled mixers and booze. On the large teleprompter, It's the Great Pumpkin, Charlie Brown played as the music echoed over the crowd.

"Jack!" she screamed, jumping into my arms from the stage. Pulling me in closer, she yelled into my ear over the loud music and crowd, "Let's get out here," and took my hand, dragging me through the celebrating mob.

We ran outside together, holding hands down the metropolitan streets, hearing an occasional, "There's two of them," and we fell into a small alleyway between two brick buildings. She laughed and put her arms around my neck, looking up at me while we made bullshit statements, like, "What a great night," and, "I need another drink."

She ran her hand over the top of my belt buckle, and looked up at me, asking, "Have you ever thought about kissing me?"

I didn't hesitate a second before moving in. Months of pent-up frustration came to a head. I kissed her, hard. We made out for a few minutes, and I moved my hands along her sides. She pulled me closer by my belt, which made me crazier. A first kiss with someone is always exciting because of the unknown. She bit my bottom lip gently and ran her tongue over it after. There we were: two Waldo's kissing in an alley. It was exciting.

She pulled away first, putting her hand up against my chest, and said, "Stop. We can't."

I said, "Right. I know," and started kissing her neck, behind her ear.

She whispered "Stop" again, and I did.

We walked back into the crowded area, costumed people still yelling and raising their drinks at us. Before we left the alley, we agreed to keep the kiss a secret and to never tell anyone, but her lively demeanor changed to serious contemplation after a block. I smiled and tried to stay in the moment, hoping that she'd leave Cambridge for me as soon as possible. I figured that she had a rough week ahead, but I wanted to remind her why I was the better choice, so I danced and laughed, hoping that my carefree mood would appeal to her.

But it happened.

I kissed my dealer's girlfriend.

The five of us regrouped in the middle of the packed street. A skeleton band was on stage playing "I Put a Spell on You," and Cambridge and Rabbit were dancing in the front, spilling the contents of their red solo cups. Jessica was near, grinding on a guy dressed as Harry Potter.

"Let's go home," Came said, putting his arm around Riley.

She hugged him, staring off at nothing.

We all took a cab back to their house. Riley and Jessica went to bed immediately after taking selfies in the bathroom. Rabbit, Came, and I sat on his front porch, smoking a blunt, while watching the chaotic traffic.

"My dude in Cali got popped...so no more mail," Cambridge said," I'll have to find another source. Idiot got pulled over with a pound in his trunk, so he's done."

I said, "That's horrible." At the time, it genuinely surprised me that I was able to sit with him after I kissed his girlfriend not too earlier. I guess that I compartmentalized the entire situation over the past few months. I was knowingly trying to steal her, so some slight social conditioning, on my part, must

have occurred. I just hoped that we could still be friendly after she left him for me.

He said, "He is a big boy. He knew what he was getting into when we started it up." He and Rabbit continued to talk but I couldn't help but repeat that phrase in my mind. The disconnection from the reality shook me. Would he say the same words if I got caught with this "train" thing?

I went home that night, collapsing into bed with a fulfilled smile and an excitement in my gut, and passed out.

It finally happened.

Finally.

The next morning, I found a text from Riley that said, "Remember. Don't tell anyone," but Rabbit also texted me to call him immediately. On the floor, my damp Waldo outfit reeked of smoke and booze. I slowly sipped some coffee and called him.

"Dude," he said. "Riley told me about last night."

"Shit," I said, rubbing my face, "We agreed to keep it a secret."

"She's going to tell Came today. You better say something first, bro, so you don't look like a complete asshole."

"Dude, she started it."

"Well, she's saying that you just randomly kissed her and she's upset about it."

"That's bullshit." I was too anxious to explain the full context, so I kept repeating, "It was her."

I called Riley.

She answered, sounding like she didn't sleep at all last night.

"I'm at work and can't talk long."

"Riley, are you going to tell him?"

"Yeah," she said, "I can't look at him without feeling bad. He needs to know."

"We agreed to keep it a secret. Whoever doesn't tell him looks like an asshole."

"He's my boyfriend," she said.

Apprehensively, I paced around my bedroom, rubbing my messy hair, and asked, "Are you going to break up with him?"

She laughed like I never heard her do before, and said, "No! Of course not."

"...but...what about us?"

"Are you serious? You kissed me, dude. Oh, did you seriously think there was something between us? I have a boyfriend, Jack...who is your friend, supposedly."

"Riley..."

"God, this always happens," she said. "Did you actually think that I was going to break up with Came for you?"

"I don't know."

"...you got to deal with the consequences of your actions."

I said that I was sorry and hung up, feeling beyond defeated and utterly confused. Did I make it all up? What else would "Have you ever thought about kissing me?" imply?

I texted Cambridge to meet up with me for breakfast, on me, and waited for him in the parking lot of the taco place on 4th and Cedar. I sat there, repeating what Riley said to me over in my mind. Of course I thought that something was going on between us. My heart broke seeing this side of her, hearing her abundantly capable of being so distant and cold. My chest hurt so deeply that tears welled up in my eyes until I let out a pained wail.

I sat crying, with my head on my hands, until he showed.

I got out and said, "I have to talk with you about something."

"Let's wait until we're inside," he said, and with that, I knew that he knew.

Sitting at a booth, he said, "I know it's unlike you to behave like this. I know you're a good guy, so that's why I'm not going to beat you ass. It's so out of character of you, that I'm chalking it up to being wasted, but Riley is pissed. I'm pissed."

"But..." I said.

"Just don't do it again and it's settled."

I weighed the choices. I could tell him my side of the story or let it be.

"Okay."

I accepted to the role of a drunk asshole to squash the drama. I wasn't about to present my case to him which would make her yell at me more. She was better at it and I was brokenhearted. Imagine me pleading with her, repeating, "...but you asked me if I ever thought about kissing you?" and her laughing it off or saying that she never said that.

"Plus," he added, "This isn't the first time. Two other of my friends tried to kiss her."

I bought Cambridge's breakfast burrito, and another quarter from him, and left. I continued to cry at the traffic lights, in my keyed-up car, holding my chest in emotional agony. Everything that I thought about my relationship with Riley was wrong and I would look like a jerk to everyone at that house.

I continued to hang out there, despite what happened. It was the social scene and, despite what happened, I wanted to leave the group on good terms, so I showed up, bought pot, got drunk, and acted as normal as possible, but was always on my mind. I slowly started to go over less and less. No one ever mentioned it, but I got the feeling that people knew. Riley and I never talked about what happened. I took the full responsibility for the kiss and, even though I was quite drunk, I remember what happened.

I remember what really happened.

A few months later, I heard that Riley left Cambridge for Rabbit.

About the Author:

Mark Massaro received a master's degree in English Literature from Florida Gulf Coast University with a focus on 20th Century American Literature and also profound personal respect for 18th Century British Literature. He is an English Instructor at two universities, teaching Creative Writing, Composition, and Literature. When not reading or writing, he can be found at concerts, watching his stories on the couch, or in his black Chucks at a bonfire in his home state of Massachusetts with his friends. His works have been published in Literary Juice Magazine, The Pegasus Review, Jane Austen Magazine, and The Mangrove Review. His happiness is being next to his wife, with their son in his arms, and their golden retriever curled up nearby.

THE CLIENT

by Catherine Lin

The first thing Debbie noticed when Hilaria Wigotsky got into her car, was that she didn't look like most clients. From the thick, blonde hair elegantly coiled on the back of her head, to the gaudy, golden belt cinching a waistline impressive for Wigotsky's age, she appeared better suited for hiring a chauffeur than a contract killer. Yet, Debbie waited to hear it straight from the horse's prettily painted mouth before she shooed good business away. Murder-for-hire wasn't the most lucrative field to be in, believe it or not.

Debbie pushed the hair from her face, her edginess making her impatient as she did so. The damned hairdresser had given her bangs, and now she looked like a sock puppet. No one would take her seriously now. Sighing, she turned the key in the ignition, pawing at her stubborn hair as it encroached on her field of vision again and listened impassively as the decrepit taxi sputtering to life. The decommissioned cab's top light was perpetually dark, and the 'five' in the 235 embossed on the side had chipped away until it was a backwards 'C'. In spite of its wear and tear though, it was a meeting place that provided a suitable enough alibi should this woman not be who she said she was. Ms. Wigotsky looked like the most contact she'd had with a taxi was watching them streak down Edgewood's streets from her penthouse window. And yet, she still got in.

"Where to, ma'am?"

Debbie checked her rearview mirror carefully, before pulling out from between two cars and heading down North Quantock Street. Edgewood bustled at this time of day. There were so many potential witnesses to their secret, little cab that there might as well have been none. Like whispering a confession into a stampede.

Ms. Wigotsky cleared her throat daintily. "5610 Brown's Hill," she replied.

It sounded practiced, as if Ms. Wigotsky were reading from a script, and Debbie heavily suspected that there were few things the woman said or did, that wasn't.

Debbie's husband devised the passphrase. Being a former Navy cryptographer, he'd been enthusiastic in his creation of it. '5610' referred to May 6th, 2010 – the date he and Debbie had gotten married, while Brown's Hill had been a juvenile attempt at humor. 'Brown's Hill because the target will shit their pants by the time they realize what's happening,' Arroyo had said. Debbie thought it stupid even then but laughed anyways. Her targets would never realize what was happening; by the time it would've occurred to them that they were being stalked, a bullet would be firmly lodged in their brain. That was a stipulation of marriage though, wasn't it? To laugh at your husband's dumb jokes? To love him in spite of them?

"Ms. Wigotsky, what can I do for you?"

"I have a job for you, if you're interested."

"I picked you up — " Debbie's glanced at Ms. Wigotsky " — I think it's safe to say that I'm interested."

The corner of Hilaria's mouth twitched, and the human gesture looked strangely wooden, like an old, pulley system was hoisting the muscles in her face up, instead of her own nerves. Debbie wondered if she'd had work done. Debbie had an eye for those types of things; her instincts were sharp even when not behind the scope of her Tango 51 rifle. A woman of Ms. Wigotsky's standing could probably afford plastic surgeons akin to modern day Michelangelo's opposed to some butcher with a scalpel. Ms. Wigotsky's true age had been revealed in the background check Debbie had asked her client liaison to run when she'd originally come to her with the lead. Not much surprised Debbie anymore, but finding out Ms. Wigotsky was approaching the cusp of forty had done it.

"Who's the job?" Debbie asked, turning right again. One block was usually enough time to get all the pertinent details of a hit.

"A good...friend of mine, shall we say — " Ms. Wigotsky's eyes narrowed " — is trapped in his marriage and it's causing some trouble for us."

Debbie raised her eyebrows. "Your friend's marriage is troublesome for you?"

Ms. Wigotsky studied Debbie for a moment, as if deciding whether or not she was truly so stupid. The implication of her irrelevance to the matter offended her, but the flaccid remark rolled off Ms. Wigotsky's hairspray-stiff locks like water on duck feathers.

"Anyways, everything you need to know is all in here," Ms. Wigotsky said as she unclasped her purse – snakeskin, Debbie would venture – and procured an envelope. "Name and address. Those are all you need, correct?"

"A picture would've been helpful," Debbie replied, her voice sharp. Thankfully, the customer was almost never right in her field of work. "And I'll be taking my seven-thousand up front." She pulled into the drop off lane of the Vertex Baron Luxury Apartments. With lavish, gold carvings around the entrance and gaudy, vintage lights, the drop off area itself was so dazzling, no one would bother sneaking a peek at the envelope's contents as Debbie unfurled it in her hands.

"I think you'll find that a picture isn't needed in this particular case," Ms. Wigotsky said with an edge to her voice.

"Payment is, though."

"Certainly." Ms. Wigotsky smiled curtly before dipping a manicured hand back into her bag.

Debbie scanned the stationary in her hands. It felt thinner than computer paper and had 'Hilaria C. Wigotsky' stamped front and center, in prominent, shimmering letters. The pencil scrawled across looked bizarre in its jagged plainness.

"Hang on, this address is the old distillery — " Debbie cocked an eyebrow " — Ms. Wigotsky, did you lure the target there?"

"Does that matter?"

Debbie frowned. Maybe you should just do the job yourself then.

"It does to me," Debbie explained. "If the target has already been lured, then I have to act right away. Not to mention, if you've lured them to a place that'll appear suspicious to investigators, and I'm traced back to said place, I'm already as good as caught."

"Why do tomorrow what you can do today? Carpe diem," Ms. Wigotsky replied, flippantly.

"And what about being traced back to the distillery?"

A car honked behind them, but neither women paid it any mind.

"Well now, that seems like it should be of your concern, rather than mine, but let's say — " Ms. Wigotsky tipped her handbag forwards, so it fell open for Debbie to see. It reminded her of a certain fantastical nanny's bag; looking at the stacks of cash bound inside, Debbie could hardly believe it could hold so much. "An additional thousand for the added risk?"

Debbie sighed, exasperated.

"You're just like my husband - you don't seem to take 'no' for an answer."

Ms. Wigotsky's smile was wooden.

"With all due respect, I'm not terribly interested in your personal life. Take it or leave it," she said, and Debbie felt an abrupt cold front hit her.

Tossing a look over her shoulder, Debbie scanned the windowpanes for wandering eyes. A car honked again, louder this time, and Debbie noticed the doorman look in their direction.

"Sure, fine. Just... get it out of sight, will you?" Debbie hissed.

"Don't worry Mrs. Pinto, I'm a careful woman," Ms. Wigotsky reassured.

Debbie caught the tail end of Ms. Wigotsky's serpentine smile, before the woman opened the passenger side door, and stepped out. Debbie watched Ms. Wigotsky's form disappear behind the large brass doors. Blood, like ice water, coursed through Debbie's veins. Through the churning, dense flow, Ms. Wigotsky's voice cut through the slap of water and into her brain with the precision of an ice pick.

Mrs. Pinto.

Dusana knew better than to use Debbie's real name when hunting for clientele, and in the past twelve years she'd been at it, never had a client learned her name before. Shaking off ice chips, Debbie put the cab into drive, and flicked on her blinker again. This time, she'd continue straight down Quantock and onto the main expressway heading towards the northmost edge of town.

Clenching the steering wheel like she had talons instead of hands, her knuckles were bone white as she thought of how Ms. Wigotsky had gotten her name. It was sort of like in the exorcism movies, where a demon was expelled using its name – hitmen worked much the same way. Knowing her name meant a potential prosecution. Debbie would have to finish the job today, and then look into moving again. Arroyo would be surly; he hated moving, given how extensive the process was for them in their line of work. New names, new social securities, even a new face in her husband's case. Their relocation guy wasn't cheap, and if she were being honest, both Arroyo and Debbie were rather fond of his current visage. A

strong brow, nose, and jaw, with prominent cheekbones carved out in the warm brown of his skin. Admittedly, he was more handsome than when Debbie had married him. While Arroyo himself would never admit it; his pride would be bruised to part with that winning smile.

Debbie glimpsed the instructions scrawled onto Ms. Wigotsky's note once more before she shoved it into her jacket pocket. She could burn it later, along with the purse — after she'd dealt with the cash. She pulled into a vacant, unpaved lot at the address. Despite the nondescript vacancy of the desolate location, the distillery was somewhat of an urban legend in Edgewood. An age-old tale of another fat cat Icarus who flew too close to a gold sun that shone over the most exquisite of island vacations, and plummeted into bankruptcy. The distillery slumped along Ann Causeway in decay like roadkill rotting in the gutter. She left the taxi parked haphazardly in the corner of the empty lot and gravel crunched underfoot as she made her way to the old Pear Systems Distillery. It sat like a large, concrete, skull staring blankly out from its long forgotten grave. The building loomed large and square before Debbie, with tin and concrete for cartilage. There were but two windows spaced out like eyes at where she'd guessed the second floor would be. The entrance and its shut doors made the building look as if it were baring its teeth at her, and graffiti tattooed where Debbie imagined the left cheek and temple might've been. She met its stare readily as she approached the entrance. By the looks of it, the padlock on the front door either rusted off, or had been smashed off by vandals, long ago.

Debbie unholstered her Glock 19, having opted to leave her Tango in the trunk, and stepped through the front entrance. One good thing about Wigotsky's 'ingenious' plan to lure the target to a desolate location was; there was no need for the usual setup. No other structures in the vicinity were ideal for sniping. Just as well. There was no one but a few grazing cows to hear the gunshots.

She held the gun at the ready, with both hands wrapped firmly around the handle. Broken glass skittered softly across the ground, up-turned by the rubber soles of her boots. Debbie paused every few steps and listened intently for other movements, her thumb nudging the safety off. The open main area of the distillery was barren, save for the crumbling concrete, and scrap metal that was deemed useless by even the most innovative of scavengers.

First order of business: clear the floors. Debbie knew her target should be somewhere in the building, presumably on the third floor, according to Wigotsky's elegant script. Debbie couldn't take any chances, especially when she was following someone else's plan. She drew in a slow, deliberate, breath and held it tight, her body taut like whipcord despite the fluidity with which she moved. Careful to sidestep out of the light slanting through some high windows, Debbie kept to the shadows and tried not to cast her own. Another potential announcement of her arrival, and yet without a means to engage in any potential opponents.

Debbie cleared the foreman's office and two closets when unease prickled in her gut. Her gaze swept the surrounding area and Debbie sighed in relief when the search yielded nothing of interest. She waited a few moments in expectant quiet before the distillery caught up to her heightened vigilance. The last unchecked closet tucked opposite of the foreman's office held flutters on the inside; Debbie could hear them as they rustled in the dark.

Debbie pressed herself close to the wall beside the door and took a deep breath. In one smooth motion, she kicked the door open, flooding the cramped space with light. The rustling exploded into a squealing cloud of brown-black, flapping viciously, like a vengeful autumn wind stirring up withered leaves. Adrenaline, coursing hot and cold through Debbie, had her wrapping her arms around her face for meager protection. She stood terse and blinded for a few trailing moments after the bats had vacated the area. When Debbie's own timpani heartbeat quieted, the icy fear that locked her joints thawed. She eased herself forward with a sharp mental kick – here's hoping she hadn't potentially alerted the target of her presence, in her panic.

Fucking bats.

When Debbie told Arroyo about it later that night, he'd probably claim it was a 'bad omen'. Perhaps she could use it to appeal to his superstitious side and coax a willingness to move from him.

Debbie resumed her guarded stance, gun at the ready as she listened intently. Dirt and pebbles skipped across the floor, as a bone-dry wind whistled through the hollow carcass of the building. No heaving breaths or pounding footsteps. Still though, Debbie was on a job. Ideally, she wasn't alone, and she wasn't referring to the bats.

With the first floor cleared, Debbie began her careful ascent up the set of steep, concrete stairs tucked in a narrow hallway. The shoddy, wooden railing had long since fallen off, and it lay across the stairs like it was hoping for someone to mourn it. Debbie stepped deliberately over it. The second level was as derelict as the first floor, albeit, less open. Light fought through the caked grime on the windows and broke against looming shadows cast by narrow corridors and hideaway offices. Like the ice cap pictures Debbie had seen on National Geographic; brilliant, jigsaw-pieces of ice chunking across the inky expanse of water.

Debbie weaved in and out of the offices, peeking in just enough to reassure herself there were no witnesses before moving on to the next one. With each office that passed with no incident, Debbie's heart rate normalized, until another creak of wood or rustle of debris leapfrogged it into a stuttering run.

Another door, shoved agape by crumbled slabs of concrete, housed a flutter of color that waved at her from her peripheral vision. Stomach swooping as the last of her steel nerves jumped ship, Debbie spun on her heel and aimed the barrel of her gun at the motion's source. Her finger tensed at the trigger; a hint of a squeeze without the commitment.

Hot adrenaline turned cold and the vigilant tension that held her taut seeped away, leaving Debbie feeling like rubber. Caught on the splintered backend of what had been a chair, was a colorful piece of fabric. It danced enthusiastically in the draft, rags with the vain hopes of being a flag one day, instead of a gunman waiting for Debbie in the dark. She should've felt foolish – she wished she had. Instead, she tasted sawdust and felt the bite of her nails around the gun handle.

Upon closer inspection, it was a scarf; teal silk with red flowers embroidered onto it. Debbie found herself transfixed as she ran the crook of her finger along the soft garment. It reminded her of the one Arroyo gave her a couple of years back. The same color, same softness – it wasn't her style at all. Too loud for someone trying to live under the radar, and too distinctive for someone whose livelihood depended on remaining unnoticed. Butterflies stirred in the pit of her stomach and she brushed the cobwebs off her timeworn affections for her husband, all the same. Debbie bunched the fabric between her fingers once more before she left it to fall gently to the ground. Perhaps this sort of scarf was destined to be abandoned.

Even as she left it in the old, dilapidated office, Debbie wondered who'd left the scarf. For her, leaving it unworn in its immaculate, ribbon clad box, meant allowing the dust to settle on her marriage again. The days felt shorter and the nights stretched long when there were no greater mysteries in the man miles away on the other side of the bed, than what he'd eaten for lunch that day. Debbie wanted to speak to the woman who'd left the scarf, and for one fleeting moment, she wondered if it could've been Ms. Wigotsky. Hilaria must have been to the distillery before she deemed it the perfect killing room, had to have worked her way up to the third floor, just as Debbie had. Although she liked to think Hilaria did so with a bit more apprehension.

If Debbie recalled correctly, Hilaria wasn't married. However, she also struggled to reconcile her client's exquisiteness with being a spinster. The kill Hilaria hired Debbie for was one born of envy; that much was clear. But what of the woman who coveted what Hilaria wanted so desperately that she'd hire someone to kill for it?

How long had Debbie been with her own husband? The thought was as intrusive as the intent behind it was poisonous. How long until it

had begun to feel more like a life sentence than a partnership. Debbie craved the knowledge that she wasn't alone in this loneliness, as contractually binding as the jobs she took. To know that the woman who'd left this scarf, had done so because her marriage was strong enough to not rely on tawdry gifts to bridge the distance that had formed through years of routine and increasingly lukewarm anniversaries. Maybe it was Hilaria, the man would be leaving, and not his wife. Debbie tasted the lie in her mouth, though she hadn't spoken it aloud.

Debbie thought of her own husband; it was funny, really. Arroyo used to get his face 'tuned' every five years or so, back when he was mixed up with The Pseudonymous, and Debbie had found her closest confidant in every single one. Now he'd been with the same face for almost seven years, and as another one came and went, he became more of a stranger.

When Debbie ascended the final stairwell, she vaguely noted how her heart seemed to slow, rather than race. Her blood felt viscous, like it was hesitant to flow, her chest tightened and burned with the breath she detained. Her footsteps were nearly soundless - either that or she couldn't hear themit over the static screaming in her ears. When she rounded the corner, her entire body seemed to resonate with a note of finality. Hell, if this was to be her last job as Debbie Pinto, then maybe she could make it her last job, period. She used to think she and Death were good friends; like she'd been able to give him gifts few others could afford. Now it felt like his company had overstayed its welcome. It made her stomach churn.

The static roared in trepidation as her eyes swept around the empty room. She scanned the cracks in the wall and the broken glass lining the lone window in the room, like the layers of teeth in a parasite's mouth. Debbie pivoted in a shaky three-sixty, a piss-poor pirouette. But the room was silent and unfeeling. With no one there to stare into the quivering barrel of her gun, Debbie unwrapped one hand from her weapon, and reached it into her jacket pocket. The folded paper softened in her sweat-dampened grasp.

Shaking it open, one hand still holding the gun even, her eyes ceased searching for a target, and turned instead to Hilaria's instructions for guidance.

Go to 973 Ann Causeway

Target will be on the third floor .

Take her out

In their vagueness, the words left both little margin for error, and giant question marks bubbling in Debbie's thoughts. 'Take her out'. Take who out exactly? Debbie's eyes circled the room again, this time more frantically. The target may have caught on to the hunt and had used the time Debbie spent consulting her client's directions to take to the hunt herself. But Debbie was still alone in the room – the singular room without a crack or crevice for anything larger than a flea to steal away to. A room, empty save for debris so weathered, Debbie couldn't make out its original form, and a mirror propped up against the wall.

Her attention jerked to the mirror as if it had reached out to grab it on its own. It was full length, and very out of place as Debbie stepped out in front of it, her entirety contained within it at her current distance. The golden frame was unscratched, undinged – mysteriously new in the disarray of the abandoned distillery. Debbie was drawn to this outlying detail. Who had put it there? How recently?

She could only think of two people other than herself.

Debbie whipped around, her heart vaulting at a pace that left her breath floundering to catch up, as if she expected her unseen target to be stalking her. There was no one else in the room but her.

She looked back to the mirror now and edged closer.

Hilaria's instructions felt white hot in her feverish hold.

Take her out.

The woman in the mirror looked blanched, her eyes bugged out and eyebrows cinched together like a caricature of fear. Debbie barely recognized her.

Take her out.

Her memory retreated safely back a few years, spinning a safe haven from that damned scarf she'd found. The Debbie from two years back curled up on their living room's loveseat in the now-Debbie's mind. Arroyo leaned in to press a chaste kiss to her cheek as he passed her a navy-blue box, the silky red ribbon shining softly in the light. The old Debbie lifted the lid and tossed it carelessly aside. She looked more excited than Debbie recalled feeling as she gathered the fabric gently in her hands, her eyes coveting the intricate stitching of each red petal.

"It's lovely," she'd murmured, bunching it in her hands.

"I'm glad you think so, I had it custom made."

The real Debbie's stomach dropped, scattering the memory into dust that collected at the fibers of the crumpled scarf, where it lay just one floor below. The one-of-a-kind scarf that Debbie had left in her drawer to collect that dust. When Debbie looked to the mirror again, her gaze was splintered with shock.

Take her out. Take her out. Take her out.

The 'her' that was married to Hilaria's "friend". Her, the 'other woman' to Hilaria's other woman. The her who was supposed to be waiting in a place where the custom-made scarf Debbie's husband had gifted her was also waiting. Her.

The lead in Debbie's stomach felt too heavy paired with the light-headed spell that had suddenly overtaken her. She felt as if it were tearing through paper tissue, muscle, and bone. News with this magnitude had a warpath, and that path was currently ripping through Debbie as the synapses in her brain fizzled and popped her understanding of what was happening. Years of marriage and an unknown number of them shared with Hilaria Wigotsky in secret, shattered like glass, the shards eviscerating her. She felt all of this with exceptional rawness but was still startled by the realness of the crash and trailing tinkling sound of glass fractals scattering to concrete.

Debbie blinked at her empty fingers, dazed – a resounding echo to the hollowness that gnawed on her bones like a junkyard dog on a mealy carcass. She had hurled her gun at the mirror. She felt stupid, although no one had witnessed the act. And small, as if everyone had witnessed the sham that was her marriage. Maybe Debbie hadn't broken a mirror at all, but a one-way window. She waited for the vultures to emerge out of the emptying frame to pick her bones.

Bile welled inside Debbie, chewing at her from the inside out. Arroyo —that rat bastard.

Rage swept through her, white-hot. When the burn settled in a few moments later, it came to her.

The venomous, green-eyed basilisk thrived off Debbie's inadvertent pull on her husband despite his betrayal. She supposed that was another stipulation of marriage - she was his, and he was hers, even most despicably. When the basilisk passed through Debbie's throbbing veins, like blood beneath a bruise, her own hallowed voice came pounding from inside her skull. What about me? Even when the butterflies in her stomach withered away, and her nerves stopped electrifying the moment she stepped into the same room as Arroyo, Debbie never forsake him.

It was done. Her marriage was done. And through it all, laughably, the job was not yet done. Take her out. The wife. Debbie didn't much mind the idea of killing the wife, she might be putting the poor, stupid thing out of her misery. It was supposed to feel new, but all Debbie had really done was finally acknowledge the gangrenous limb as it rotted her. She thought back to one of those late-night specials she had been addicted to in her twenties. There had been one about mountaineers getting lost in the frigid wastes tucked in the summits of mountains — closer to the unfeeling sky than she was in that distillery. When the climbers had been found and brought back to civilization — if they had — their ice crusted gloves were removed to reveal grotesquely engorged appendages, more charcoal stick than finger where the frost had bitten them black. The rest of the episode was about how the fingers were lopped off; the doctors amputated dead limbs.

Regardless of the fact that Debbie would relish it, she had a duty to kill the wife.

She slunk over to the mirror, where her handgun lay dusted in glass crumbs. Plucking it up with two fingers, she ignored the sharp pricks at the pads of her fingers. Most of the glass fell from it in a light snow as she holstered the gun again.

From this point on, the wife was dead. Debbie Pinto would be dead — first she'd have to contact her relocation guy again to dot all the i's and cross all the t's. The 'fresh start' fee would be no trouble; so long as she didn't confront Arroyo about his affair, their accounts would remain joined and he'd be none the wiser until she was long gone. The last time she'd moved, she hadn't changed her face — vanity was more of her husband's vice, the pretty man that he was. She might perhaps invest in a new haircut though. Whoever she was to be next, she wanted to start without any deadweight. Perhaps in Europe somewhere? Or Asia. Anywhere that put an ocean between her and her husband.

Debbie descended the stairs again, leaving the wife in a grave of glass shards and dirty concrete. Taking a detour through the second floor, she didn't leave the distillery until she had a pocket full of silken, red flowers tucked safely in her jacket.

About the Author:

Currently working towards her BA in English at the University of Illinois at Chicago, **Catherine Lin** intends to pursue her PhD in the same course of studies. She daylights as a tour guide at the Willis Tower's Skydeck attraction, while working on her novel and short stories in her spare time.

STREET OF ANOTHER WISH

by Judson Blake

They discussed it several times. How it would be straightforward and might even be fun, moving, really, only across town. There would be more space than they had now. Ailana was looking forward to it and Howard had taken off work to help with packing. But in the midst of it he was called away. They just couldn't resolve something from what he said over the phone. Some important party was upset. He left the big plastic bag of old papers, things to be thrown out, in the middle of the floor. When he was gone Ailana planned to make a quick twist and wire it up with the others--but then she saw the unopened letter. Without thinking she stuffed it in her purse. Then she wired up the bag and put it by the door. Moving was a convenience, Howard said; you got to get rid of so much stuff.

From the first time she met him Ailana had made a simple sizing up: Howard was an ox-like man. He was steady. He was dedicated to his work, often enthusiastic about it and not about much else. He was a safe man, the man you held onto. He planned things; he remembered dates and anniversaries. He knew the names of all her friends. He took his umbrella when he probably would not need it. They watched television together; they had similar opinions. Ailana admitted that she liked the routine; she liked his steadiness, the freedom from idle jokes and excursions that might go nowhere. In five years they were a couple that marriage had established, suited in their quietude.

But now there was this detail, this simple letter she probably should have ignored. That gnawed at what she had thought before. It sat in a fold of her purse with no purpose or meaning, or none that she wanted to delve into. She could wait, as if the envelope with its secret contents were something dead that could no longer act and was no danger anymore, something she could attend to if she chose. And if she got tired of waiting. Waiting for what?

The move in fact was easy. It had gone smoothly and Ailana felt adventurous finding new shops and people. She enjoyed walking along streets that were structured the same but were still very different from the old neighborhood. They settled in. They felt their way into their old familiarity in a new way in the new space. It could have been a change in which nothing changed.   But the letter stayed. It somehow asked her: don't throw me away for then I'll be gone forever and you'll never know who I am.

As she lay awake at night sometimes the thing would capture her imagination, like a distant relative she had found out about but never known. The relative, now known to exist, still could not be found, could not be met. It was a face behind a blank curtain. And what if this creature, her husband, ever found out about her theft? Her intrusion? What would she do then? Why, she thought in the night, she would simply own up to it, that would be all. But he would not find out; she wasn't going to tell him. As she lay awake beside him she watched his breathing and she felt the soft motion of cloth and air in the gray tones of the dark. Could you love a man more when his back was turned? You might love him more. For then you saw what he never sees. And seeing the same facts for years as she had, how was it different now? At quiet times in the semi-dark and at times when she was alone Ailana was sure of one thing: she would never accuse him. She would never hint. And she would never act like she knew something special. And in another space on the shelves of her reflection she had decided something else that seemed foreign but just as certain: she would never open the letter.

Finally one October day she decided that enough secrecy was enough and she confided in Julie. They met at an upstairs café that was too obscure to attract a busy crowd. It had a musty air, a polite venue for people who read the newspaper for hours, even the obits.

"What would you do?" she said, having shown the letter to her friend.

Julie fingered it and turned it over again.

"Well, it was returned to his office at work. That's stealthy enough. Then he brought it home. Hm."

"Well, it was in a pile of other things. All junk."

Julie was pensive, not wanting to say too much.

"You've had it for a while, since the move. It nags on you."

"Yes."

"Well," she said straightening her frame, "you're sure he doesn't see the woman. I mean, aren't you?"

Ailana almost bit her lip, but she looked directly at Julie and said instead:

"Yes. I'm sure. I don't see when he would have time. He's always with me. I call him, he's always there."

"Then throw it away."

Ailana had thought all along that that was exactly what she should have done. She had that thought the first day. But from the first the letter had taken on an existence of its own. She was sure: throwing it away would have been a degrading failure, a personal failing of her own, all the more if it was impossible to define. Throwing it away would have been disownment. The thing belonged to something else.

Or to someone else. Well, that was simple: it belonged to the woman it was addressed to. That was its implacable fact.

"And who is this Raphaela Fabrice, anyway," Julie asked. "She's probably dead and that's why it's written like that: Return to sender. Or it's the wrong address, one of the two."

Ailana corrected herself for thinking that her friend was being obtuse. Julie wasn't seeing something but Ailana did not want to say: Howard would not make a mistake about the address. He was steady. He didn't make typos. And why had he not thrown the letter away himself? Why did it sit around somewhere until the jarring focal point of moving came to a head and he must have idly put it in the trash with a bunch of other stuff, if he saw it at all, without thinking more? Without noticing even. The steady man was throwing it away. As Ailana should have done.

Julie seemed to collect her friend's doubt. It was bad to be undecided, to be between two things without really knowing either one.

"Maybe the letter isn't so important," Julie said. "What's important is the woman's address.   You know where she lives. You know the street."

Julie relaxed back and laughed.

"Well, that's it. You could become a sleuth, Ailana. You could just go there and see. If there is a Raphaela Fabrice who really exists, you could ring her bell."

Ailana backed in her chair.

"I wouldn't. No, I couldn't do that. And even if I could, it's absurd. Why? Why would I do that?"

Julie thought easily, waiting to form her words:

"Because, well, it might be a side of the man you really don't know. Maybe that you'll never know."

Julie had touched a thread of nerve that wound somewhere she could not see. Did not want to see. Ailana obviously did not know something, and how far could that other thread reach? She wanted to avoid going further. Her friend had been too successful.

"How can you be married to someone...." Ailana began but she could not finish. She put the letter back in her purse. It was stolen goods.

They let the matter die and talked about the new neighborhood. Now, having sought out her friend, somehow Ailana did not want to expand. She looked around for something else to see. Glancing in a corner of the shop she admired a sleeping boy leaned over on a storage bin, sprawled so discomfort no longer mattered. She imagined he had worked a double shift.

The fact of the letter, the deeper fact that she would never accuse Howard, still traced its way into her thoughts each night. Now it was worse than before because she had talked about it. The address was right there. It was in another part of town, not near where they used to live, not near anything really. It was a strange street she had never seen. If she were tracking down a man she would have felt no fear at all and what she felt now was not so much fear as misgiving, as if she did not trust her own curiosity, her own anticipation. She knew where it was. She could go there and merely look. Raphaela Fabrice would not stop her on the street. No one would even know she went.   It would be a trek of another form, not of distance nor even of time, but of something else she felt growing in her thoughts: resolve.

--Better go now. Will you wait forever? No. I'd better go now.

As she walked down the strange street she wondered what Howard might have gone through walking here. There were large trees and attentive doormen who watched her pass. Leaves caught the wind around her feet. Was this place, this reputable slightly decorous old street, similar in many ways to their own, was it secretly true to the ox-like man? Another truth? Was the place knowing?   Did it contain a secret side that no one saw? Was this, these trees, these doorways, were they all the accoutrements of a side of him she had never seen, never guessed at, a side hidden not out of cunning, for she still did not believe, not entirely, that he would turn to that. No, it would be from simple dismissal, ignorance, even blankness of his own that he did not really see. She watched the solidity of the bricks and trees she passed. Did these solid facts mean the street was the path to another way of life?

--Some life he could not have with me?

She passed a disheveled man crouched on a civil bench. He might have been a derelict, huddled from the new cold, but his look, his open willful eyes, did not say he wanted spare change.   Had that man seen her husband? Had he watched Howard enough to know his purpose or his gait? Would he have a smoky memory of her husband, of details she did not know? If he were a regular on that bench, an artifact as some people could become, did he inhabit this street like the trees and doorways and the sameness of people walking dogs? Would he be part of a memory Howard would have? Ailana felt she should come close and touch this stranger, offer him her hand, pierce his solitude and breaking the ice within, breath it into herself and end it forever. But no, her resolve was narrow, directed down the hollow of the street and only that.

She got to the address and the door to the vestibule was open. No one was watching her; it was past the time when people would be rushing home. Ailana looked carefully over the panel of buzzers. The name Fabrice froze in her sight.

--You must not walk away, she thought. This moment can't be broken off or it will become a dead thing that will weigh upon you, stick with you more than it has already. You have come this far and what did that take? It is here and you are here.

Without waiting she rang the bell.

After a moment a woman's voice answered on the speaker.

"Yes. Who is it?"

"You don't know me. I'm Ailana Verzan. Howard' wife. I have a letter for you."

Ailana was astonished at the firmness in her own voice. It sounded confident and direct.

--As if I know what I'm doing.

The matter had taken on a moment of its own. It was more solid than she was, more on its own path. There had been no daring, no impulsive leap. There had been hardly a shred of hesitation. Now she only had to wait, since the woman would have to think. Wait for refusal if that was what the matter would lead to, but still just wait.

"I'll come down," the voice said.

Ailana waited out in the street so crowding of the vestibule would not push them together more than either would want. The woman when she appeared was tall and had a stalwart air. She eyed Ailana with what seemed for an instant to be admiration but then shifted to the consenting cast of formality. They shook hands. Ailana felt a sly blush of relief that the woman was not terribly pretty. She kept herself well, but she was too stalwart, less feminine than Ailana felt herself to be. But then that made it worse, didn't it? For then he had seen something else in this woman. Something he had not found.

"I could just give it to you now," Ailana said. Her fingers extended in her purse as if burning their place there. Raphaela looked around blankly staring then looked back.

"Yes. If you like. Or… maybe, well, if you like … in some more private place."

She met Ailana's peering. She was nervous and trying not to be.

"Come with me."

Raphaela Fabrice acted as if this was not a surprise or that, in some quiet way, all that she experienced was a surprise. She was open and gentle where she led. It might have been that she expected this, for she seemed in some gritty way to be ready for it. A hotel lobby down the block was guarded by a man in a black coat who spread his arm beside the door.

--She has done this before, Ailana thought. How could I think that?

The woman chose a writing desk with stationary for guests and a conical light designed for solitude away from home in a strange city where one regretted anonymity: it could never be used enough. Ailana produced the letter.

"It seems you are not dead."

Raphaela Fabrice fingered the letter in a tentative way, blinked at being alive and seemed in the gaze she returned to Ailana to be refreshed and accepting.

"I should take back what is mine," she said. "Not lie. I lied when I wrote Return to sender. That wasn't fair of me. Evasive. I'm guilty of evasion. And now you've, well, you've found me out."

She looked directly at Ailana as if to deny her eyes might fill with tears.

"Well. Are you going to open it?"

The other paused and pursed her lips. Her voice was steady and hoarse as she spoke back:

"I'm no threat to you. Ailana. Not at all. It was months ago. A year almost. It would not have worked. And now we've met…. I… I'm glad we met. I'm no threat. I'm no threat at all…."

The woman's voice choked and a flush came into her face. Her hand came up to cover her face but stopped and would not allow even that defense. Ailana was stunned with the awful thought: that was what he had seen in the woman, her courage.

"It would not have worked," she said again.

--Why? Ailana thought. I could ask. Now is the only time. I won't be able to ask again. Not call. But what I would learn would be only details. It would be tiny facts. Facts of how it began, more facts of how it ended, what she saw of him. All wasted details to clutter more nights.

"I'd better go," Ailana said.

The woman leaned over the desk and grasped her wrist.

"Yes. Yes. It would not have worked. It couldn't. I should never…. I should take it back. You did right to bring it. Absolutely. I'll take what is mine… mine." Her fingers clutched the letter still unopened. She barely looked at it.

All the walk down the strange street Ailana heard an echo, the soft secret refrain of the woman's words:

--I should take what is mine. I should take….

About the Author:

Judson Blake: BA, Literature, UC Berkeley; MS, Mathematics, UNM. Long experience in Wall Street (didn't save a dime) and the scientific community, technical writing and programming. For several years he directed and acted on stage in New York. His full-length play Perversion ran for five weeks in the West Village. Two of his stories were selected for the 2019 American Emerging Writers Series. His work has also appeared in Don Webb's Bewildering Stories, The Literary Yard, and Freedom Fiction literary periodicals.

THE YOUNG WARRIORS

by Steve Slavin

1

The day before I left for basic training, I sat in Katz's, a massive family style delicatessen on the Lower Eastside. Widely known for its delicious pastrami, corned beef, and roast beef sandwiches, Katz's fare was considered "kosher style."

What's the difference between kosher and kosher style? While the food is identical, truly religious Jews — strict Shabbos observers — do not patronize restaurants that stay open on Friday evening and Saturday. Those restaurants are labeled unkosher no matter how many rabbis supervise the preparation of their food.

All of this is to explain how I happened to be eating an overstuffed pastrami sandwich with sides of cole slaw and potato salad at Katz's. Henry's, located just down the block, had a flashing window sign — the only kosher deli in the vicinity.

Henry's was kosher; Katz's was just kosher style. Well, kosher style was good enough for me and for my friends, who had thrown me a little going-away party. There was a sign on the back wall, which led me to believe that mine was not the first such party. The sign read: "Send a salami to your boy in the army."

2

It was drizzling when I got off the bus at Fort Dix, which served as the basic training post for those of us from New York City and most of the surrounding area. It's about an hour and a half down the Jersey Turnpike, not far from Trenton.

The year was 1961, there were no serious wars going on, and I had signed up for what was known as "the six-month deal," which consisted of six months active duty and five and a half years in the active reserve. That seemed a lot better than waiting to get drafted and having to serve on active duty for two years plus two more years of the reserves. Of course, you needed to be able to do the math to make the comparison.

Within days we were provided with uniforms, assigned to basic training companies, and taught how to march in formation. The sergeant running our company might have had a successful career as a stand-up comic, except that he was actually quite serious, like when he addressed us as "Mens!" When he felt the need to take us down a peg, he called us "college boys."

My favorite term — and perhaps his — was "young warriors." Most of the sergeants had combat infantryman badges — a rifle and a wreath — sewn on their uniforms. Because we were in the peacetime army, they often reminded us that we had it way too easy. None ever told any war stories, but the sarcastic term, young warrior, pretty much said it all.

3

Sergeant Sudyc, who led our platoon, looked like GI Joe. A tall stocky bald-headed man in his mid-forties, he loved climbing up on a footlocker and addressing us once or twice a week after dinner.

He meant to scare us, but his warnings often had the opposite effect. Another of his themes was that while we were suffering through basic training, he could at least get away on weekends.

"While you're stuck on base all weekend, I'm gettin' on that bus tuh the Port Authority terminal, and then I'm gettin' on the subway tuh Brooklyn. And when youse guys ull be sittin' in the barracks dreamin of yuh girlfriends, my beautiful wife ull be drawing a nice warm bath for me. She'll pull off my boots, unbutton my shirt, help me outta my pants... And then she'll whisper, 'Get your big Russian ass into that bathtub!'"

We looked at each other and burst out laughing. And Sergeant Sudyc was soon laughing the loudest. We truly loved the man!

Another time he got on the footlocker and yelled, "Listen up!" He was ready to scare us. Up until now, we had had it much too easy. But this coming Monday morning it would all change. We'd be getting up an hour earlier because we'd be riding out to the rifle range to practice shooting at targets with our M1 rifles.

In theory, we would get eight hours sleep every night, with lights out at 9:30 pm. But often we had to stay up somewhat later, whether to clean our rifles, polish our shoes, or take care of some other mundane business. But beginning Monday morning, we'd have to get up at 4:30 a.m.!

Well, as promised, that dreaded Monday morning did arrive. The lights went on, and our sergeant was happily screaming, "Hit it! Hit it!"

We had learned that this was short for, "Hit the floor!"

But he was just getting warmed up. "I warned youse guys that things were going to get tough around here."

Indeed, he had. "It's 4:30! It's Monday morning." He paused a few seconds for dramatic effect. "And it's raining!"

There was a big smile on his face. In his entire life, the man had probably never been happier. He had warned us! But the weather gods had made it worse than even he had predicted.

We saw how happy he was. And that made us happy. If all it took was our misery to make him happy, then we'd gladly be miserable. Wasn't that the way of the young warrior?

We happily got dressed, stood in formation in the pouring rain, grabbed some "shit on a shingle" (chipped beef on toast) – reputedly the worse meal the Army had to offer – and then clambered onto the open "cattle trucks" for the hour-long ride out to the rifle range. Our sergeant was smiling for the entire ride.

4

A day or two before Passover we received some great news. Those of us whose religious affiliation was "Hebrew" would be getting two days off. We could go home to celebrate this great holiday which, after all, did commemorate the freeing of the Jews.

But everything had to be done by the book. We couldn't just stroll over to the orderly room to pick up our passes. No, this was the Army. We had to march there in formation.

About a quarter of the members of our company were, as we identified ourselves, "Hebes."

So we formed ranks and marched to the orderly room calling out our cadence in Yiddish: "Eins, zwei, drei, fier... Eins, zwei, drei, fier.

The absurdity of basic training, the Army, and perhaps life itself, seemed to come into sharp focus. How could any of this be taken seriously?

Some of us imagined the next-to-last week of basic training like the "hell week" of a high school or college fraternity, when the brothers tested us to make absolutely certain that we would make worthy associates. That week we bivouacked in a remote area of Fort Dix, and then marched back to the barracks just after dinner on Friday evening.

For us, this was twilight walk through the Jersey pines. We had our gas masks at the ready, because we had heard a rumor that there would be a gas attack. Canisters of tear gas would be shot into the air, and we would need to quickly remove our helmets and correctly place the masks on our faces. We had practiced this operation dozens of times and were confident that we had it down right.

After having walked four or five miles, we saw the canisters being shot into the air as the call went out, "Gas attack!" Within thirty seconds, we all had our masks on. We resumed our march, and then, after a few minutes someone yelled, "All clear!"

As I took off my mask, I could smell something just a bit off. But that was it! Our last test had been passed. For the rest of the way back to the barracks, we just enjoyed that beautiful evening. It would remain my fondest memory of the Army.

After nine weeks of basic training, we would go home for two weeks, and then head off to some other military post for another three and a half months of specialized training. And that would be it, more or less.

We'd still have five and a half years of reserves ahead of us, and there was always the risk that we might get called up to active duty. Still, that was sure a hell of a lot better than spending two years in the Army, and maybe even having to fight in a "shooting war."

5

Suddenly, everything changed. President John Kennedy and Soviet leader Nikita Khrushchev got into a pissing contest that would go on for another year, culminating in the Cuban Missile Crisis.

Perhaps to demonstrate his toughness, Kennedy called up hundreds of reserve units to active duty. Now being in the reserves did not seem like such a wonderful deal. At first, we thought to ourselves, we already are on active duty. So what did it matter if our reserve unit was called up?

But then we realized that when our six months of active duty was up, we would rejoin our reserve units. And if they were on active duty, that's where we would end up.

Thankfully, my unit had not been activated. So as long as we didn't get into a shooting war,

when my six months were up, I'd be a free man.

As things turned out, I would be able to serve out my remaining five and a half years in the reserves, just going to weekly meetings and summer camp. After President Kennedy's assassination and President Lyndon Johnson's escalation of our involvement in the Vietnam War, there was again some concern that there would be a massive reserve call-up. But it didn't happen. Johnson demonstrated his macho by fighting a full-scale war without having to call up the reserves. What a hero!

6

Overall, I enjoyed my days on active duty, but by the end of my six months, I had had quite enough of it. And as our involvement in the Vietnam War expanded, like most of my friends I railed against the war, marched for peace, and joined a couple of anti-war organizations.

But until national sentiment began to turn against the war in 1968, there seemed little we could do to stop it. Some young men fled to Canada, got student deferments, and went underground while many more just resigned themselves to being drafted, hoping they would not be sent to Vietnam.

Like almost everyone else, I was enjoying my life without thinking too much about the war. One Friday evening, as I was putting the moves on a nice young woman, my phone rang. It was my friend Josh, whom I had met in the Army Reserve.

Could I talk? Instead of answering, I just put the woman on the phone. I figured that if she were really interested in me, she would just blow him off. I remember her stating her full name, which somehow struck me very funny. To this day, I can't remember her actual name, but it definitely was not "Barbara Schleperman."

They chatted for a few minutes and then I got back on the phone with Josh. He told me that our friend Zach's nephew Ben was going into the army, and they were taking him out to enjoy his last night of freedom. I explained that

I'd love to come, but I was otherwise occupied. He understood and hung up.

Five minutes later, my downstairs bell rang. It was Josh, Zach and Ben. They came upstairs. The woman seemed glad to see them. She and Josh resumed their conversation. Oh well: easy come, easy go.

We decided to drive out to Bensonhurst where the woman lived. It was close to midnight when we entered Famous Cafeteria, just around the corner from her house. They served dairy dishes, and like Katz's Delicatessen, it was kosher style. Although it was Shabbos, the place was packed.

We sat there for hours. Ben's mom had grown up in New York, but she married a Jewish guy from Iowa, and that's where they raised a family. Ben had dropped out of college and received his draft notice two weeks later.

"Yeah," observed Zach, "the college registrar and the draft board must maintain a direct line."

Ben had an eight a.m. flight out of Kennedy. He would spend Saturday with his family and report for basic training on Sunday.

At five a.m. we were on the Belt Parkway on the way to Kennedy. The woman came with us. She sat in the front with Josh.

Ben seemed OK about going into the Army. They promised him that after basic training, he would be trained in computers, and that he would remain in the United States during his entire two-year tour. They even put their guarantee in writing. Josh, Zach, and I didn't believe it.

7

I checked in with Zach every few months. Apparently, the Army actually did keep its word. Not only had Ben never left the country, but he was one of the few people being trained on some kind of top secret Defense Department project that might have civilian applications.

Two years after our going-away get-together, Ben was back in New York. He had been hired by a computer start-up company and would stay with Zach until he found his own apartment. He was working on some kind of hush-hush project called an internet. I just hoped all that training would not go to waste in another lame-brain government boondoggle.

Ben's timing was excellent in at least one respect. He would arrive just in time to attend a wedding. In fact, it would be a reunion of sorts since the last time we saw Ben. He, Josh, Zach, and I would all be in the wedding party. Josh and "Barbara Schleperman" were getting married.

8

A few years later I was driving across Staten Island on the way to my teaching job in New Jersey. I had to leave my house very early to beat the traffic, but on the plus side I had just a two-day week teaching economics in a community college. Although I had to get up at 5 a.m., I worked just sixty days a year.

The traffic was all going the other way — towards the Verrazano Bridge; It was still dark, and I could see the headlights of backed-up cars extending for miles. This put me in a great mood. In fact, I began to laugh so hard, I feared that I might lose control of the car.

If a traffic cop saw me now, he'd probably throw the book at me. He'd make me get out of the car and try to walk in a straight line. I might not be able to because I'd be laughing too hard. If he asked me what was so funny, how could I explain it to him?

"You see, officer. It's still dark outside. It's Monday morning. And it's raining!"

About the Author:

A recovering economics professor, **Steve Slavin** earns a living writing math and economics books. The third volume of his short stories, "To the City with Love," will be published in September by Fat Dog Books.

A BORING LIFE

by Barbara Borst

"You're not really going, are you?"

Laura wasn't sure which of the guests milling about her living room had lofted that question over the din.

"Of course not," she replied to them all with a laugh. "Not until next week." She spun around as a man leaned in and kissed her on the cheek. "Andre, mon amour."

Her daughter Isabella forged her way through the crowd to scold her mother. "We're out of guacamole."

"Check with Jeremina. See if she's making more."

"Hey, baby," Paul said with a Western twang, slipping his arms around her from behind as she answered Isabella.

Laura sashayed in his arms for a moment, careful not to spill her Jameson's. "I'll be back," she promised as she escaped to check on the bar arrayed on the porch. Ezekiel had it all in hand, except he needed more beer.

Citronella candles lined the edge of the porch, to ward off mosquitos carrying malaria. Laura leaned against the railing and surveyed the garden. The last rays of equatorial sunlight sliced through the avocado and mango trees and made stripes across the lawn. More things to miss when they reached Boston, along with the world she had built for herself here out of the ruins of a marriage.

Laura forced herself out of such reflections. After all, few things tasted worse than anti-malarial medicine. She turned her attention back to her guests. She stepped down into the garden and went around to the kitchen to ask the staff to bring out more beer, cold for the Westerners, warm for the Kenyans. She checked with Jeremina about dinner preparations.

"Me, I shall have everything ready. You don't worry," Jeremina assured her, adding a little quiz, "Which of those boys you going to miss most?"

Laura laughed off the question, but she did think to herself about calling them boys. As the foreign press corps cycled through Nairobi, they were getting younger, and she was not. She moved on through the dining room, where the sideboard was set for a buffet and the long table waited for a crowd, and back into the living room.

Gracefully winding her way among her guests, Laura dished out hugs and kisses-on-the-cheek to diplomats and rebels, aid workers and opposition leaders, macho journalists and the young women of the moment some had brought along.

"Assistant foreign editor," Martin, a junior diplomat from Britain, congratulated her.

"The title's nice. Don't know about the job yet," she replied as she stopped to chat with him and his wife, Sarah.

"But you're moving up."

"And leaving all this." She gestured to the guests, the house, the gardens and beyond.

"When you Americans go home," Sarah remarked, "at least you have open space and wildlife, whilst we must return to our damp and crowded island."

"Now, dear...," the diplomat began.

"Yes, plenty of wildlife in Boston these days," Laura interrupted to save the woman from being 'corrected.' She noted how proper Martin tried to be, unlike the United Nations diplomat she had married, who had brought them all to Kenya, then run off with another woman, denying his wife even the dignity of a divorce. A diplomat above the law, or at least outside its reach.

But that was old news. And look what she had done on her own, she thought as she turned to survey the gathering. Friends. A career. Three brave daughters, though she wondered if they were ready for the change.

Reverend Njoroge, who often spoke publicly about the failings of the Kenya government, came up to wish her well in her new job and to introduce his wife, Rose. The leader of the Kenya national women's group, Edwina, joined to say how much she appreciated Laura's reporting on women's initiatives.

A young freelance journalist named Bart popped up to announce to Laura, "I have lots of story ideas to pitch to you."

"Probably good to give me a day or two to get my bearings," she told him, glancing toward the ceiling. "But do pitch them."

A grand entrance drew their attention to the front door. The Reuters bureau chief, a tall Nigerian with a voice as big as his personality, greeted each guest as if he were the host, gradually making his way over to Laura, resting an arm around her neck and inquiring for all to hear, "Why are you abandoning me?"

"You had your chance to hire me as news editor, Muhammad," she reminded him, knowing she would never have taken a job as his vassal.

Nick, an Australian photographer with a new girl tucked under his arm, stepped in. "We'll miss you on those endless jeep rides to nowhere."

"I'll leave you my silk cushion," she joshed.

Jeremina's son came up and spoke to her quietly. "Madam, the dinner is ready."

"Thank you, Jeremiah. Please tell your mother we are coming." Turning to the gathering, Laura clapped her hands loudly to draw attention. She stood before them in a safari shirt wide open at the neck, tight-fitting khaki slacks and long brass-and-bead earrings, and called out, "My friends, my friends," as the conversations gradually stopped.

"Welcome. Karibu. Thank you all for coming. A bit of a last hurrah, or at least a last drunken revelry. Please join us for a buffet supper, or at the bar, whichever is your poison. Then find a seat wherever you please."

The crowd split, some to the food and others to get another drink to fortify themselves as they waited in the buffet line.

Cara and Emily ran into the dining room.

"Guests first in line," their mother reminded them.

"We know."

****

Andre waved a goblet of red wine in front of himself as he regaled the guests at the dining table, along with Laura's daughters.

"We were all creeping through Kampala after Museveni's child soldiers took the city. Spying around corners," he said, demonstrating how they ducked and peeked out, "trying not to get shot. We'd seen all the bullet holes in the walls. We were ready to put those holes in the headlines of our stories..."

"Yeah, I got a lot of photos of them," Nick chimed in.

"...and then Laura said, 'Those holes were here last time I came to Kampala, two years ago,'" Andre continued.

"Saved our asses from a rookie mistake," Nick agreed, holding up his empty beer bottle in salute. "Laura, tell 'em how you got the exclusive interview with Mahdi in Khartoum," he urged her.

"And stared down Mengistu at that press conference," Paul added, remarking to the man next to him that the Ethiopian dictator was about as tame as a rattle snake, and just as likely to strike.

She just laughed.

"What about that time we all rode with the Sudan rebels, hotter than hell, dust in every pore, bouncin' on our butts in those Land Rovers," Nick started anew. "Finally we get to some little hut to spend the night, and we smell so bad, and we all stripped down and..."

"Excuse me just a moment," Laura interrupted. She turned to Cara and Emily and said quietly, "Time to tuck in."

"Do we have to?"

"Say, 'goodnight,' girls."

They did and followed their mother to their shared bedroom. Laura could hear her guests carrying on while she supervised the girls' preparations for bed.

"Why does Isabella get to stay up?" Emily demanded.

"Because she's sixteen, and you two are a bit young for that crowd."

"No fair."

"We'll be good," Cara promised.

"We've stayed up late before," Emily added.

"But not this time. Get some sleep so you're ready when all your friends come over tomorrow." Laura kissed her twins and then hurried back to the dining room to rescue Isabella from whatever braggadocio was under way.

"Did you manage to keep things civilized while I stepped out?" Laura asked her older daughter.

"Didn't try," Isabella said, glaring at her mother.

Muhammad boomed, "I kept them in line."

The others roared at that fib.

"And then there was that Somali warlord you had an affair..." a journalist named Rob began.

Martin interrupted to say that he and Sarah needed to head home. The Njoroges also said good night.

That peeled the group down to the hardcore drinkers and tellers of tall tales, often true, much embellished.

"Let's go relieve Jeremina," Laura said to Isabella as her colleagues threatened with a raunchy tale.

"No. I wanna hear what you've really been doing while we got stuffed away in school," Isabella snapped.

"Hope you're ready."

"So we're flying in a Polish Army helicopter, worst tin can I ever rode in," Nick started on a story the others knew because most of them had reported on the famine in Ethiopia that killed a million people. Maybe it was more for the girl who was with him, though he hadn't even introduced her by name.

"And the government minder is trying to tell us some propaganda but we can't hear a damn thing over the noise of the chopper. They won't take us to the places where people are actually starving because the government won't let the aid groups in, 'cause those are rebel areas. They got three civil wars goin' at the same time.

"We land on the edge of a camp. The minder keeps trying to tell us that people are happy they've been moved to greener areas where they can get food handouts and grow some of their own. Their faces tell a different story. Like prisoners. But none of us can get them to talk. Except Laura.

"When we get back to Nairobi and we all publish our stories, she's got the big feature that all the papers pick up. How'd you get it?" he demanded.

Laura just put up her hands as if she didn't know. Not her fault if the guys missed a story because they never thought of talking to the women. The minder had ignored her, too, because she was just a woman, so she had used sign language and a few words gleaned from the local tongue to ask the women about their families, how many children, whether they were well, whether any had died of hunger. They took her into their huts to meet the children. She remembered talking with one boy who looked to be about five years old. The mother held up her fingers to show that he was eight – the age of Laura's twins, but only two thirds their height. The famine had done that much harm to him.

"Tell us about the Somali warlord," Isabella insisted, leaning back in her chair at the dining table.

"Not a warlord, a rebel leader," Muhammad boomed.

"It's my story," Rob insisted.

Muhammad ignored him. "Four of us, we are in Dire Dawa, Ethiopia. We want to go by road to Hargeysa in Somalia where the Somali dictator Siad Barre has bombed his own people. We are needing security. Laura made a 'friend'," he said, exaggerating the word, "who helped us out. He protected each and every one of us," he emphasized, pointing to his three companions on the trip, Laura last of all.

The rest guffawed, even Rob.

Maybe they were trying to embarrass her, Laura thought, but she was not ashamed. She was unattached and free to have a fling with anyone she wanted. Just as they were. There was a slight chance they saw her as one of them, the foreign press corps. She had proven herself as bold as they were in war zones and famine camps, with dictators and rebels, in capitals and the back of beyond. She had beaten them on enough stories to earn respect. Or were they too sexist to give her credit? And, she admitted only to herself, there were a few places she might not have gone alone but felt she could go with one or more of them as company.

Still, she had a correction to make.

"I never had an affair," she paused to specify, "with a source."

They roared at that parry.

Laura glanced at Isabella to see her reaction, but the girl had turned away.

"Never lonely, that's true," Paul added, grinning at Laura. "Even when they made her eat alone – too exalted to eat with the women, but not high enough to eat with the men."

"I got the interviews, anyway," she countered.

****

As the drinking and storytelling continued, Laura turned to Isabella and said, "Let's relieve Jeremina."

Isabella got up reluctantly and followed her mother. In the kitchen, they found Jeremina working her way through a stack of dirty dishes.

"You've outdone yourself tonight, Jeremina," Laura said. "We can finish up."

"I am not tired," Jeremina said. "I can say that I am angry."

"About what?"

"About you. You are the one taking my girls away," Jeremina replied, turning an exaggerated pout toward Laura.

Laura paused, leaning her head to one side. "I suppose they are yours as much as they're mine," she admitted. "I will miss you every day." She moved to hug Jeremina, who lifted soapy hands from the dish water to return the hug. "You'll make me cry."

"I am crying already," Jeremina said.

"So, why are you making us go, then?" Isabella grilled her mother, hands on hips.

Laura sighed. "We've talked about this. It's the right time. Even your little sisters are ready."

"They just think it's gonna be Disneyland or the beach every weekend, like when we visit."

"Just like you think everything here is safaris and poolside parties."

"You're making us move for your career. But I know I'm never gonna fit in."

"I am saying 'good night' now," Jeremina interjected, stepping out of their dispute.

Isabella gave Jeremina a big hug, then watched her go.

"I need the job," her mother said. "How else can I pay for you three to go to college?"

"Who asked you to?" the girl replied, turning to scowl at her mother.

Laura looked at her daughter's angry face. She wanted to remind Isabella how hard it had been to pick herself up after her husband deserted her. She hadn't had the money to take the girls home, nor had she wanted to return in defeat. She had dived into reporting to build a career for herself and a life for the four of them here. Laura paused to realize that tale was just about herself. It wouldn't help Isabella find the courage to forge her own future.

"Izzie, I love you," Laura offered as her daughter walked away.

****

The storytellers were just beginning to head home when Laura returned to the dining room.

Nick stood by the door with his arm around the girl, but it seemed that she was holding him up and maybe should do the driving.

"Hope you didn't mind all the ribbing," Rob said. "Really gonna miss you."

"Thanks. I'll miss you, too," she said and gave him a hug.

Muhammad wagged a finger at her and told her she would be back soon to cover the next bush war.

Andre whispered in her ear, "I must see you again before you leave."

She left that hanging but gave him a kiss on the lips and a pat on the butt.

Paul waited until the others had cleared out, then offered to help her clean up. She took it as a proposal to spend the night, thought about it, felt the temptation, then told him she had fifteen adolescents coming the next day for the twins' goodbye party.

He kissed her deeply. "Monday?" he asked.

"If you want to help us pack," she teased, hoping he would.

****

Laura sat in the empty living room. The furniture still in the wrong places but the glasses and ashtrays and napkins all cleared away. She propped her feet up on the zebra-hide ottoman and leaned deep into the cushions on the sofa. She noticed that someone had left a pack with one cigarette inside. Although she hadn't smoked since she was pregnant the first time, she lit the cigarette and took a puff.

Was she doing the right thing taking this job, wrenching her daughters away from the one home they knew only to return to a homeland they had barely seen?

Yes, she told herself. This was a real opportunity for her, but it was a necessity for them. Not so much a question of money, though that was the part she could explain to others. It was more that they needed a place they could call their own. Here, the girls felt comfortable, but they were expatriates, foreigners living the high life in someone else's country. So many friends at the international school from countries all over the world. But those people were transient, too, moving on as their parents' careers took them to the next emergency or diplomatic post. Life in a bubble. Leave before it burst.

And for herself? Could she manage a conventional life, leaving all this freedom behind? She had done harder things, she supposed. Maybe she could do this, too.

She stubbed out the cigarette and took another sip of whiskey.

About the Author:

Barbara Borst teaches at New York University in the Journalism Institute and in the master's program at the Center for Global Affairs, where she leads study groups to Ghana, South Africa, Tanzania and Uganda. Previously, she was an editor on the international desk at The Associated Press and frequently reported from the United Nations. While based abroad for a dozen years, in Nairobi, Johannesburg, Paris and Toronto, she wrote for Newsday, The Boston Globe, The Dallas Morning News, The Los Angeles Times, Inter Press Service news agency, and others. Her recent work appears on her website, CivicIdea.com, as well as on The Huffington Post.

HOW TO BUILD A BRICK WALK
by David Landsperger

It was a beautiful Sunday morning in July and he knew exactly what to do with it. Doing nothing would give him too much time to think, and he didn't want that. He decided to immerse himself in that project he and Dan had planned over the winter: a new brick walkway from his front porch to the driveway. It would replace the existing bland concrete slab walkway, adding a bit of character to the place. He had learned how to do it last summer when he'd helped Dan install a brick patio at his house down the street.

The two of them had developed a special bond in a short time. They both moved into the neighborhood, a new development in a suburb of Pittsburgh, the same time a few years ago. They grew up as only sons with two younger sisters. They both always wanted a brother and he felt that perhaps these coincidences helped draw them together. They both loved Catch-22 and referenced it in poking fun at their respective bureaucracies. Dan Wade was twelve years older, tall and muscular with thick, wavy brown hair while he was short and paunchy with a prematurely receding hairline. The neighbors even good-naturedly took to calling them Mutt and Jeff. Dan nicknamed him Zink, jagging him that Sylvester Zienkowski was too much name for anyone and he'd gotten along fine with two syllables, thank you very much. Neither of them ever said it out loud, but he was sure Dan felt the same emotional attachment he did. He felt they were almost brothers.

Dan had taught woodworking and metalworking at the local Vo-tech School for the past twenty years, and had developed a talent as a metal sculptor as well. Dan could build things and knew how to fix things. He discovered one thing Dan couldn't do and loved to tease him about his Achilles heel. Dan couldn't pick up a dime from a smooth surface because he gnawed his nails down to stubs. "Dan, you're going to need band aids if you nip those nubs back any more," he'd remind him.

"Hey, these are a real worker's fingernails, not like those pretty, manicured bean counter fingernails of yours."

"Well, it's not just for looks; we bean counters never want to leave any money on the table," he shot back.

When Dan mentioned he was putting in a brick patio, he offered to help. He didn't count on the blisters or sore back he got in return but they were temporary and what he learned from Dan would always be there in the permanent record in his head.

Dan couldn't help him today, but he knew what to do. First he'd have to dig out the existing flat, tombstone-like concrete pavers. They were heavy, maybe 80 pounds each, too heavy to hoist into his wheelbarrow alone so he flopped each one on a heavy duty tarp and dragged them one-at-a-time step by step around to the back of the house, stacking them into some kind of rickety monument. It was hard work and he saw himself as a draft horse mindlessly dragging his heavy load but it felt good. It was a far cry from the tedious work he did auditing clients' books at the CPA firm, working long hours and hoping to make partner in a few more years. He was good at it, yes, but it felt good to use his hands and back as well as his head.

He marked the contour of the new walk, widening it and replacing the walk's right angle turn with an arcing curve. Next, he set about excavating the dirt to the proper depth, chipping and scalloping it out with a medieval-looking mattock he'd borrowed from Dan. He shoveled the loose dirt into the wheelbarrow, and periodically checked the depth and flatness of his excavation with his spirit level to make the trench just right.

The day was warming up, or at least, he was. His wife brought out a pitcher of iced tea and easily convinced him to take a break. He gulped down two glasses and stretched out on the cool cement floor of the shaded front porch, letting his body slowly relax for the first time that day. He closed his eyes and slowly exhaled, moving into the Savasana, or corpse pose, he'd learned last fall when he and Dan took a yoga class at the Y with their wives. Maybe it was his relative youth but he'd been more flexible than Dan, better able to achieve the plethora of pretzel shapes into which they'd twisted their bodies. He wasn't bashful in chiding Dan that he'd finally found a way to outdo the old geezer. Their wives kept reminding them it wasn't a competition but, in an unrelentingly chromosomal sense, it was.

If Dan were here, he'd be jabbing him, telling him his break's over, time to get back to work. Preparation was the foundation of any job, Dan always said. Plan your work and work your plan. It sounded simplistic, even corny, but it was true. Just as true for financial auditing as it was for metalworking or building a walkway.

Back at it, he trimmed and laid down the landscaping cloth that would provide water drainage while preventing weeds or grass from growing up through the bricks. On top of this went the base for the bricks. Most people used sand or gravel but Dan preferred crushed stone, and not just any crushed stone; it had to be 2A Modified, a mix of coarse and fine granules that packed to a tight, even base. He'd dazzled Dan last year when he quickly calculated in his head how much crushed stone and

sand he'd need for the patio, a side benefit of his facility with numbers.

The quarry had delivered the stone two weeks ago, dumping it on the tarp he'd spread on the front lawn. He'd planned to do the walkway that day and figured a few hours wouldn't hurt the grass, but other events transpired to cause postponement after postponement. Now he'd have dead grass to deal with, as well, but that didn't bother him. His wife didn't even raise a stink about it.

After repeated leveling and tamping, the base was ready. He spread an inch of sand on top of the stone, creating a long, soft pillow into which each brick would nuzzle for its final resting place. He thought of Dan again and the freakish events that had pulled them even closer last winter. Dan had been having intestinal issues he couldn't shake, which led his doctor to order a colonoscopy. It indicated two possible Stage 3 or Stage 4 malignancies and required immediate surgery. A week later, Zink was in a freak accident that put him in the hospital with a collapsed lung, a pain in his side, and blood in his urine. X-rays showed a mass on Zink's left kidney that wasn't supposed to be there. The doctor said he was lucky to have the accident because it triggered the bleeding that led to the discovery. He didn't feel very lucky but knew the doctor was right. He and Dan were operated on within a week of each other and sent home to recuperate over that cold, dark winter. When they were well enough, they walked slow laps around the neighborhood to build up strength. At their post-workout recovery sessions at Dan's, they tackled everything from the Steelers to spring projects and summer vacations. It was at one of those roundtables that he decided on a brick walk. Dan gave him his masonry hammer, suggesting he keep it displayed in a prominent place as a reminder of his commitment. Naturally, he'd kept it on his venerable Wiley GAAP , the book of Generally Accepted Accounting Principles,.

He picked up the masonry hammer in his gloved hand and felt the heft of it, hoping he was up to the task at hand, hoping he could do it justice. The bricks he was using were not ordinary home handyman 2:1 paving bricks.

These oversized, red-orange mottled bricks had for years been Green Street in the next town upriver where he'd grown up. They'd endured a century of horses, motorists, pedestrians, winter freezes, and spring thaws until the town decided to modernize the street by paving it with asphalt. The dense bricks with their smooth, naturally sculpted faces were ploughed up and unceremoniously dumped along the riverbank. He'd rescued enough for my walkway that spring, hauling them in Dan's ancient, rusty, mustard-ugly Chevy short-bed pickup. Working alone, he made three trips and stacked the bricks around the back of the house. Now it was time to restore them to their rightful purpose.

One by one, he planted the bricks in the sand, tapping each into place with the blunt end of his hammer and periodically checking for flatness with his spirit level. Using the chisel-end, he split enough bricks in half to allow him to create the staggered stretcher pattern he wanted. For a while, he succeeded in concentrating solely on the task at hand. But, his mind kept drifting back to those daily winters walks with Dan where he slowly regained his strength while Dan's condition seemed to stagnate after an initial improvement. But, Dan's surgery was more extensive, after all. Even so, he found it to be very un-Dan like when Dan began to talk about hoping to reach age fifty.

After three weeks, he was able to go back to work on a reduced schedule, coming home dead tired but happy to be back doing what he did best. He still stopped over to see Dan once or twice a week when he could, offering encouragement and waiting for that turnaround he knew just had to be coming soon.

It was late afternoon when he tapped the last brick into place. He then worked stone dust into the joints between the bricks with a broom to further stabilize the walk, followed by a light hosing down to further pack the stone dust in the joints. The brick walk was finished and a fine, sturdy walk it was, he told himself. He'd done it, built something that would likely outlive him, a brick walk that would make Dan smile.

The call from Dan's wife that woke him early that morning meant Dan would never see the brick walk. Those last few weeks, they both quit kidding each other that there was going to be a happy ending. He knew it would be over soon, knew the call would be coming. Dan, the guy who could fix anything could not, in the end, fix himself.

And what could he have done? He was Yossarian patching Snowden's wounded leg while Snowden's guts spilled onto the floor of the plane. He did what he could but he couldn't fix him.

Deciding he wasn't yet done, Zink bent over and worked free one of the bricks that abutted the driveway. He pushed a dime into the sand and carefully reset the final brick.

About the Author:

David Landsperger is a part-time bicycle mechanic and tungsten guru who splits his time between Sarasota, FL and Pittsburgh, PA, depending on the weather. His fiction has appeared in The Loyalhanna Review and his essays have appeared in the Pittsburgh Tribune-Review and various cycling publications.

WHEN'S MOM GETTING HOME

by Alex de Cruz

I slowly drove the car with my three young children along the frozen-dirt road that ran between the rows of trees. We were at a Christmas tree farm, an hour north of the Twin Cities in Minnesota, where we lived. On a Sunday afternoon in mid-December, I thought getting out of the house and cutting down our own Christmas tree might help cheer the kids up, and myself too. The excursion was a flop and adding to the forlorn mood though.

The weather was bleak: cold and windy with gray skies and snow flurries. As soon as I spotted a half decent tree, I tried to drum up some enthusiasm for helping to cut it down. None of my children had the least interest in getting out of the warm car. Who could blame them, when I felt the same way myself. I jumped out of the car, grabbed the saw from the trunk, and quickly cut the tree down.

As I tied the tree on the car's roof, I recalled the wonderful time we had the previous year. The weather had been much better, but the big difference had been that Marie, their mother was with us. Marie was the center, the heart and soul of our family. It felt very lonely without her. When I'd committed to solo parenting several days a week, I hadn't anticipated how difficult it would be, and how much we'd all miss her.

Marie had left that morning to return to Cedar Rapids, Iowa, a four-hour drive away. We wouldn't see her again until Friday afternoon. Sundays were the hardest time, especially during the four to five months of wintry weather

in Minnesota. During the week, the kids went to school and I'd be at work.

Ever since Marie decided to go back to school to become an orthopedic physician assistant, I tried to be supportive and encouraging. I owed her that. She'd been a full-time mother up until then, which allowed me to concentrate on realizing my goal of becoming a tenured professor at the University of Minnesota.

I'd been an old-fashioned father, parenting more like my father's generation than the somewhat more equally-shared approach of my son and two sons-in-law. If I'm being honest, I probably changed less than two dozen diapers in total with my three children. I'd been spoiled.

Marie had been the one who'd almost always gotten up in the middle of the night, when they cried in their cribs. She'd potty trained them. Much of my parenting involved fun activities, such as making snowmen in the winter and raking leaves in the fall and jumping in the leaf piles. One of my favorites was telling them bedtime stories, which I made up myself.

I shouldn't completely disparage my role. When our children were young, there were more than enough parenting duties to go around. Both of our parents lived in California, so we didn't have grandparents nearby to help. In fact, when we'd arrived in Minnesota, we hadn't known a soul there.

The only school offering the orthopedic program Marie was interested in was Kirkwood

Community College in Cedar Rapids. Our children ranged from eight to twelve years old, when Marie started the two-year program at Kirkwood. Our youngest daughter was old enough so that her mother's absence wouldn't be traumatic. Our two older children were not yet involved in lots of after-school activities, requiring shuttling them around. Much of the time Marie arranged her courses, so she had no Friday classes. She'd get back home either Thursday night or Friday morning.

The kids and I developed a routine for weekdays. They were old enough they got themselves up, dressed, and fixed their own breakfasts, usually just cereal and orange juice. All three rode a school bus to and from school. They got home at around the same time and had a key to the house.

I didn't worry about them being home alone until I got back around 4:30. Our house was in a safe community-oriented neighborhood. We lived close to campus and I could be home in minutes. Our golden retriever put on a ferocious show, if a stranger showed up, but it was only an act. I did all the cooking and usually had dinner ready by six o'clock.

In the evenings there was homework, showers, and getting ready for bed, which required minimal help from me, usually on homework. I had time, after they were asleep, to get ready for my classes the next day. Sometimes I was too tired for my mind to function by then, and I'd have to set the alarm for 5:30 the next morning, which I hated.

As a university professor, I had more control over my schedule than most people. I could take someone to a doctor's appointment for example, as long as it didn't interfere with my teaching a class. Marie didn't have classes during summer and worked at a medical clinic in Minneapolis that first year.

During bumpy times, the kids' favorite refrain when things weren't going well was some version of, "When's Mom getting home?" And when I got frustrated trying to help with something she'd always done, I regularly snapped, "If Mom were here, she'd know what to do."

One night I prepared a nice dinner: pork roast, mashed potatoes and string beans. I was darn proud of myself. I went to let the kids know that dinner was ready, and then headed back to the kitchen. I went ballistic when I saw what had happened.

Our golden retriever had helped himself to the pork roast, which was now on the floor. Some rather colorful language ensued, which got cut short. The dog choked and then vomited up a large chunk of meat, which it had gulped down.

I booted the dog out the back door. I yelled at the kids to stay upstairs and that dinner would be delayed. Staying mad wasn't a luxury I could afford. I needed to cool off and get busy. After cleaning up after the dog, I was going to toss the pork roast into the trash.

I then surprised myself. I trimmed off the part of the meat the dog had eaten from, ran the roast under water from the kitchen faucet, turned the oven back on, and cooked it for another ten minutes.

There were many great times too. The kids and I had a few favorite TV shows we watched together. Sometimes as a break in the evenings, I put a record from a Broadway musical on the Hi Fi. We'd sing and dance to the show tunes. The favorite was "Fiddler on the Roof." I used to belt out, "If I were a rich man."

We celebrated when Marie graduated and became an orthopedic physician assistant at a local hospital. Becoming a two working-parent family brought its own demands, but I was now ready to shoulder my share. Ever since my solo parenting, I've viewed the role played by mothers with new respect.

BLUEBEARD'S TREASURE

by Joseph Albanese

There was treasure in those woods. He knew it. Even at five-years old, he knew it. There were ghosts in those woods as well. He knew this too.

The Boy knew this because it was what he was told. At such a young age, the Boy didn't question bedtime stories.

They weren't just stories though, they were legends.

The woods in question were no more than sixty yards behind his house's back fence.

Hundreds of years before, after Bluebeard found the treasure in his own right, he kept it for himself, and his crew turned on him. This is the story the Boy was told before he'd go to bed.

Bluebeard had to hide out, hide from his crew. Hide from other pirates. Traditionally pirates did their deeds at sea, but the Boy's home was at least forty miles inland. Bluebeard's port was in the middle of South Jersey, according to legends. The Boy accepted this as truth.

Bluebeard hid his treasure in those woods. Jewels and gold and who knows what else, so the legends went. He stayed in hiding until he died, deep in those woods behind the Boy's eventual home. The Boy could see those woods through his bedroom window at night.

Bluebeard's treasure was waiting somewhere in there, in those deep dark woods. So was his ghost. And there they would stay...

Spring meant the Boy's family needed to do some cleaning. So they cleaned. Every room they cleaned. Even the attic.

The legend of Bluebeard and his treasure was not a single family's story. No, this legend spread through the neighborhood. The Boy told someone. That person told another. Soon every kid on the street knew of Bluebeard and his hidden treasure.

It was not odd to the Boy, nor the other five to seven-year-olds, that they all needed to be in the attic to help the Boy's father clean it out. But they were there, huddled and hunched over, searching through random and needless things.

And in that attic they found something. A map. A map to the treasure.

It was an old map. Hundreds of years old probably. They could tell it was old because it was discolored and the edges were burnt. Yes, this was indeed a pirate's treasure map.

The map must have been left by the previous owners of the house. The owners before that must have left it too. Lost in the clutter would lead to the treasure lost in the woods.

Bluebeard must have left it before them, before he died.

And this group of kids knew they had to find that treasure. They had to find that gold and those jewels.

This would be a dangerous mission, going off and find the treasure, deep in those haunted woods. They needed the approval of their parents, like all treasure hunters do.

It would take a few days for everyone to prepare. Treasure hunting was not something to do in haste.

A day before the hunt would take place, the Boy and his father followed the first two clues on the map themselves. According to the map, at first there would be a hill. There was only one hill near those woods, and it happened to be right behind the Boy's house.

So they started there.

They went during the day. Hunting a ghost's treasure is too dangerous at night. Everyone knows this.

The map said to start at the tree with four trunks.

The Boy knew this tree well. The whole neighborhood did. One tree on that hill among many trees was one that stood out, for it had what looked like four trunks coming out of a single base.

The Boy and the neighborhood kids called it the "elevator tree." You would stand in it, and the elevator tree would take you away. Childish fantasies that got in way of grown up business - the treasure.

The Boy and his father followed the map from the elevator tree. Pace after pace they counted. Down the hill. Through the field. And to the entrance of the woods.

There they would stop. It was too dangerous now, just the two of them. And no weapons? They were not that dumb, not that careless.

They'd wait for backup the next day. And backup did come. Treasure hunters. The whole neighborhood of kids. The Boy was the youngest, but this was his hunt, his story.

Kelsey was his best friend by his side. They were too young to know boys and girls couldn't be best friends. They were way too young to know they could be much more than best friends.

There was Pete. Pete was a year older and several years crazier. But he was prepared. He had a metal shield and swords, as metal can kill a

ghost. This was a known. He had crosses around his neck and he had holy water he blessed himself. Impressive for a six year-old.

Sam and Brandon were the tough kids of the neighborhood, six and seven respectively. They both played it cool, but they were scared out of their minds. They could rough up the kids on the lawn, but a ghost was a whole other story.

There were other kids there that day of the hunt. They were mostly there to not be left out. Leaving out others is how Bluebeard lost his crew to begin with, the Boy's father explained.

They were all geared up with water guns and plastic weapons, ready for whatever the woods and Bluebeard could throw at them.

All the parents were there. Some had video cameras. Who would not want to capture this expedition on film? Some followed, some stayed behind. Pete's dad stayed back. Sam's dad, Big Sam, came along with rope. You never know when you need rope.

The Boy's father took them the long way to the woods, passing the big kids sitting on the electric box. The cool older kids always sat there. They were barely teens but to the treasure hunters they were adults. The young kids always wanted to sit there and couldn't wait to be old enough to. But for now they were too young and not cool enough. But they did have a treasure map. That was enough that day.

The Boy, his fellow hunters, and a few witnesses with their cameras followed the map. They followed it to the elevator tree. They followed it down the hill and through the field. They followed it to the edge of the woods.

The Boy took a breath. This next part would be new to him.

There was another hill down into the woods. It was steep. Thank goodness for Big Sam and his big rope. He tied it around his big belly as an anchor. The hunters used the rope for support as they descended the hill and into the darkness of the woods. As dark as five P.M. would allow.

Just into the woods and they lost a member of the group. Sam, the tough kid they all knew, he could not go down the hill into those haunted woods. Fear got him. And he was left behind.

The rest of the kids continued on, following the map, keeping their weapons at hand. Bluebeard's ghost could be anywhere.

They trekked those woods. Deeper and deeper they trudged, but always in sight of the entrance. And then there was a tree. A handprint edged into the bark. It was clearly a handprint as long as you were told that's what it was, as the map told them.

According to the map, it was here that they could find what they sought.

The Boy's father did the digging. He was the only one strong enough to use the shovel. The rest of the hunters stood guard.

He dug and dug and dug some more. And then... he hit something.

"We've found it!" the father shouted into the air.

And there was about to be amount of celebration from all the hunters and the witnesses, when all of a sudden, a great booming voice echoed out from deep in those woods.

"GET OUT OF MY WOODS!" the voice bellowed.

Bluebeard.

There was no time to wait around. Bluebeard had them and their weapons would be useless.

"Run!" the Boy's father cried.

And they did run. Through the woods. Up the hill, using the rope still anchored to Big Sam. Through the field and around the houses.

It was in their escape they made sense of what was happening. This was all real. There really was a treasure map. There really was a treasure. There really was a ghost chasing them.

At five years-old, this could be reality.

They regrouped back in front of the Boy's house. Hearts raced with fear and excitement. They had made it back safely.

Of course the adults were not scared, nor should they have been. Only children are vulnerable to such ghosts. But they were out of

breath, chasing the treasure hunters with their video cameras.

Minutes later the Boy's father finally arrived. He made it back as well.

And he had a box.

It was no larger than a shoebox, but it was old. You could tell it was old because it was made out of burnt wood.

A treasure chest.

It was closed tight and the Boy's father had to open it with a hammer. He banged it. And the lip opened.

And it was everything they imagined. Jewels. Gold. Chalices.

Treasure.

They found what they sought. They found the impossible.

Even the big kids left their electric box to see what the commotion was about.

These treasure hunters had succeeded. And for that summer he basked in the glory of what they accomplished.

This was real to the Boy. It was real for a long time. The hunters divvied up the takings evenly. The Boy kept his share of the treasure in his room. He brought it to school to show the other kids.

He was proud of his accomplishment.

At night he looked out at the woods, wondering if Bluebeard would ever leave its refuge to come after his treasure, to come after the Boy.

In the end, Bluebeard never came back.

The treasure hunt was as real as anything that would happen to the Boy after it, even if it wasn't. But for that day, there was magic in those woods. The magic a father can give his child. For that day, ghosts were real, and their treasure can live with you forever.

About the Author:

Joseph Albanese is a writer from South Jersey. His fiction, nonfiction, and poetry can be found in publications across the U.S. and in ten other countries. Joe is the author of Benevolent King, Smash and Grab, Caina, For the Blood is the Life, Candy Apple Red, and a poetry collection, Cocktails with a Dead Man.

MILK DUTY

by John L. Stanizzi

St. Mary's was a tiny, predominantly Irish-Catholic school – first through eighth grade. There were thirty-one kids in my graduating class -- 1962. There was Armstrong. Flaherty. McGowan. Lynch. O'Connor. There was Father Shanley. Monsigneur Drennen. And there were the nuns who may or may not have been Irish. Who knows? They all changed their names. Sister Mary Bernardo. Sister Maria Richard. Sister Grace Mary. So who knows?

And then there was me – Johnnie Stanizzi. I'm not Irish.

One time, for a reason that really does remain a mystery, someone decided that it would be a good idea to allow Greg and me to take care of "Milk Duty." It was a short stint, and during that very, very short stint on milk duty I took part in a miracle. Figures, right? Catholic school, and all.

I guess I sort of understand what they were thinking, but how could they have been that naïve. Greg and me? On milk duty? The two absolute worst kids in the school. It was unbelievable. I remember thinking, This is unbelievable! But I think I understand how it happened. The nuns were with us every day, so they got the full force of our obstinance. Daily. But Father Shanley only got the stories, from the Sisters' point of view. I really think he underestimated how much disruption we caused because on more than one occasion he'd intervene and dole out the punishment, and it was never as bad as what the sisters would give us. They'd keep us after school writing a thousand times I will not take the Lord's name in vain.

Or I will not talk in class. Or I will not bother Teresa. But Father Shanley would do things like make us go the rectory after school and vacuum or dust or something. And he'd always be there, joking and talking like a normal human being, things the nuns never did, ever. That's why I think the "milk duty" idea was his. It had to be. There was no way the nuns would ever let Greg and me go anywhere alone, unsupervised. That was guaranteed trouble. Guaranteed. And the milk duty fiasco was typical proof.

There was no cafeteria at St. Mary's. Everyone brought their lunches to school in small brown, grease-stained bags. Everything wrapped in useless waxed paper. Soggy sandwiches. Bruised apples. A couple of Oreos. We left our lunches in the "cloak room," which was a long, dark corridor directly behind the classroom. One door opened out to the hallway. The other door opened into the classroom. Mornings, we'd file from the hallway and into the darkened cloak room, toss our lunches on the floor, hang up our "cloaks," and enter the classroom at the other end.

As the morning wore on, the smells from all those bags would waft out of the cloak room and begin to permeate the air in the class. All those different lunches...peanut butter and jelly, bologna, salami, last night's leftovers – meatloaf, chicken, some kind of "American" macaroni -- all those smells hung in the air of the classroom which I swear got up to a hundred degrees by May. And we ate in the classroom at our desks. It was disgusting. I will never, ever forget the smell and foul taste of a wilted lettuce, rancid tomato, hot mayonnaise, bologna sandwich, on soggy white bread. I will never un-see that slick tomato and greasy lettuce dripping from that flattened, wet sandwich. Wonder Bread. Helps build strong bodies twelve ways. Look for the red, yellow, and blue balloons printed on the wrapper. Right.

Also stashed in our greasy brown lunch bags was a nickel. That was for milk, which was delivered to the school at lunch time. The milk guy would drive up to the door at the back of the school which opened to the basement. There was a long corridor that led to a big open area where the church held bingo and spaghetti dinners. The corridor had boys' and girls' bathrooms on the right side, and a couple of storage rooms on the left. The storage rooms held the Boys' and Girls' Brigade uniforms, props for the Christmas Minstrel, reams of papers, folding tables...things like that.

It had to be somebody's job to go down and meet the milk truck. It was always one of the "good" kids, someone Sister deemed "trustworthy." But this one time, after Greg and I had gotten into some trouble – I don't remember what exactly -- Father Shanley must have made the decision to give that job to Greg and me. I know. Right. Don't ask me! This was 6th grade. We had already been in every kind of trouble you can imagine, though as I think of it, the infractions that made our reputations legendary were so innocuous, so silly, that all the drama that swirled around me all the time was entirely unnecessary and a creation of the nuns and their own cockeyed view of how to treat kids. The nuns and my parents; what a team! There wasn't an ounce of patience or understanding among them, and their preconceived notions about us traveled with us and grew from grade to grade. But what had we actually done wrong in the first place to derail this train? Talk back? Probably. Not do our work? Yeah, I guess. Pick on kids at recess? I suppose so, but not too much. Vandalize the school? Yup. Once. But, man, the way they treated us, the way they explained it to our parents, we were like wild animals, careless hoodlums who terrorized the school, in the classrooms and on the playground. I never really thought of myself as a bad kid. Not at

first, anyway. But you know, if someone keeps telling you you're bad long enough, you not only start to believe it, but you start to act on it. Anyway, for whatever reason, Father Shanley thought it might be a good idea to put the two biggest gangsters in the school on milk duty.

Here's how that went.

The milk guy brought all the milk down to a little room off the hallway in the basement. It was very remote. No classrooms. No people, except maybe our janitor, Frenchie, whose real name was Mr. Thibodeau, naturally. There was nothing else down there. Just the smell of sawdust and Pine-Sol, and a whole lot of emptiness...a long, empty corridor...a few empty rooms. And that's where the milk man rolled his hand truck...down that hallway, and into a room where we were waiting. He tossed the plastic milk crates onto the table and left.

And there we were. Milk duty. Oh geez.

It was our job to divvy up the milk. Fourteen milks for Sister Anthony Mary's class. Nine white. Five chocolate. Sixteen for Sister Maria Richard....and so on. Then we'd traipse all over the school, delivering the milk to each classroom. Totally unsupervised. It was amazing to me. An absolute invitation for trouble. I just couldn't grasp being so completely unsupervised. I also couldn't handle it.

On our last day of milk duty – the second day -- I discovered that if you aimed one of those cardboard milk containers at someone, and squeezed it firmly, quickly, the milk would spray out in a nice, hard, thin stream. I don't remember exactly how I figured it out. But I do remember saying, Hey, Greg. And when he looked up from milk-divvying, I shot him. Squirrrrt!!! Chocolate milk right off the chin.

"You fucker! What the fuc....."

But before he could get the words out, I shot him again.

Instantly. I mean instantly, Greg picked up a carton and shot me.

And that was it.

We were off. Unloading milk at each other with complete abandon. Consequences?

Whatever! Squirt!! Squirt!!

When we were both drenched in luke-warm milk, Greg had had enough, ran out of the room, cackling, and headed for the exit door at the end of the hall, maybe twenty yards away. I have no idea where he thought he was going. That door opened to the parking of the apartment house next to the school. What was he going to do out there? But I started to follow him out, chocolate weapon in hand.

And that's when the miracle happened.

Greg made it to the exit door. Pushed it open with all his might. And screamed with laughter, anticipating being hit. In fact, he not only made it to the door, he made it out the door!

That's when I let my chocolate grenade fly. I threw the container the length of the hallway, as hard as I could. And when the airborne carton reached the door, Greg was all but vanishing out to the safety of the parking lot. The door was nearly completely closed. Greg was safe. But somehow that little eight-ounce milk container passed through the five-inch crack of the closing door, smacked Greg directly in the back of his escaping head with an audible SPLAT! OW!! and exploded in a glorious spume of utterly slow-motion chocolate milk. This remains one of the single most amazing, impossible, remarkable, startling things I have ever seen in my life. It was an impossible throw. Incomprehensible. Not doable. But it happened.

OK. Count. One-one thousand. Two-one thousand.

That's how long it took for Greg to open the door and come back in, soaking wet, out of breath, hands on his hips. That's also how long it took for the two of us to realize what we had done. And what would come next.

And it would not be good.

About the Author:

John L. Stanizzi is author of the collections – Ecstasy Among Ghosts, Sleepwalking, Dance Against the Wall, After the Bell, Hallelujah Time!, High Tide – Ebb Tide, Four Bits, and Chants. His newest collection, Sundowning, will be out this year with Main Street Rag. John's poems have appeared in Prairie Schooner, American Life in Poetry, The New York Quarterly, Paterson Literary Review, Blue Mountain Review, The Cortland Review, Rattle, Tar River Poetry, Rust & Moth, Connecticut River Review, Hawk & Handsaw, and many others. His work has been translated into Italian and appeared in many journals in Italy. His translator is Angela D'Ambra. John has read and venues all over New England, including the Mystic Arts Café, the Sunken Garden Poetry Festival, Hartford Stage, and many others. For many years, John coordinated the Fresh Voices Poetry Competition for Young Poets at Hill-Stead Museum, Farmington, CT. He is also a teaching artist for the national recitation contest, Poetry Out Loud. A former New England Poet of the Year, John teaches literature at Manchester Community College in Manchester, CT and he lives with his wife, Carol, in Coventry.

TALES OF PEPPER
by Bettina Rotenberg

June 27, 2018

Pepper was my heart, my soul, the spirit of my life. He animated my bed, the red easy chair in the living room, his bowls on the kitchen counter. He left a half-eaten bone on the carpet in my study. Gina came in from the balcony and Pepper knew the peace of gnawing his own bone was over because Gina would soon commandeer his bone remnant. He rushed Gina with an angry growl and I rose from my seat and closed the doors to separate them, to sequester Pepper with his bone in the study. But soon there were scratching noises on the double doors of the study, and it became apparent that Pepper preferred my company and Gina's presence over sole possession of his bone. This was Pepper. He'd let Gina take possession of every one of his bones so that he could challenge Gina when she came close to me. And Pepper possessed my heart.

At the end of his life, he was scraggly. Hair fell down and eclipsed his lovely eyes. His fur was locked in tight ringlets from being exposed to successive rains. The bones of his back protruded when I tried to stroke him. His plump belly had receded from keeping up with Gina on many long walks. He looked scrawny and frequently refused to eat his kibble, so I heaped on wellness wet food for breakfast, and small pieces of chicken and steak for dinner. I hoped that these foods, which he gobbled down, often choking and coughing because of his speedy ingestion, would encourage him to eat the more healthful dog food. Towards the end

of his life, I'd pick up a handful of kibble, bend double, and hold my hand to his mouth. This method worked from time to time, and the last time he ate, he licked my hand for a long time, I thought to taste the steak juices, but I realized that he was just licking my hand, kissing me.

He said goodbye in so many ways. On the Sunday before he died, he was uncharacteristically lethargic, and rested on the brown leather chair in my study without moving. He did not jump down and follow me wherever I went, as was his wont. This was the sign that something was very wrong. I congratulated myself afterwards that I did not leave Pepper that day to go with Gina to her second obedience class. There were heavy rains and so I had that added incentive to remain at home with Pepper.

He told me silently that he was dying. Such devastating news, I didn't know whether to believe our telepathic communications. But he was preparing me. And he went through my list of friends, telling me who to avoid, because he or she wasn't kind to me or Gina, and who to befriend. It was his parting gift. He took care of me all the time and part of that care involved imparting advice to me about how to deal with the people in my life.

Now he's gone and his sweet eyes are not visible to follow me everywhere I go. I feel lost. My confidant and advisor is missing from my consciousness. Gina lies on the furreted floor of the vestibule or on the carpet in my study. But her eyes are closed, and she dreams of Pepper. Pepper, who sniffed her constantly, and put his little furry paws up on her haunches, humping her tail, or the thin air. And Gina would look around at her eager lover, and growl briefly. She would try to bite Pepper's legs, which were small enough for Gina to take in her mouth. But Pepper deftly jumped aside and avoided Gina's teeth.

I am bereft. My little dog died and now he is an invisible spirit of holiness, healing my hands and wrists so I can walk his beloved dog Gina on a leash. He quietly tells me secrets only for my ears. He tells me what to do. He is my guide. He tells me he will heal the pain in my body, the extravagant pain of his loss.

Pepper, who watched me constantly. He would leave my side and my petting him just to lie opposite me and look at me. I was cared for all the time, awake and asleep. I used to watch Pepper completely relax with his head down at the foot of our bed; and then five minutes later, his head was up again and he was awake until I fell asleep. I'd watch him, his back to me, the black swaths across the white of his body, and I'd feel great pleasure just in looking at his back as he lay on one side of the bed or the other.

I longed to touch him, to stroke his back or his belly. And he loved to spread his legs and have me pet him. But at night he didn't want me to touch him. He wasn't that much of a physical dog. He was an eager spirit, and when he was excited to see me enter the door after I had been away, he'd jump up and down against my legs. I always felt missed and welcomed home again. It was a lovely feeling even though it seemed like Pepper must've suffered from my absence but he was so joyful to see me that I could forget about the pain I'd caused him by leaving him.

Pepper had a serious case of separation anxiety. It manifested itself in his getting very upset and anxious when I was preparing to go out and his howling as soon as I closed the door, or even before I left. It was heart wrenching and I could never be sanguine about him after I heard his cries. If he was being held by someone else on a leash and the look of extreme distress came over his happy face, and he jumped towards me, straining at the leash, I'd hurry away to do my business without him as fast as possible and never let him out of my mind.

I went to Yorkdale shopping centre to find a winter coat and Henry, my caregiver for my dropped foot at that time, drove me and Pepper there. Pepper wasn't allowed to enter the mall, so he had to stay behind with Henry. He looked so panic stricken that I rushed through the mall with the sense that my presence was urgently needed back with Pepper. I was very worried about him. When I got to the store, there were shop helpers standing around. Rapidly I picked out the colour I wanted and asked one of the young men to bring a coat in my size immediately because a friend who was not well needed me. I found the coat, bought it, and was out of the store in a matter of minutes. I had memorized the place where the exit was and rapidly returned to Pepper with a terrible sense that something awful was happening to him. When I saw him, he greeted me with great joy, and to my anxious questioning, Henry assured me he had been all right. I didn't believe him. In my heart, I knew that Pepper was attached to me as much as I was attached to him. That was the state of affairs.

In the last couple of months, Pepper would lift up his head and howl shortly after I got out of bed in the morning and was briefly absent from the bedroom or the study or the living room. I grew to like the sound. It was so pure. But the neighbours were disturbed at an early hour; so I rushed back to Pepper and put my hands on both sides of his body, and he stopped his lamentations. Most mornings this occurred, and I never figured out if it was because I was briefly gone from the room or I hadn't petted him enough when I arose or because he was suffering some pain that I didn't understand. Frequently Gina came running to Pepper too with the natural compassion that dogs feel for each other. But it was always my hands on Pepper's body that intercepted the howling.

Pepper was a favourite at our local Starbucks. Henry would walk with us if we awoke by 7 o'clock and frequently paid for my coffee. He was a sweet man who was in love with me for a while, and initiated taking us to dog parks on Saturdays and not charging me for his time. He loved Pepper, who returned the favour royally. At Starbucks, they agreed to allow Pepper inside, come the cold winter months, and he got a lot of attention and praise from the staff, in particular, Deborah, who was an older woman with dyed red hair cropped short who loved my little dog and always greeted him.

The squirrels that appeared on the front lawns of the houses we passed on our walks were initially my bane. Gina would stop her ambulation and stand very still, or sit, and even lie down to watch these little furry creatures. They would often stop too and there would be a standoff between Gina and the squirrels. In the first couple of months, I would quickly become impatient. First I tried yelling, "come, Gina, come!" She was impervious and wouldn't move. Then I pulled; but frequently I hurt my thumbs or my wrists. Pepper cautioned me to be patient and wait for Gina who usually only moved when said squirrel was out of sight. When it became very hot, I was angry at the squirrels, and sometimes had the misfortune of encountering a squirrel, or even a rabbit who wouldn't move. I'd yell at the squirrels and this outbreak had the opposite effect that I wanted. Often the squirrel wouldn't run away in fright but actually approached closer.

But lately, since Pepper died, and I'm in communication with him constantly during our morning walks when the squirrels most frequently appear, I have more patience, and I watch the squirrels with Gina, trying to figure out what about them fascinates her.

Yesterday I spoke silently with a squirrel, and to my amazement, he answered me. He said, "we heard about you. We've been waiting to see you." I countered, "run up a tree and disappear, so we can continue our walk." The squirrel did what I said!

This morning a squirrel sat by the edge of the road and munched on a berry or a nut. He said, "we heard you didn't have breakfast; so I'm eating for you." He sat there, eating, obviously relishing his meal. He ran towards Gina, and then ran up a tree, and Gina moved on. Gina was particularly pushy this morning, and initially pulled me along at a fast pace. We went to a park in front of a church that smelled of garbage as we came closer to two large garbage cans with open holes. Uncharacteristically Gina

pulled me as she got closer and closer to some squirrel she must've seen in her vicinity. I was able to leave the park eventually, only to encounter a fat beagle that Gina played with. She crouches very near the ground, then jumps and crouches again. I'm fearful that she'll pull a muscle in my wrist or my thumb, so I don't like these sudden movements when she naturally acts like the puppy that she is.

Towards the end of our walk, Gina broke away from walking with me and pulled me into a yard with red poppies. To my dismay, the local rabbit was sitting in a flower bed. Gina charged the rabbit and she ran to the end of the flower bed with Gina following. I got a little angry because she was really pulling me, and yelled, "bad girl!" And she hates that. I was able to pull her out of the garden and continue our walk. Later on she looked really distressed and I told her she was a "good girl" and she relaxed. When she's upset, furrows appear on her brow and her eyes look very sad.

Gina is a wonderful bed partner. Before she goes to sleep and when I wake up, she licks my lips and my nose, and sometimes my ears. One gesture I love is she puts her paw on my back, as though she is holding me. Since she came into our lives, I've been able to fall asleep without sleeping medicine. My dreams are not so disturbing either. Last night I dreamt that I jumped over two wire fences with a woman friend. I didn't think I could make the second one because it was very high; but in my dream I realized I made it, for I was on the other side. In the middle of the dream, I ran into a woman that I knew, but my friend told me not to worry because my appearance had changed so much that I was unrecognizable. We had made it over the fences into foreign territory, but somehow a woman from our former lives was there. The fact that I was unrecognizable was an accomplishment. I had passed through experiences that had changed me.

Often Gina leaves the bed in the middle of the night or early in the morning. When she returns, she's up for kissing me. She frequently puts her head on my pillow and her legs extend to my back. If I turn around, to give her the message that she's in my space and I want her to move to the other side, she usually doesn't respond, or she leaves the bed altogether.

Then between 4 and 6 AM she returns and barks at me to get up. I'm usually awake and resting and she's in a hurry to see the squirrels. When Pepper was here, I'd hurriedly get out of bed because Gina's whining betokened a need to pee, and if I didn't respond with alacrity, she'd often urinate on a rug in the living room. Lately Gina's vocal missives do not mean a need to pee right away, just a pressing eagerness to go on a walk out in the morning air.

After Pepper's death, I went to Starbucks somewhat reluctantly. I had the feeling someone would ask me where Pepper was. Sure enough, Deborah was taking orders, and she leaned over the counter, looking for Pepper. She asked, "where's my friend?" I answered, "he died." She was shocked and aghast and said, "I am sad." I said, "me too." I ordered an American Blanco and went outside. A tear fell on my cheek as I thought of all the times Pepper had gone there with me. Everywhere he protected me from sadness and loneliness. Now Gina and I really miss Pepper. I have pains in my knee and my ankle – Pepper says they are from grief.

I went next to get a pedicure at Nail Boutique. Mio gave me a very good very gentle pedicure, and she too asked for Pepper. He used to jump up on my lap when I had a pedicure. One time he insisted on getting on my lap when I had both a manicure and pedicure at the same time, and the soapy water that the manicurist was using fell over onto my hip. Everyone loved him, and they continued to ask about him long after his death.

Pepper was the most loving presence wherever I went. We would go to a woman's dress shop together, and like Shuggie, my former dog, he'd encourage me to buy some of the clothes I tried on. He'd lie on a couch covered with a black fur cover, and always drape himself over the clothes I took off to try on store clothes. He was loved by all the sales girls for his sweet demeanour and his way of looking so lovingly at me. Even where there wasn't a couch to lounge on, Pepper would enter the cubicle with me where I would try on clothes and pronounce judgements about different outfits. I always followed his advice about whether to buy pants or a top or a skirt or a dress. Sometimes he knew ahead of time, before I actually

tried on boots, for example, whether they'd fit. I bought a pair of shiny silver boots last winter that fared very well and took me trudging in the snow and ice without any ill effects.

When I was very angry with my father, Pepper encouraged me to go to the dress shop on Yonge Street. I bought an expensive green leather jacket but I felt guilty about it afterwards, and returned a dress and a blouse and some pants to accrue some credit. There had to be a psychological reason for dealing with fury with my father by buying something that he'd disapprove of. Pepper knew the justification – I just indulged the rebellious spirit.

Pepper advised me to do some things that were very surprising. For example, I spent a lot of time drafting a series of course proposals for Continuing Studies creative writing department at the University of Toronto. Finally, the director approved one of my proposals and invited me for an interview. I was accepted as an instructor to teach a philosophy and experimental poetry course the following winter. Then one night Pepper told me to email the guy and cancel. I was very shocked. I told Pepper, "it's so prestigious." When I was invited to teach, the prestige meant a lot to me. I'd suffered the previous year from depression and been bedridden for months because of dropped foot. A succession of caregivers left me with an impaired sense of confidence in myself, and getting a university course to teach was something that impressed everyone I knew.

Pepper asked me, ""is prestige the only reason you want to teach the course? Do you really want to teach the poets you chose? You'll hate it and you won't like your students. There's something else you're going to do. You need to make room for it." I was more or less convinced. In any case, I trusted Pepper, so I emailed the guy that I had other priorities than the course, and wanted to postpone it. I wrote up a statement about communicating with dogs, and tried to figure out where I could conduct a class with dogs and dog owners about talking to animals.

As with every one of Pepper's startling pieces of advice, I waffled, and wrote the director a second time, asking to teach a poetry course.

He agreed to hire me a second time. Yet again I turned the course down, enrolled in a fiction writing course which I suffered through for eight weeks. I hated the way the teacher and most of the students critiqued my stories, and abandoned one story after another, without "correcting" any of them, with the sense that my interiority wasn't comprehended or appreciated. I came out of it with ideas about teaching psychological dreamlike fiction, but Lee Gowan by this time was fed up with an applicant who shifted her expertise from poetry to nonrealistic fiction, a category they didn't entertain in the creative writing department anyway. So I wrote Mr. Gowan one last time, asking to teach the original poetry course he'd accepted, and he summarily turned me down.

I had thought that fiction writing was the pursuit that was replacing the teaching of a university poetry course. At the same time, I became very absorbed in looking for a second dog. I had learned a few months prior to this that Pepper was diagnosed with heart disease and only had a year to three years to live. Pepper knew that his days were numbered and we threw ourselves into the search for another dog. I was popular because I already had one dog and I was a stay-at-home "mom." I now realize that having two dogs, which all of a sudden made me very busy, was one of the things Pepper had in mind. He knew he was going to die; we didn't know when; but he wanted me to have a companion for when he was no longer here.

Pepper also advised me concerning the friends and help that I had. He kept me up-to-date about the way the dog walkers and housecleaner treated him and Gina. Some of my friends and family he disliked for the way they treated Gina or their patronizing attitude towards me. On the Sunday before he died, he went through a list of my friends and told me whom to reject and whom to embrace. Once again, I was very surprised. He criticized people who I thought were devoted friends and guided me in sending angry and critical emails to them. Some of them wrote back and asked me what they should do, or told me I was right. I felt kindness and gratitude toward these people. In others, I saw clearly the flaws Pepper mentioned and tried to refrain from

apologizing to reestablish contact. The people that Pepper told me to see immediately started calling me and setting up dates to get together. As usual, Pepper had shown wisdom and foresight.

One of the people Pepper counselled me to stay in touch with and go visit was my mother. We had gone together to see her two weeks before Pepper died. It was a day I regretted because I walked Pepper a couple of miles from Yorkville Avenue to our apartment, only stopping at my mother's house for a short while. It was hot and I felt guilty one night after Pepper's death that I had exerted him too much and caused his death. But Pepper walked without difficulty. I was glad he saw my mother, who adored him, one last time. While we were there, mommy wanted to see Pepper jump up on my lap, the way he had before. But he stayed down by my feet.

In the middle of our visit, a terrible storm erupted and there was a crashing downpour and heavy winds. We left as my mother was yelling in pain at a caregiver, and I had an awful sense of old age and failing health. We went downstairs to her living room and stayed inside until the storm passed. Then we walked out Cottingham Street down a back way to St. Clair Avenue. Many branches had broken off from the storm and blocked our way. Trees had split as well, and the walk was scary. Cars lined up on the back street we walked along and the exhaust fumes bothered me.

I was wearing a white skirt and the sleeveless black-and-white check top I had bought, and was still hot. The June weather in Toronto was oppressive, frequently rising to 90°F. But my companion walked along beside me with no apparent trouble. After his death, I worried that this walk caused a resurgence of Pepper's cough; but I'm not sure. The vet asked me if Pepper had been coughing when I brought them into the clinic the day that he died. I said, "yes, the same cough you examined him for." But afterwards I berated myself for not bringing Pepper in to be examined again.

I wrote Dr. Franklin after Pepper's death, asking him if there was anything he could say to help me deal with the awful guilt I felt. I'd wake up in the middle of the night and remember some pain or symptom that Pepper had and be attacked by guilt feelings. I remembered that I had similar feelings when I learned about Shuggie's death while I was in the hospital.

Thankfully Ryan Franklin wrote me an email that consoled me. He said that Pepper's death was sudden, rapid, and couldn't have been foreseen. He wrote, "Pepper was exquisitely lucky to have you as his owner, you did EVERYTHING for him. There was nothing that you could have done to prevent it." My friend, Annie, in Berkeley told me, "Tina, you're not God. You can't control death." Those two assuaged my spirit and I stopped being tormented by guilt. Pepper's spirit joined me and we resumed our talks. When I walked around my apartment, lost and bereft, he guided me to sit down and listen to him.

I miss Pepper sorely. Gina sleeps most of the day, and when she isn't sleeping, she is prowling around the apartment like a young panther. She looks for diversion in her toys, but unless she has a satisfying bone she's never entertained for very long. She often barks at me and whines to be taken out. She is very insistent; and then when she gets outside, she is very happy.

She turns her head from side to side as she walks, looking for squirrels I suppose, noticing everything around her. On our walks together, Pepper watched me and Gina, and was not concerned with squirrels or even other dogs. I remember the days when he trotted along ahead of me, faster than I walked. Then he slowed down, and when we walked with Gina, she slowed her pace to accommodate Pepper. Now she walks fast, pulling me along, her powerful back legs ready to spring into action.

Tomorrow I go to the Pet Memorial building to be with Pepper's body. I'm nervous. I don't know if it's going to be painful or whether there will be an opening to being with him. I wrote a prayer:

May I always be with you, Pepper.

May you come close to me.

May I feel your tender and passionate love always.

May you join Gina and me in our loneliness for you.

May you find peace and joy wherever you go.

May you accompany us on our walks and protect us.

May we feel your presence with us waking and sleeping.

My dearest Pepper.

Pepper followed me everywhere. If I went from the bedroom into the dining space, he'd come and lie beside my chair or directly under my chair. When I went to the living room, he'd lie down on my left side or jump onto my lap. When I adopted Gina, he set up his quarters on my lap, and he was so warm and cozy. But when Gina came close, he growled at her, and my lap became the scene of a quarrel between them. When I sat at my desk, Pepper lay on the purple pillow at my feet. If he had secured a bone, he gnawed on it which attracted Gina to his spot. She would consider him and the bone for a few seconds, then let out a loud bark. Pepper would growl, and then abandon the bone. All this activity took place so close to my feet that I'd have to leave my desk chair and try to manage their quarrel at a safer distance.

But Pepper growled much more furiously if Gina approached while he was lying near me on the bed. Pepper would climb on top of me and growl at top speed from his perch. Just before he died he was beside himself, growling repeatedly, jumping off the bed and making as if to bite Gina, he was so angry when she approached. Gina partially capitulated and, instead of lying at the head of the bed beside me, lay at the foot of the bed. Pepper even slept one night on the pillow beside me, which he never did.

Pepper knew he was dying and told me so two days before he actually did. Perhaps he wanted sequestered time with me at the end and that's why he objected to Gina entering the bedroom.

Whenever I spoke to Pepper in my mind silently, he always responded and concluded with "Tina, dear one." Immediately after he died, I could still hear him clearly. Then his silent voice became very quiet and barely discernible. There was a period when I thought that he had gone somewhere else. Then he told me he was in the "hollows" and this is the place that I could look forward to being after my death. There was another time that I thought that he had disappeared altogether, and I grieved. But I called on him a little later and he responded again.

It has come to me recently that the divine spirit entered Pepper when he came into my life. He comforted me as no one else has, assuring me that I would never enter a hospital again. And when he died, Pepper the dog disappeared, and once again he was the divine. But I can't think of God, if Pepper was God, as an abstract Spirit of heaven. He remains my little poodle mix animal I love so much.

About the Author:

Bettina Rotenberg grew up in Toronto, attended Radcliffe College, studied painting for three years, and received her PhD in Comparative Literature from University of California, Berkeley. She taught art, literature, and creative writing at colleges in the Bay Area, and between 1995 and 2015 was the founding Director of VALA (Visual Arts/Language Arts). She sent visual and performing artists into public schools in the East Bay to work with poets to teach low income minority children poetry in conjunction with the arts. She wrote a book about her work, I Dare to Stop the Wind, which was published in 2010. She now writes, draws, teaches, and takes care of her dog.

SURVIVE. LIVE

by Edward Lee

Like too many fathers across the globe I only get to see my daughter every second weekend. Out of 336 hours, I get 30. Before, as a stay at home dad, I saw my daughter every day. I got her up for school in the morning, fed her, dressed her, walked her to school, and outside the school, hugged and kissed her, told her I loved her before she went in. After school I would pick her up and we would spend the afternoon together, playing, doing homework, drawing, watching television and reading. Then, at night, her mother, home from work, would take her to bed, and before she went upstairs I would hug and kiss her, and tell her I love her.

Every day I do not see my daughter is a half-lived day. My morning did not begin with seeing her. And my night will not end with me checking on her asleep in her room before I myself go to bed. Though myself and her mother separated over a year ago, I find my daughter's absence no easier today than I did in the first weeks after the end of the relationship. If anything it is as though my daughter's absence weighs heavier on my heart with every reminder of her, be it in the cry of another child, or in the sight of another girl the same age as her, or even hearing a song I know she likes on the radio; there are moments, sometimes only minutes long, sometimes hours, when I simply cannot function, so undone am I by such reminders, combined with the knowledge that I will not be seeing her for 'X' amount of days. I feel as though, were once part of my existence was defined by being a father, that now I am

nothing more than this half-being I have become since I was removed from the everyday workings of my daughter's life.

Every day, simply put, is a struggle, one I do not know how to overcome, beyond setting my sights on the next time I get to see her, what we might do across those thirty hours, how we might make up for all those missing hours. This is not healthy, this struggle, this feeling. I know this. But I find myself unable to shift my mind from this thinking, a feat made all the harder by the depression I have suffered from all my life, a depression which, like a snake endlessly eating its tail, increases, and is increased by, all those empty days. I am not existing. I am not living. I am surviving. That's all: surviving.

Out of all those empty days, the Monday following my weekend with my daughter is the emptiest, the hardest. For those 30 hours I have re-experienced what it is to be a present father. I have become responsible again for her well being, directly so. From 11 a.m. on Saturday morning, when I pick her up from her mother, and we embark on whatever adventures she wishes, until 5 p.m. Sunday evening when her mother picks her up and takes her home, I have once more become a regular part of her life, playing with her, feeding her, minding her. On the Saturday night I put her to bed, read some stories to her, and when she has fallen asleep, simply watch her, drink her in, for a few minutes, a half hour, and, once, near the beginning of this seemingly endless journey, for an hour and a half. Come the morning I wake and she is there for me to see. Some-times she wakes before me and I am woken with a body slam and an excited 'Daddy' while other mornings I wake her, just as I did when I lived under the same roof as her; there is an all too apparent cruel irony when she is the one to wake me, when before, I would dread being woken by her at some ridiculously early hour, but now, I cherish the sound of her no matter the hour. Both of us awake I give her her breakfast, get her dressed, and again, we do whatever she wishes to do.

I feel like a father again. Complete. I feel like a human being once more. 30 hours out of 336.

In the hours after she has gone home with her mother, I still feel relatively happy, com-plete. Normal. I have hugged her and kissed her and told her I love her. I have helped her strap herself into her car seat, and then stood at the gate and waved and blown kisses at her as they drive off, my daughter waving and blowing kisses at me. I am, I freely admit, tired, pleasantly so; while obviously impossible to cram two weeks into two days we have achieved much in our time together. Never the best sleeper myself, even before my world was so savagely rearranged, I sleep reasonably well that night. But come the Monday morning, and not only has the emptiness returned, it has expanded, widened itself to the point where I am more that abyss than I am a man; what I had been missing for two weeks I have experi-enced only for it to be gone again for another two weeks, and the pain of it is as bright and new as if freshly inflicted, like a wound almost healed, suddenly, and violently, pulled asunder again. My eyes are barely open and already I wish to close them again, and stay in bed and not rise until it is a morning where my daugh-ter greets me.

That Monday after my weekend with her is my own private circle of hell.

I cannot help but imagine that this will always be the case, this dark emptiness, this immova-ble nothingness. I do not know how other sin-gle fathers endure it. I do not know how any man, or woman, can endure being separated from their children for such long periods of time. But, that is what occurs across the world every day. I have spoken to other fathers in similar circumstances in the hopes that I might find some comfort there, possibly even learn how they endure their own enforced absences. But all I feel after these conversations is a sharper sadness, one on par with how how I feel on those threaded Monday mornings. I have never be one to fully open myself with strangers, and doing so makes me uncomforta-ble, but it is discomfort I am willing to endure if it gives me some ease. Even talking to friends about it, I feel myself overwhelmed by its weight, emotions constricting my throat, tears coming to my eyes, and again I feel worse than I did before I began speaking. Even as I write this, hoping that maybe resorting to my be-loved writing will ease my pain in a way no amount of talking ever will, I am crying, and there is a solid blackness sluggishly turning in the pit of my stomach; if it were not for the fact that I am alone as I write I doubt I would be able to keep putting word after word. May-be when I reach the end of this piece I will feel better in the satisfied way I feel when having completed a poem or a short story. Maybe. As I write, it just feels as though I am pouring an ocean's worth of salt into a wound the size of the Grand Canyon, my nerve endings launching fire into my heart and mind.

On my phone, in the clock app, there are four different times set for the alarm, all saved and ready to be switched on as needed; three of them get used at various points during each month, and so it is easier to simply leave them saved. The fourth one was for when I was still a stay-at-home-dad and my world still made sense, the one that would sound at 7.33 a.m., for me to rise and wake my daughter on those occasions she slept beyond that point and hadn't already woken me with an elbow to the ribs, or a foot to the head. I have not used that setting since I moved out of the home I shared with my daughter and her mother, the home they both still live in, the home I still own but will never reside in again. But I will not erase it, no more than I would erase the first photograph I have of my daughter, taken mere minutes after she was born so various family members could see this beautiful new addition to the family, a photo that has transferred from that phone to every phone I have had since. Every time I have to switch on one of my regu-larly used alarm times, I see it there, and am saddened by the sight of it, which, some days, is simply an extra weight upon the sadness which permanently dwells within me, while on others it is a crippling punch to my mental equilibrium; there is no rhyme nor reason to what my reaction is going to buy, it simply strikes as it strikes, and I hurt as I hurt. If I were to erase it I might spare myself this unnecessary addition to my already manifold pain, but I would rather this extra blade to my being rather than lose one more connection, no matter how tenuous, with my daughter.

This coming weekend is my weekend with my daughter. I will ensure she has a good time. I will hug her and kiss her. I will tell her I love her, repeatedly. I will spoil her and feed her. I will play with her and draw with her. I will put her to bed, and read to her. I will watch her sleep. And I will smile when she says "daddy" on the Sunday morning, as I will smile when she hugs me and kisses me, when she tells me she loves me. This weekend I will, if even only for those 30 hours, do more than survive. I will live.

About the Author:

Edward Lee's poetry, short stories, non-fiction and photography have been published in magazines in Ireland, England and America, including The Stinging Fly, Skylight 47, Acumen and Smiths Knoll. He is currently working on a novel. He also makes musical noise under the names Ayahuasca Collective, Lewis Milne, Orson Carroll, Blinded Architect, Lego Figures Fighting, and Pale Blond Boy.

His blog/website can be found at https://edwardmlee.wordpress.com

EXCERPT: A REVIEW OF "ABSOLUTELY, POSITIVELY 4th STREET"

by Brenda Yates

...as for the title poem, it, too, keeps to itself. In fact, nothing is known of "I" at the outset (perhaps expected by now of this author). Strangely, nothing is revealed in its course, an oddity offset only by a growing sense of narrator presence. What are we to make of fragmented references to Pessoa, Dylan, Rushdie, Wallace Stevens, Borges, Unamuno, T. S. Eliot and the Oxford English Dictionary? But let's begin with the title. Call up a famous song by arguably one of the 20th century's greatest songwriters, and already a reader is alert or perhaps even slightly hostile; imitation so often breeds weakness.

The second notable choice is no better—an epigraph from Fernando Pessoa: Am I thinking about everything,/Or has everything forgotten me? It is worth noting that Pessoa wrote a lot about identity and, in fact, created several. None were mere pseudonyms inasmuch as they wrote in different styles, critiqued or reviewed one another's work, and had entirely separate biographies.

When venturing into Pessoa territory, witticisms spring to mind, such as: "The self-division of the I is a common phenomenon in cases of masturbation." Or "the more I worked on The Book of Disquiet, the more unfinished it became." Or that language was a scalpel to cut to

the heart of truth, which he did not believe in, and to the heart of himself, which he also did not believe in. He did, however, consider himself animated by various ideas not the subject of this review.

Yates seems haunted by a concern that one's angst may be sophomorically self-indulgent. (Don't forget Dylan's classic line "you got no faith to lose and you know it.") The speaker, like Pessoa, has "lost all respect for the past," and aspires to "factless autobiography"—demonstrated by a self-aware beginning that exists only to set up the recursive mechanisms in play throughout. First, the strategy steeps the body of the poem in religious allusion. "Faith," "God," "anoint," join images of shroud, rain, roses, fisherman-like spiders, a heavenward-leaping worm, as language slips back to its sacred-seeming origins. Speaking in meditative fragments, the "I" moves through its cruxes in the form of an inclusive, indirect discourse, an effect used to draw the reader in.

We become "I" knowing, for instance, that faith, a gift, can never be an act of will, that some of the most powerful tragedies in western literature concern its loss. We get inklings of Eliot's "Ash Wednesday;" of Unamuno's "San Manuel Bueno: Martir," of Stevens'

"Sunday Morning," of the Borges character drawn into an encyclopedia entry about another world, as well as his book review of a tome that never existed (which now we want to read).

We know belief is not unwavering, that even saints struggle with doubt. But worse is Unamuno's parish priest who continues to nurture, to save others though he, himself, is beyond salvation because he has lost his faith. We are kin to him, to that writer—who sought truth in life and life in truth, even knowing he would never find them—and to Yates' speaker, given to seeking. We understand paradox—Salman Rushdie noted there was no vocabulary to speak of the spiritual except the religious, yet religion is the poison in the blood as well as the great solace and inspiration. We know art began as sacred—and that sacred, "at its best, brings about great masterpieces, and at its worst, murders."

Though Yates has been criticized as descending into indifference, I would argue instead that in this book and its title poem, she evokes the way we know what only humans can, eyes open. This despite the fact that rain, spiders, shrubs, cats and of course, the universe, don't care about struggles to understand the world or to label its parts in order to bring ourselves some comfort.

It may be that her "I" weighs in with a Buddhist sensibility of mindfulness, or can be seen as having some spiritual relationship with nature, but even so, we aren't allowed to forget the sadness and futility that accompany consciousness. We keep in mind how frequent these thematic arcs are, as in, say, Defoe's Journal of the Plague Year or Camus' The Plague." And of course, we must consider etymologies.

There's a history of confusion between imminent and immanent—that indwelling or abiding, as of the Deity. Consider, too, the latter's secondary denotations that make the distinction of acts performed or occurring within, rather than outside the mind of the subject. Implicit is the fact that one of the earliest gods was the sun—which carries through history, as in: "May the Lord bless thee and keep thee.

May the Lord make his face shine upon thee." Attending to roots in the hypothetical proto-language of origin wherein words like shine, sheen or show have connotations of behold, of radiance, of brilliance, we find they begin to define one another, adding illuminate, glisten, shimmer, luminous, glow, along with beam, ray, halo, as in the appearance of...which are then often compounded with deity or divine.

And so a speaker weary of trying to find an expression lacking that, concludes in the only vocabulary available—a likeness to God.

Even a word such as beautiful can't be fully unlocked from beatific, and thus to bless, where the OED makes an aside thusly: "Hence, a long and varied series of associations, heathen, Jewish, and Christian, blend in the English uses of bless and blessing."

I would argue that these are in fact blessing poems.

From Reviews and Essays, 2000 to 2015 by Willes Christian

About the Author:

Brenda Yates is a prize-winning author of Bodily Knowledge (Tebot Bach). Her reviews, interviews and poems can be found in Chaparral; The Tishman Review; KPFK Radio 90.7 (Why Poetry); The American Journal of Poetry; Mississippi Review;City of the Big Shoulders: An Anthology of Chicago Poetry (University of Iowa Press); Angle of Reflection (Arctos Press); Manifest West (Western Press Books); The Southern Poetry Anthology, Volume VI: Tennessee (Texas Review Press); Fire and Rain: Ecopoetry of California (Scarlet Tanager Books); Unmasked: Women Write about Sex and Intimacy after Fifty (Weeping Willow Books); and Local News: Poetry About Small Towns (MWPH Books) as well as journals in Ireland, the UK, Israel, China and Australia.

A WASTE OF BREATH

by Roberto Loiederman

November, 1967 -- Da Nang, Vietnam

I looked over the railing. I'd just smoked half a joint after having swallowed small, measured amounts of Dexedrine and Valium, so I was hypnotized by the scene: oil slicks, left behind by ships like ours, created a constantly-shifting color palette just beyond the shoreline.

Small, wiry Vietnamese children used casket-sized Styrofoam casings in order to float on the gentle surf. It took me a few seconds to realize what these casings were: they'd been used to cushion the stowed bombs, big ones, during the SS Del Alba's trip across the Pacific.

Bob yelled from the bridge: "Hey, Maynard, someone looking for you. Top of the gangway."

My visitor was Dana Stone, a photojournalist. Before the Del Alba had left San Francisco, Theresa told me to look up her friend Dana in the war zone. I'd left a message for him at the Da Nang Press Club, where a wire service reporter told me, "Dana? Probably in the boonies."

The next day Dana, in his mid-20s like me, showed up at the Del Alba. He wore U.S. Army camouflage fatigues, but he used an Australian bush hat, cocked at a jaunty angle, signaling he was a civilian. He was short, compact, energetic, wore glasses, with a thin nose that came straight down from his forehead, eyes close together, giving him a rat-like look.

"I'm Dana."

"Maynard."

We shook hands.

"So you're a friend of Theresa's," Dana said. "I call her Big Red."

"Tall, maroon hair. Yup. Big Red. She was my old lady for a couple of weeks."

"She was my old lady for a few weeks too."

"Homosexuality once removed," I said.

"What?"

"That's what Leslie Fiedler calls it. Us, having had the same old lady."

Dana laughed uncomfortably.

He had a nervous, intense manner, and he asked to see the bridge, the engine room, even the fo'c'sle I shared with my two watch-partners. He said he had worked on merchant ships before becoming a photojournalist. Dana peppered me with questions. Did I like working on ships? How did I feel about being on a ship full of napalm and other bombs?

I shrugged it off. "You must know," I said. "You know the joke about ammo ships: If anything happens on this ship, she ain't going down. Uh-uh. She's going straight up."

"Yeah, right," Dana said. "Shit happens. But it's not like going into battle, right?"

I said the tough part, for me, about working on ships was the solitude: on lookout on the bow at night, scanning the sea for lights, standing by at 3:00 am in the messroom, or working alone all day on deck, removing rust or painting. I said that life at sea had taught me how to be alone.

"Yeah," Dana said, looking at the rigging. "Is that useful?"

"Well, it's what we really are, all the time, isn't it? Even when we're with others?"

I said I'd memorized lots of poems, mostly by W. B. Yeats and Wallace Stevens. That way, I said, when I was alone, I had "good company."

"Far out."

We left the ship, went down the gangway to the pier, and walked through a U.S. Army depot where there were hundreds of broken tanks, LSTs, amphibious craft and other large military machines, kept there so they could be cannibalized for parts. At the end of this area, I pointed out a small, empty wire-mesh trashcan that had a sign on it: Please help keep Vietnam clean.

"Americans... we're good at unconscious irony," I said. Dana didn't react. It was hard to tell if he had even heard the remark.

Once outside the depot, Dana led me toward a jeep. "A Newsweek reporter lent it to me. I get to use it when he's in the boonies."

As he drove, Dana rattled on about the war.

"You get a rush when you're in battle. I mean really in it. Man, I'm telling you. Not just for the grunts, for me too. Something inside you takes over, and you know, you take chances. You have to, if you're going to get a good shot. You get hooked on risk, you know? After a while, it's like there's no limits. You want to go all the way. Get closer to the action. Artillery goes off, grunts get killed, gooks get blown up. And after every firefight, you think, shit, I made it past another one."

Dana was telling me how much further than me he'd gone on the road to personal freedom, and I nodded.

Water buffaloes sloshed in the paddies next to the road, a C-130 zoomed low. Dana swerved past checkpoints manned by U.S. soldiers who waved us through.

"There's a guy I normally go to the boonies with, my close pal: Sean Flynn. Son of Errol Flynn. Sean was in a couple of movies, like Son of Captain Blood, then he gave up Hollywood to come here. He's fearless when we get into a fire zone..."

At the Da Nang Press Club, we drank beer with a dozen reporters and photographers. Like Dana, they'd come to the war-zone to seek adventure and make a name for themselves.

"Did you hear about old Adams?" said a Time reporter. "He caught the green weenie in the air." George Adams, a Marine colonel had been shot down in a helicopter. "Yeah," the reporter went on, "he's the highest-ranking officer to take the Big Plunge."

"Just another day at the job," Dana said.

"You guys are pretty cynical," I said.

"You let yourself get emotionally involved, and you stop taking risks," Dana said. "You stop taking risks, then you can't go all the way."

We left the jeep parked outside the Press Club and walked through Da Nang, a city pock-marked with bombed and crumbling buildings ringed with sandbags. People on the street were selling back-scratchers, stone pendants, filigreed fans, sexual potency powders, marijuana, carved tusks.

A woman with a scrawny, deformed child in her arms begged for money. Her mouth was rouged-out from betel-nut chewing. A blind man, playing what looked like a home-made guitar, was led around by a little girl who held out a tin can for coins.

"The way I see it," said Dana, "Vietnam is like some grotesque amusement park. Disneyland for the weird. An E-Ticket in an alternate universe. Surreal. Sir-Real."

Dana chattered about himself in a rat-a-tat-tat hipster manner. He had studied photography in Maine, he said, then moved to "the coast," where he got a seaman's document and worked on a couple of ships to Vietnam. Back in San Fran, he met Theresa, who convinced him to try his luck as a war photographer. So he flew to Saigon on his own and started taking pictures.

"Theresa got rid of me the same way," I said.

"What?"

"Yeah. She suggested it was time for me to catch a ship back to Vietnam. What's she do, send all her old men here?"

"Yeah, well…" said Dana. "So you've been here before?"

"This is my third trip to the Zone."

"Ah, right, the Zone. Double base pay when you're within fifty miles of the Zone. Bonus cargo."

I nodded. "You know… it's all about the paycheck. Ten percent more of our base pay while there are 50 tons or more of ammo on board, any kind of ammo." I changed the subject. "So you came out here as a freelance photographer. Then what?"

"Yeah, see, some of my pix got picked up by the wire services, you know. As soon as that happened, man, I was on my way. That's when I kind of hooked up with Sean. He looks like his father, you know, tall and handsome, so when I'm with him there's always a lot of attention from the ladies. From guys too. He's got this movie-star charisma and everybody's drawn to him."

As if on cue, whores came up to both of us at that moment, pinched our arms and offered a variety of services. I was always ready to go to a massage parlor, but I hated group pinching and waved the whores away.

"I wonder if all wars have been like this," I said. "People whoring themselves to the invading army."

"We're all whores, man," Dana said. "You, working on ammo ships. Me, taking pictures. I mean, we chose to come here, and we choose to stay. We're all whores. That's what Graham Greene would have said."

Dana had two touchstones. One was the outrageously handsome Sean Flynn, who sent young girls' hearts aflutter. The other was Graham Greene, who had spent years in Vietnam during the 1950s. Dana pointed out places where Greene had slept or eaten or been entertained when he was a journalist here.

We walked past the American NCO Club, where dozens of yclos waited for business. Dana

gathered some of the drivers and gestured as if he were smoking a long pipe. He said, "O-peen, o-peen." One of the drivers, ancient-looking, nodded and gestured for us to sit in the cyclo.

A few minutes later we were being pedaled deep into a warren of very narrow streets where most of the residents wore black pajamas.

"Does the clothing mean anything?"

Dana laughed. "Hey, it could mean they're VC. But, you know, I respect the little yellow bastards. Far as I'm concerned, they're not Charlie. They're Charles. Look, nothing's safe. Nothing here is safe. You can't protect your ass all the time, you know. We're the invaders. They can move around like shadows. We can't."

In a narrow alleyway -- no way in the world we could have found our own way out of there -- the driver stopped and pointed to a doorway. Dana jumped out, knocked, and a toothless papa-san came to the door.

"O-peen?" Dana said. Papa-san nodded and waved us into the house.

I signaled the cyclo driver to wait for us and we went inside.

One by one, Dana and I lay down on our hips on top of the wide, bed-like platform, covered only with tatami mats, that took up most of the small room. Then a pipe-preparer joined us, also lying on his hip, facing us, a kerosene lantern in front of him.

"This is the origin of the word 'hip', you know, meaning 'cool'," Dana said. "You lie on your hip to smoke opium." I doubted the etymology but just nodded.

The preparer slowly stabbed pellet after pellet with something that looked like a pick-up stick, held each pellet over the lantern while it hissed and became distended, then -- while still very hot and gummy -- jabbed the pellet into the small aperture of a large, elaborately-carved pipe. The pipe was then inverted over the lantern so that the opium could be inhaled. It was an unhurried ritual. I stopped after we'd smoked four pellets.

"You hedge your bets," said Dana. "You go only so far and no further."

"I'm as stoned as I want to be," I said.

"Yeah, well," Dana said, "the idea is to fill up the last corner of your brain with smoke. Keep sending out your mind till it stops coming back." He laughed as if he were exhaling smoke.

Dana smoked and smoked: ten pellets in all.

An hour passed, maybe more. I drifted in and out of the present, dreams mixing with the reality of the room. I felt peaceful, surrounded by a loving lava flow of warmth. Lots of nods, smiles, touches. Mama-san brought in some tea and cookies.

When we finally left, it was dark. The cyclo driver was outside, still waiting. We got in, and he cycled us toward town, ringing a bicycle bell when pedestrians scooted in front of him. I felt a quietness of spirit, as if I were on the other side of things, a feeling that nothing needed to be done. Not by me, at least. The dim lights of this neighborhood -- its narrow streets throbbing with life -- took on a tranquil aura. We rode in silence during most of the trip.

I finally said, "We headed to some restaurant along the water?"

"Nah," Dana said. "I never eat next to the water. This coast has funny tides." He meant: bombs, explosions. "We'll go to Graham Greene's favorite place."

Once inside, he ordered entrecote and I had fish wrapped in banana leaf. Both of us washed down our food with bottles of 33 Beer.

"Tell me something, man. You gonna go on working as a deckhand?"

"It's a living," I said.

"You know what I mean," Dana said. "I got out of it. You can too. You went to college, right? All that shit about memorizing poems... what did you major in, English?"

"I don't remember," I said.

"No, seriously, man, you're like some wacky character in a novel, exiling yourself into downward mobility. I mean, we all do some shit like that for a while... but, you know..."

In a strange way, he sounded a bit like my parents, which was unsettling.

"Hey, I'm like you," I said. "A voyeur. This is the outer edge of the known world, isn't it? Where humanity's doing itself in? How could I live through this era and not see it for myself?"

"Ah, that's pre-packaged shit. What about the name 'Maynard'? Where'd you get that?"

"Guys on my first ship, a couple of years ago, they thought I looked like Maynard Krebs from The 'Dobie Gillis' show."

"But I got the note you left me in the Press Club. It didn't say Maynard. Your real name is what, Leaderman, right?"

"Loiederman."

"Ah. Loiederman as in 'oy'. As in oy gevalt. Bizarre. A nice Jewish boy like you," Dana said in a mock Jewish accent. "Bringing shame on your family! A shonda! Feh!"

I laughed: my Jewish origins seemed very distant from the person I was now: a muscular deck-hand, high on opium, on the shores of the South China Sea, in a war-zone where artillery illuminated the night sky.

But he was dead-on: my family was embarrassed by me. My parents were ashamed by what I'd chosen to do with my life so far. I changed the subject.

"I tell you what I'm ashamed of. Every time I join one of these ships I have to go past anti-war groups outside the docks. Protesters holding up signs and yelling 'Stop delivering napalm! You're baby-killers!' And they're looking at me in a van going into the docks with other seamen, and my shipmates are saying, 'Commie scum' and 'We should stick napalm up their asses'. But the demonstrators, they're my people, not the fascist seamen I work with."

"So... you feel guilty about working on ammo ships... ever think about taking direct action?"

"What? What're you talking about?"

"Mutiny... Or sabotage. Why don't you organize other seamen and hijack an ammo ship?"

The idea took my breath away. "Whoa!"

"I know, I know: you'd never go all the way..."

"Hey, I'm willing to do a lot of crazy shit, but I'm not going to throw my passport into the drink..."

"Okay, then: What would you throw into the drink?"

I thought for a moment. "My past," I said finally. "Parts of it."

"The nice Jewish boy part?"

I was getting tired of his needling.

"All those times I hurt others, whether I meant to or not. Those times I betrayed people. Those times when people counted on me and I didn't come through."

"Okay..."

"What I wouldn't throw into the drink is my future. I like to keep options open."

"Fuck options. Fuck the future. Trouble with you is, you're still carrying your parents inside of you. All that guilt shit. That's what keeps you from going all the way. Unless you go all the way..."

Dana held his palms up, head cocked at an angle. The rest of his thought was clear: Unless you go all the way, there's no personal redemption, no hitting bottom, no breaking through to the other side -- which is what we optimistic Americans believe happens when you hit bottom.

"There's a poem," I said, "a poem by Yeats. During World War I in Ireland. Yeats is middle-aged and he's got a friend, Lady Gregory, she has a son who volunteers for the British forces and learns how to fly a plane. Ireland was still a Brit colony then, so he didn't have to fight in that war. It was his choice, right? He's in his mid-20s -- our age -- and he goes off and flies a combat plane in World War I... and gets killed. And of course, Lady Gregory is devastated and Yeats is heartbroken. So he writes a poem called 'An Irish Airman Foresees His Death'."

"You aren't going to recite the whole thing, are you?"

"Just the last couple of lines. Yeats is trying to figure out why Robert Gregory, a young man with his whole life ahead of him, would risk death doing something he didn't have to do.

Yeats says it wasn't because of a sense of duty or because political leaders told him to. No..."

I closed my eyes and recited slowly: "...'A lonely impulse of delight drove to this tumult in the clouds. I balanced all, brought all to mind: the years to come seemed waste of breath, a waste of breath the years behind... in balance with this life, this death.'"

I opened my eyes and Dana was looking at me in a quiet, inscrutable way. He nodded, not saying a word. Like a ship knifing through calm waters, the poem left silence in its wake.

After dinner, Dana and I walked back to his jeep, then he drove me to my ship. Since ammo ships weren't permitted to berth on the inland side of the protected harbor, we had to drive miles all the way around, to the other side of the port. We passed a couple of checkpoints on the way, manned by U.S. troops. I could feel Dana getting more belligerent with each stop: not with me, but with the jumpy American soldiers, rifles ready, who shone lights on us. One checkpoint soldier fired a rifle up in the air after we left, and Dana laughed with delight.

But as we got close to my ship, Dana's delight quickly turned on a dime to something else. Loosened by -- by what? The bit of poetry I'd recited? More likely, by the beer and opium -- Dana tempered his cynical stance and talked about the war he'd witnessed.

"This thing, this war isn't what you think. It isn't what they say. Our soldiers... they aren't winning hearts and minds. You know what I've seen? Massacres. Massacres, for Chrissake!"

This was before My Lai and other horrors became public knowledge.

"I've seen two massacres. Twice Sean and I were there when the grunts got orders to shoot anything that breathes. I mean, they didn't know if there was any Charlie there. They just wasted a couple of villages. Wiped them off the fucking map. No questions asked. Okay, in a firefight it's grunt versus gook and may the best side win. But those villages... that wasn't war. There was no fighting back. They were massacred... men, women, kids..."

"So this war's getting to you..."

"Yeah, I guess, man, I guess. I take pictures and some of them are so gruesome and bloody that I never get to publish them. But I got 'em. And I got 'em here." He tapped his temple with his index finger. "I'll always have them here." He seemed on the verge of tears.

We arrived at the base of the gangway. Dana inhaled/exhaled loudly, pulling himself together.

"What was the line from that poem? A waste of what?"

"'A waste of breath.' Weighed against that moment when life and death hang in the balance, it's all a waste of breath. All of it: past, future…"

"Yeah," Dana said. "Yeah. I guess that sums it up. Everything else… just… a waste of breath."

We hugged each other warmly and wished each other the best possible future.

As it turned out, Dana Stone's future did not last very long. A little more than two years later, in early 1970, he and Sean Flynn were taking photos in Cambodia, on the trail of a big story, and both disappeared, presumably captured and killed by the Khmer Rouge.

There is no definitive evidence of what happened to them.

But there is evidence of what happened to me.

It took a few more years, but in time I became the nice Jewish boy Dana foresaw I'd become. Wife, children, house… like Zorba says, "the whole catastrophe." A respectable middle-class father and husband, a quiet unexciting life with family, friends and a mortgage.

I've lived forty-some more years than Dana… but has it been a waste of breath?

I don't know. I really don't know.

About the Author:

Roberto Loiederman has been a journalist, merchant seaman, and TV scriptwriter (Dynasty, Knots Landing, etc.); has had more than 100 articles and stories published in L.A. Times, Washington Post, Baltimore Sun, Penthouse, and many other publications. One of his stories, "Before Me Today," is included in the recently published anthology about Hollywood, The Way We Work. He was nominated for the Pushcart Prize in 2014 and 2015 and is co-author of The Eagle Mutiny, a nonfiction account of the only mutiny on an American ship in modern time: http://www.eaglemutiny.com

LITTLE MAX MOUSE
by James Padgett

James Padgett:

I was born in Clearwater, Fl. and grew up in Seoul, Korea. My father was stationed there while working with the NSA. I also served four years in the USAF as a German linguist. I was stationed in Berlin, Germany where I met my wife, Renate. We have two beautiful children: Max, the poem's namesake who is now 22 years old, and Lili (15 yrs). The attached image is of me and Max when he was just three years old. A time of my life that was the fertile ground where the seeds of Little Max Mouse were lovingly planted.

It was a warm, sunny day in Willowy Wood.

Little Max Mouse ran as fast as he could.

He had to get to the Oak by the stream.

It was his turn to pick the winning team!

He saw Billy Bear-cub and Sammy Squirrel too.

He knew he'd pick first, but he wasn't sure who.

Ricky Rabbit was fast and Sally Sparrow could fly,

He thought of Tommy Turtle, but he wasn't sure why.

Tommy was nice and he was Max's best friend,

But he always made an out, again and again.

He could kick the ball with all four of his feet,

But when raced to first base he'd always get beat.

Billy Bear-cub could kick the ball far into space.

Sammy Squirrel seemed to win every foot race.

Felicity Fawn was pretty quick too.

WHO TO PICK FIRST! If Max only knew!

Suddenly Max grinned as he spoke up and said,

"I pick Tommy," the others shaking their heads.

What Max finally realized when it came to the end,

Is that it's hard to beat sticking with your only "Best Friend."

HE PRETENDS TO BE A SENATOR

by O. Howard Winn

HE PRETENDS TO BE A SENATOR

but it is clear
he is really a Mock turtle
from Capitalist Wonderland and
his song is a serenade to
the Red Queen running
the nation pretending to be
a strong but twittering leader
or is it Humpty Dumpty with
its brittle shell for skin
neither male nor female
while the Mock Turtle takes
money from his Chinese father-in-law
as if it is earned
to enhance his own career
of singing the Mock Turtle melody
and the confused Kentucky voters
wonder who he is really representing
or is it all for the Lobster Quadrille
choreographed by the simulated senator
to satisfy the Monarch in the White House

THE POET HAD FAITH IN FORM

for he knew that without form
it was not poetry
since his masters of the genre
preached with the sonnet or
the villanelle where control of
form was mastery of the poem
and therefore, of life itself
and even the Limerick design or the
simple couplet was a serious
poetic device when in the hands
of the significantly creative poet
although an unsophisticated aspiring
bard cannot substitute form for
a simple mind and construct an inspired
original perspective to create a poem
that is unique and complex for
intelligence is vital for authentic creativity
and an Emersonian impulse cannot
provide the truth that intellect seeks

MY GRANDAUGHTER HAS DECIDED

she is not my granddaughter any longer
although in her discovery she is also
not my grandson either and wants to
be referred not as she or he or him or her
but them and their in clear violation of
standard grammatical usage but a linguistic
scholar has suggested in a letter to the New York Times
"one" could be used with clarity and in keeping
with standard English grammar although in
realizing neutral gender do not use sex
which seems to be a concept too prickly
than just gender which does not suggest the
damp and slippery moisture of cohabitation
and desire when she wishes to crop her coiffure
in ways despite her desire she appears closer
to being an adolescent boy than the female
person she clearly is attempting to escape

About the Author:

Howard Winn's writing, both fiction and poetry, has been published by such journals as The Galway Review (Ireland),Dalhousie Review, Descant (Canada), Break The Spine, New York Quarterly, Southern Humanities Review, Borderlands, Beloit Poetry Review, Xavier Review and Toyon. His novel, "Acropolis," has been published. His B. A. is from Vassar College. His M. A. is from the Writing Program at Stanford University. His doctoral work was done at N. Y. U. He has been a social worker in California and currently is a faculty member of SUNY as Professor of English.

BEES

by Robin Ray

Steepest of Hills

Who can sing
when the water's edged,
mouths are paste dry,
fruit trees stand barren
as virgin tides?

Step after step
up that steepest of hills,
hungry vampire stones
live off the burst blisters
of innocent seekers.

Kippers in the sand,
raisins in the rocks –
cruel mirages with
more lessons to teach than
grades of right or wrong.

Bees

These industrial bees
outside my window
getting amusingly drunk
in the nectar of jasmine
reminds me of one thing –
our inevitable differences
are the crash test dummies
of history: better to savor
the sweetest juices on our
tongues that urge the pains
in our fragile bones.

Two Hearts

I can continue guilt-free about adulting,
spitefully neglect the child itching to
burst from my insides, but I sense this
isn't the appropriate me to digress.

Peace is lackadaisical now, a troubling
afterthought at best. I find relief in the
knowing, the concealment of my own
autocratic ingenuity, deodorized, free.

Two hearts collide in a conflict; I dive
beneath a table to avoid the sparks that
can ignite a water-logged bridge.

You wished an anger management class
from me; instead, I signed up for the
course, Exploring the Afterlife. Should
have known it was fake when the
instructor wanted his fee up front.

Trust, a fleeting kiss on a bridge in a
monsoon. We romance each other,
wonder if the moment was heightened
by lightning and thunder, routine
Hollywood gaffer/key grip nonsense.

I wanted to be your false god, your
slingshot hero. You smelt a ruse from
the distance, could've conspired to turn
and walk away, but you had your own
sleeved tricks, didn't you?

Disposable Me

The specter of our bond is an illusion, spans
further as if dust upon pollen spurned by a sneeze.
I've trusted my eyes blindly so long I'll loathe
the day they rise to betray me – yellow turns to
black, me believing canaries are a threat to my
cornfields, marigolds are bat orchids in play.

As a child, I was denied unlimited access to new
feelings, drifted in and out of obligations beyond
my reach. Aging, I couldn't hate myself as much
as gravity already did. Death, the trivial cousin
transplanted from picture album to shadow, palls
over laughter, trembles in brevity's wake.

I dive in the lake near Half Moon Bay, surface
with a conch of our histories, listen to Tonto
gently stroking his pinto, whistle-stops of loaded
freight trains dragging millions to their doom, and
ruddy sages bowing to winter. You are impossible,
I say, like a hurricane concerned enough to rend
itself nearing landfall. Nonchalantly, you reply,
How light is an angel, her fall broken by fog? If
I'm forced to adapt to my indiscretions, I'll lose
interest in us. You remain silent, still.

My friend the cyber clown tricks hard drives into
submission, tickles secrets from their circuits,
watches generals shackled off to prison two by two.
He'd counted more scooters than waiters on the
streets of Mumbai crossing each other in the miasma
of truth. I am the man fashioned from napkins, alone.

About the Author:

Robin Ray is the author of Wetland and Other Stories (All Things That Matter Press, 2013), Obey the Darkness: Horror Stories, the novel Commoner the Vagabond, the poetry collection Welcome to Flowerville: Poetry from San Juan Commons, and one book of non-fiction, You Can't Sleep Here: A Clown's Guide to Surviving Homelessness. His works have appeared at Delphinium, Bangalore, Squawk Back, Outsider, Red Fez, Jerry Jazz Musician, Underwood Press, Scarlet Leaf, Neologism, Spark, Aphelion, Vita Brevis, and elsewhere.

THE SAME BOAT
by R. S. Stewart

THE SAME BOAT

The contraption we still cling to
has layers of catastrophe lower
than the steeper ones we sought
in our daily dreams, sailing
or swimming safely to shore
and out again, the thought of drowning
as remote as the red horizon
we knew would never reach us,
a close crew, survivors of the seminal sort,
the kind notorious for bearing good news,
brandishing bravadoes, and so incautious
of the vital sources, the power of the quiet lungs,
the ears that affix themselves
to the echoes of rescue across an ocean,
more than a mass of mere water
but a home of some kind, a coast
we once climbed up on to,
leaving our breathing apparatus behind us,
meanwhile missing the different boat
traveling on its long course through a foreign channel,
the passengers waving and waving
as some of us sank and stayed submerged,
as some of us, longing for the surrender
of our own silver surfaces,
rose blue to our aquatic calling.

THE MAIN STREAM

The stream of most magnitude
flows out of a river bound
for oceanic expanse. Who
doesn't know this, standing
on a bank and wishing water
were more abundant, disbelieving
the story of seven seas?
A stream begins as a trickle,
widens and narrows, basis
on the progress of rocks, rain, bends
in the beds of earth, depth
and height of cliffs and pools,
the cataract of wet worlds,
all of this so different
from the precipice that tumbles over us,
the spray in no furious rush to soak the earth
with us, just mild persuasion
to join a journey swiftly swept upstream.

INSERT

If it's just an insert
it's no quick fix.
Insertion's laborious
and no technique

can outdo the blank
of the page the page
is sewn to. Flipping through,
one has the urge

to paste and glue
instead of using the staple
for what it's for.
On a big spread table

stacks pile up
at twice their weight,
and slips of paper
aren't their brightest white.

Corrections are apt to add
to the flyer's flaw
but if nobody's glancing
who else is noticing how

like an angel Hamlet says
man is in action
a piece of work
left and anxious to insert.

NERVE ENDINGS

I've never seen a nerve
except as a picture.
I don't know when they end
or start or what they were

before the name of nerve
became central to what they do
inside me. Anatomy has no appeal
except when I feel askew

and know that one or more
of my nerves needs looking at.
Nerves, I've heard, are made
of something electric, a fact

I've never had the means to check.
Someone close said once that bundles
are what nerves are wrapped in
and counting them all is futile.

SOME POSSIBILITY

The care I took in the removal of error

paid off well when lines

were drawn to signal the sureness

of sensibility, its spatial core

more than mathematical, more even than metaphor

packed in bulk, heavy in the sockets

where surprises lurk and reappear

in grandiose waves to jar sureness of the surface

I'm still skating on. I'm hanging on tighter

than past remembrance, since behind my mind

I sense the sunken fear of some possibility

that all, all is in error.

About the Author:

R. S. Stewart is a native Oregonian who taught English at Christopher Newport College (now University) of the College of William and Mary in Virginia, where he also directed two seasons of plays. Three of his own plays have received staged readings at Oregon theatres. His poems have been published in many journals in the U. S. and Europe, among them Canary, Poetry Salzburg Review, 2 Bridges Review, The Same, Serving House Journal, The Journal (UK), the Avatar Review, PIF Magazine, Ink Sweat & Tears (UK), Brittle Star (UK), indicia, The Sow's Ear Poetry Review, and The Coachella Review.

INTIMATIONS OF AUTUMN
by Phil Kemp

INTIMATIONS OF AUTUMN

Sunlight fading, a chill wind drives away
last of the day's heat; in the forest
I walk through, the turning of green to red
is my life,
darkening in the dusk.

I am not where I was,
not what I had been in summer.

In the cool of evening
a quarter moon rises to
claim the night-coming sky.
All my resolutions
born in summer, left undone.

In the night, the wind changed its direction
to the north; I woke, and the trees were bare.

SOPHIA AT MY WINDOW

With bowed head, upon
the lower branch, Wisdom stares
at the window. I wonder

if I'm worthy of her presence.
She awes me.
I want her to speak.

Her servant, I'll listen. Sophia,
you survey what moves.
What do you see in my heart?

we lock glazes and then I blink.
Only an empty tree remains.
I'll remember her in darkness.

FOUR

I flew home from my father's funeral.

Four days later a car knocked
me down at an intersection.

Four months recovery
at home.

Four months solitude
and silence

Four years later, I have planted
many verdant trees.

BURIED

i

I piled
earth onto my father,
stepped back; my
duty done, and took my place with
the mourners.

I loosed his boat
into unknown seas,

returned afterwards to an empty
house as the sun set
over the stones of
our ancestors.

ii

When I was a boy my
father brought me a model train
for my birthday. He had loved to
play with a model railway when he was
a boy; I supposed it was the little
universe he could control
when all around was the chaos of the war.

I had no interest in moving
steam trains around a track,
except to hear them crash at high speed
and leave the safety of the rails.

I would rather follow the
solitary path along the river
behind our house that led
to the once-running railway
now deserted. Its
tracks were removed,
their indentations pressed into the
open fields.

Before his death three years
of silence ruled. He
might have forgotten me.

I had nothing to say
to him the day
I left him weeping
at Gillingham station.

About the Author:

Phil Kemp was born in London in 1960. He received his M.A. (Hons) in History from the University of Edinburgh and his Postgraduate Diploma in Librarianship from the College of Librarianship Wales (now part of the University of Wales) in Aberystwyth. In 2001, Phil relocated to Iowa City, Iowa, where he resides with his wife. Phil's poem River was published for Iowa City's Poetry in Public contest in 2017. He is the author of two unpublished novels, set in the UK, spanning periods from the sixteenth century to the present day. Phil is currently a member of the Triptychs, a poetry workshop in Iowa City facilitated by Jeanette Miller, author of Unscheduled Flights published by Adelaide Press earlier this year.

ARTHUR'S SEAT

What I write comes
from the Sundays
when I walked on the
higher road to
wind-ruffled Dunsapie Loch
and ascended on the well-worn
grass to the
summit of Arthur's Seat.

From this extinct volcano
on a sunny day in May
My view encompasses Edinburgh's whole,
out to the Forth bridges, across Fife's kingdom
to Highland peaks; then
east to Bass Rock
southward to Pentlands and Moorfoots.

A whole world below.
A whisper of words
elevates me to this place.

HOWEVER RICH
by Cameron Morse

Shave Gel

Theo says Mama and hands me
a hair from your head so long its ends
have twirled together. Today is
the bottle of my shave gel
he won't let go of as if it contained
some wish-granter and his wish
were to replace me forever
in the equation of mommy and me.
Theo crawls into the family
room crate, corning Sherlock,
and pulls shut the door behind him.
Pull the plume he discovers
shed hair sticks between fingers,
dog hair and cobwebs,
all the ephemera of having a baby
cricket in your afternoon's
last mouthful of ice coffee. I could see Theo
stabbing the tolerant, sad-eyed
cockapoo out of sheer curiosity
but for the distraction of a garbage truck,
salvation from the tedium of homestay
parenting, parenting home, I stay
at home. My life is an unanswered question
and every day I ask again.

Warning Label

I know my mouth is open.
I would like to close my burning
eyes in the heatstroke sun
of the first of July. But the yellow
snail kiddie pool describes
how children drown, one by one,
in language after language.
Three dusty lawn chairs surround me.
Theo carries an orange cup.
When the idea of a refill strikes him,
he grunts at the spigot, begins
to cry then comes to fetch water
from inflatable rubber lining
of the snail. I try to think
of all the things I've heard said,
or read, and what might not
yet have been written. In tree shade,
the pendulum of his child swing
veers right as if S-hooked
a link shorter on that side, his neck
flopped right. His ballcap drops.
Uh-oh, he says. One of the first words
he learned, he learned
from me.

Looking for Things to Do

However Rich

We look for things to do is how it works
with evenings like water the wilting donkey
ears of the hyacinths. Then forget it,
they'll come back next year. Things to do
like scent of spearmint. Do that,
then pull the pin oaks out of the flowerbed.
Do battle with the centipede, little man.
Snip its body segments, its fused legs,
with garden shears, releasing war cries
not baby cries, yuck! Dirty, dirty, yuck,
yuck, soldier. You look for things to do,
then watch, after the boy trooper goes to bed,
but nothing can distract from the guilty hungers
of pregnancy and I might as well be rinsing
mushrooms in the kitchen sink
as finishing the latest sequel to Halloween.

I'm afraid of protein. I'm
afraid of what aid
too many sausage links may
supply my brain
tumor. However rich my life,
I will always want more
where that came from.
The more I drink, the thirstier
I am. Last night I found
three glasses waiting
in the study. I'm always looking
for my water
because I leave it everywhere:
on the coffee counter,
the piano, in the guest bedroom,
in the mailbox, yes,
the mailbox, like when Theo
takes off and I give
chase, not wanting to carry
anything on our walk
down the lane. I can go a while
without fear, walking along
Golfview Drive as if we didn't
have to get back in time
for breakfast, but then I pick up
my boy and carry him home.

Men's Warehouse

About the Author:

I open up the blood between my toes
scratching the ancient fungus.
Hold my hands behind my back and Theo
copies me. His big head perched
on slender shoulders. My little brother
strums praise & worship storms
on his acoustic, almost
as bad as I was. Barb talks about her
women's group cancer
patients, the one in remission,
the one in hospice, her autistic grandson.
I hate the distance between Kansas
City and Spokane, man. Lili drove me
to Grand Rapids in my rented tux
to deliver a speech before the children
smashed your pinata in the church
basketball court. Our emergency lights
jammed on early the frosty morning
of our departure. I tried to buy a knife
in a gas station, couple of Armenian
guys looking back at me blankly
through bulletproof glass. In the end,
I yanked loose the entire console
just to stop the clicking.

Cameron Morse was diagnosed with a glioblastoma in 2014. With a 14.6 month life expectancy, he entered the Creative Writing Program at the University of Missouri--Kansas City and, in 2018, graduated with an M.F.A. His poems have been published in numerous magazines, including New Letters, Bridge Eight, Portland Review and South Dakota Review. His first poetry collection, Fall Risk, won Glass Lyre Press's 2018 Best Book Award. His three subsequent collections are Father Me Again (Spartan Press, 2018), Coming Home with Cancer (Blue Lyra Press, 2019), and Terminal Destination (Spartan Press, 2019). He lives with his pregnant wife Lili and son Theodore in Blue Springs, Missouri, where he manages Inklings' FOURTH FRIDAYS READING SERIES with Eve Brackenbury and serves as poetry editor for Harbor Review. For more information, check out his Facebook page or website.

IF A TREE FALLS
by Diane Webster

MALFUNCTION

Summer heat surfs up southern wall,
slithers into swamp cooler vents
to vaporize water meant to soothe
humans inside the office thus
converting cooler into heater.

The woman perspires when no one
listens to facts of cooler malfunction
so she turns it off.

The man sweats and steams
as he cranks machine to high cool
pumping burnt outside air
to the inside with dust-devil fury
and brimstone conflagration
claiming, "It's hot in here!"

CROW DREAMS

Rock perches atop the hill
where crows land,
where white poop flows
like a waterfall
cascading over
the resting site.

Crows only dream
of trout below
to scavenge
as trucks roar by
like water pounding
itself in the plunge.

DARK SHATTERS

Face your fears
as I stare down
canyon walls
echoing green river
rapids like heart
palpitations.

My fingers throb
against cold pipe
barriers bolted into rock
I'm sure will fail
after decades of freeze/thaw.

Like a boulder released
I leap, a bird too fast
to see soars passed;
the river throbs inside hearing.

Sight focuses like binoculars
until something big passes
across the lens,
something dark shatters.

THE OTHER SIDE

The fly on the mirror admires
its multi-faceted identical twin
that crawls in unison to the edge,
but only darkness on the other side.
It matches flight patterns
as if synapses fire lightning
decisions between them;
as if infinity and finite
expands/contracts between them;
as if a fishing line dangles
between them waiting
to tug someone to the other side.

About the Author:

IF A TREE FALLS

Pine tree commits suicide simply
by relaxing its roots.
It topples to lie in the forest --
a pothole of grass/roots dislodges
like a cowboy dying
with his boots on.

Did anyone hear the surrender
as it fell and scratched branches
against its neighbor as if begging
at someone's feet for a helping limb?
Was the forest too vast
to give a damn
about one passing tree?

Diane Webster grew up in Eastern Oregon before she moved to Colorado. She enjoys drives in the mountains to view all the wildlife and scenery and takes amateur photographs. Writing poetry provides a creative outlet exciting in images and phrases Diane thrives in. Her work has appeared in "the Aurorean," "Better Than Starbucks," "Philadelphia Poets," and other literary magazines.

LIFE, LOVE AND HOPE

by Ezekiel Archibong

LIFE, LOVE AND HOPE

I try to reach high to the sky
and admire the simplicity of life.
The lilting song as it floats through flowers
along a brook of fairy bowers.
Where I can't find my voice in the rhythm,
I just keep singing to the lyrics.
I live, love and hope with a will,
with loud laughter like explosives.

Life is a fickle fortune.
Like the scented nectars
spewed from the steep of radiant flowers
and sour herbs that torture the cheeks
with a shooting twinge.
The same sun that dries the wood
dissolves the ocean ice,
for one thing leads to another,
the gypsy moth Caterpillar to the charming butterfly
and the sun bringing on rainfall.

Love is a Jigsaw Puzzle.
Pieces are aliens at inception.
We keep moving them around,
shove ill-fitting pieces,
searching for the right ones,
until we find those that fit in,
until we find where they belong.
Some pieces come together and start a cold war.
Hey! there's nothing like finding a true paramour.

Hope is the crisp dew
that perches on the skin of a Lilly
with such refreshment
that sings a tune without the lyrics.
Find the words and that is what to say,
create the path and that is the way.
The wisdom of age
and the truth about all of our lives is that;
no matter what path we may take,
in the end, what will be will be.

PEACE ALERT

I rode with the wind swelling with grieve
sour tales of violence fill my ears and rings
and my nostrils a drunkard of despicable fragrance
such that could sully without reluctance.
The land overflows of river of scarlet colors
with hundreds of bodies hipped like piles of saw dust,
beckon vultures to hover and feast.
Turmoil was unleashed
from the cave,
swaddled the environs in disarray.
Tear stained face of an innocent child
in conflicts he knows nothing about.

Should it be heard that Nations search for peace
with innovations of atomic and nuclear?
Little wonder Peace becomes scarce like a dog's tear
The book of human race
is chaptered, barren of glue to consolidate,
each day slips by,
the leaves keep falling apart,
with the next volume ripped off in bits
like solvent dissolving a lactase pill.

Should we remain a walking shadow
on the face of a meadow?
Let us loose grip of the withered leaves
for anew dawn of colorful spring,
for our beauty has been marred,
and our souls twisted and scarred.
Let us not be caught
in the frenzy of shattering dreams.
Let our story be; this moment
we drop our guns and bombs
lifting our brows to behold
the perching of peace and justice.

Let's hold arms in love
and not arms to kill and destroy
Let us pick the scepter of unity
for upon it shall we find dignity.
Let the only song on our lips be song of peace,
where the rhythm of tolerance rings of bliss.

LIFE SPIRALED OUT OF CONTROL

We were kids with keen sight kits
and exceeding adrenalin
to climb trees like monkeys
and pluck from the precipice.
We listen to the birds sweetly chirping.
We cling to branches like political loyalists
When we finish devouring into our precious within
we wipe our mouth with the flip side of our fist
and gaze as the sun fades into space,
signaling the night is set to reign
and it's time to close for the day.
We back down with our faces sowed of glee
even as we surmounted our mats about to sleep.
We said our lord's prayer and shared in the grace,
and slept with such peace alien in our world of rat chase.
We were not from the lineage of Dangote
but we were still okay.

The cock caws to usher in a new dawn
The day light pierces our rotten faces
through the windows standing ajar,
as we stretch our body, yawning like cats.
Looking up, the sky painted dark sinister,
and the clouds heavily pregnant.
It began to pour in a geometry progression,
we bounced up like excited springs
peeling off our cloths like a snake discard its skin.
We carry the slaps of rain on our body,
the zinc roof plays swift beats
transcending into sweet melody
and we dance in pure ecstasy.
We flee from the shouting thunder
and chased the wind and fling.
In truth, we enjoyed every bit.

We are Adults now.
Afore dawning, we check out of our homes
hoping to fill the holes of our dreams.
We reappear late at night with weaken feet
and pores soaked from fatigue.
Like a book left the shelf,
we drift apart from family and friends,
and wear stress like a ceremonial Apparel.
Our life is spiraled out of control,
Our life is a reality show!

DIGITAL ATTACHMENT

No man has a face anymore!
With every one's head buried
on the lighten screen clutched in their hands.
A man with his eyes glazing the ground
knocks a road passer flying,
falling on his face after tripping over him.
Upon realizing he could see,
there arouses an inferno of seethe,
and he apologizes for his sins.
My fear lies more with those behind the wheels.
They could die and kill.
Once, i could have been hit.
I ran to the other side of the road
and he ran straight into a pole.
An addiction that sweeps the age
has climbed to an epidemic stage.
Like the rising of Phoenix from ashes,
we buy into a franchise that robs us of our sanity.
They are catching fire and the smoke
attracting a grip so strong over our psyche.
Twenty-four seven, we lay waste hours,
tweeting our time away, and surfing our minds off.
Even as we wear an underwear, we are still texting,
spending donkey years in the toilet no longer bored.
We are enough by the world in our hands,
caressing, cuddling and cradling it.

UNFINISHED CONVERSATIONS

I go to sleep in the night, continuing in my dream
the conversation I begun on phone with my lover.
We were perched on a lofty balcony,
discussing our trivial annoyances and petty gossips,
staring as the clouds cling to the roof of the earth.
Then there was the yellow sun with a shade of orange
that surely only angels could have sent
reflecting brightly with such ferocity.
Like a cosmic magnet, I pulled her close to my heart,
took her hand, whispered her name.
In a symphony all in harmony, we burst out a song
that transcends through the leaves and orchids,
and the breeze lending its beats and the trees dance.
We did, till the sun got tired,
tucked its head in the cloak of cloud
and darkness gave way to heavenly glow.
It's the simplest exchange,
one I would be glad to give much return to once I wake.

About the Author:

Ezekiel Archibong (Oluwasalvage) studied Law in University of Benin and was called to the Nigerian Bar in November 2018. He currently practices with Aina Blankson LP, a leading law firm in Lagos, Nigeria. He is passionate, resilient, resourceful and always digging opportunities to impact lives.

LEARN BEFORE TEACHING

by Edward Lee

TO BE THE OCEAN, TO BE THE MAN

In the ocean
I become a wave
crashing onto the shore,
pulling sand and stones
back with me,
into me.

I crash again
and again,
until I own all the stones
and sand
I want,

then I walk from the sea,
my bare feet
touching the wetted sand,
the smoothed stones,
and fall to my knees,
a once breathing man
drowned.

GONE

A long journey untaken
stretches heavily behind me,
while something akin to regret
turns my reluctant head
so I might look back
and see the multitude of steps
I might have walked,
the other many paths
I might have known.

Now, I can only close my eyes
and remain still,
my will to walk anywhere
left before my feet
gone from me,

gone.

LEARN BEFORE TEACHING

Teaching my daughter
the meaning of promises,
I can not help
but be reminded
of all the promises I made
and causally broke,
most of them to you,
my hopeful love
who, despite all proof,
believed my next promise
would be the one that
held its form,
only to see it fall asunder,
my breath still fresh
and wet on its disintegrating shape,

until you finally stopped believing in me,
and began believing
in yourself and
your manifold worth,
a worth I could never match
nor appreciate.

I realised then,
your retreating back
my moment of eureka,
that I should never make promises
doomed to only survive
in the echoes of lazy excuses,
as I realise now,
fresh promises newly broken
in my wake,
I should not be the one
to teach their workings,

at least until I better
understand their meaning
myself.

SMALL

Coffins so small
they could be carried
by one man
apiece,

yet the world,
closed eyes finally open,
watched each of you
lowered into the ground,
shoulders offered
to carry you to heaven.

TOES

Though I imagine
they would pinch my toes,
I would wear your favorite shoes
to better understand you -
everything else has failed.

But seeing as you were wearing them
when you left me,
that is another possibility
closed to me;

I know your absence though,
from the tips of my toes
to the worn edges of my heart,

I know your absence,
and the pain contained
within its heavy nothingness.

About the Author:

Edward Lee's poetry, short stories, non-fiction and photography have been published in magazines in Ireland, England and America, including The Stinging Fly, Skylight 47, Acumen and Smiths Knoll. His debut poetry collection "Playing Poohsticks On Ha'Penny Bridge" was published in 2010. He is currently working towards a second collection.

He also makes musical noise under the names Ayahuasca Collective, Lewis Milne, Orson Carroll, Blinded Architect, Lego Figures Fighting, and Pale Blond Boy.

His blog/website can be found at https://edwardmlee.wordpress.com

CHERRY FLOWER
by Daniel King

Centaur Zenith

We see the galaxy below us
Each star with azurite fire allure
Through Delta prisms they are peerless
Transformed like cerium laser light
For Titans, lemniscate with wildness,
Who slant triumphant, descend and arc
And blaze like novae with their grandeur
In steel and titanium, tain and spark.

And Centaurs are zenith Tyr-signed
And Centaurs are Aleph Null primed
And Centaurs are Delta K trined
Cantorian pearls in one mind.

Our glory magnifies the kalpas,
The endless span of exultant worlds,
A cosmos Sagitta has pierced
With stars technetium-new, and shells
A nebulosity that shows us,
In rings, infinity signs set free
Their halves to spiral and to mirror
The mystic crown that extols Kalki.

Aquaplaners Exit

Two infrared rainbows blaze on the ice:
The liquid is smooth for aquaplane carves.
The channels of Kraken Mare suffice
For exiting wide and landing my craft.

Approaching the lake I signal the plane
To check that the Point of Presence is right.
The topaz horizon's lakes of methane
Delimit my path in Saturn's gold light.

Exquisitely speed begins to increase:
Quixotic I tilt at icebergs I pass
A quincunx - I turn by ninety degrees
To equinox gusts that buffet like glass.

An hour and I head for shore and reflect
That Titan's delights are quantized, discrete
I've altered the world but much is unchecked -
As always I'll pass such chores to the Fleet.

As pixels of snow alight on the lake
I'm pleased I judged the span of the game.
This world is my image; few could mistake
That rainbows and Saturn's rings are the same.

The Attractor at Infinity

Follow my spiralling line through infinite time
The Attractor shines the ray
I, I alone,
Know the way
Learn and pray.

Freedom is blessedly mine, Cantorian clay
And lunation's wheel? I smile
You, you are bound.
So beguile;
Watch awhile.

Some with affinity, choosing me, will resile
But the rest are rust, debris
They, they are torn
Strive to be.
Seek Kalki.

Cherry Flowers

I am Kalki and I wander these shores:
They're like smiles when I surf, at the solstice, now eternally
And with the C of each surge, surfers bow -
Their arms and their legs petals for a chakra wave.

I am Kalki and I travel the world:
It's a fruit I consume, always glacé, calling azurely
And it reminds me of hard Cherry Men -
The cherries I pluck transiting around the Earth.

I am Kalki and I journey through space:
A Monoceros jaunt to the red Rosette, my nebula
What if a Unicorn Boy meets me there?
We'd look for a world, kiss and then explore its shores!

Delta Sightlines

Our legion's triangle glides in deep space.
Our craft are charged as we thirty six wait.
Our crest is delta with K in prime place.
As if tattvas of Shiva, exultant we turn
From the night with one face.

Our goal is Atria, blazing K sun.
Our sightlines lock and direct each steel hull.
Our poets rush to record the war won.
A trikona, we fall into orbit and wait
For our rivals to run.

Our warheads blast into clouds and quartz walls;
Our lasers raze as a searing light swarm;
Our mantras smash the pleroma's stored souls;
And we cheer as we chant and relight and destroy
And exalt we were born.

About the Author:

Daniel King is a prize-winning Australian writer. His poetry collection, Amethysts and Emeralds, was published by Interactive Press on May 15 2018. His hobbies include surfing, skateboarding, following the latest developments in space exploration, and listening to the music of Mike Oldfield and Project System 12." Daniel King Artist Statement: I am an Australian gay writer, with a strong interest in Hinduism (particularly pertaining to Kalki, the 10th and final avatar of Vishnu, the Preserver, incarnating now and forever together with Shiva, the Destroyer), mysticism in general, and astronomy. As a surfer, I am also strongly influenced by marine imagery.

RUNNING

by Stella Prince

Tell me now, what do you think?
I might never love again.
What can you say to me tonight?
So I'll believe in you again.

Cause I'm running now,
I guess I might come back eventually,
But I'm running now.
From all the pain that's inside of me, I'm running now.

Come on tell me what to do.
Cause I'm still in love with you.
I can try to make it through,
But it's really up to you.

Cause I'm running now,
I guess I might come back eventually,
But I'm running now.
From all the pain that's inside of me, I'm running now.

About the Author:

Stella Prince is a young writer and poet. Her articles have been published in magazines such as "Seshat Literary Journal", "Amazing Kids Magazine", "Cliche Magazine", and "Good Life Youth Journal", and her poems have been published in "A Celebration of Poets: A National Anthology" and "Adelaide Literary Magazine."

SALT

by Robert McCloy

Old St. David's (Cheraw, SC)

August pines and majestic magnolias
Stand testament to centuries
Of weddings, Sundays, funerals;
Gentle, torrid wind
Adorns the forlorn, silent yard.

What stories
Of passion, hope, faith,
Impotence, despair, bewilderment
Are sealed in the roots
Of the swaying Ecclesiastics?

Entranced by their stoic
Stillness, I gape
At the lumbering Druids.

I remember the cicada chorus
In my father's eyes,
The anger of summer
Carved in my mother's palms.
I see families of graves;
Named, forgotten,
Finally at peace.

I walk to the church window,
Pews full of shadow and illumination.
A harmonious hymn of solitude fills one's soul
As he looks in through his own reflection.

Salt

It's not what it should be,
Not picture perfect
The way I thought...

There's rock and bone
In this field of furrows,
In the flowers
Bee stings,

And day after day searing heat.
Salt is in the soil,
In the body of bread we eat.

It's not what it should be,
But it was, it can be.
There are moments of an angel passing...

When the sun is honey
And the air honeysuckle,
And the soil Eden.

We are not what we should be,
But the inconsequential days hide essential moments.
Patiently, I painfully toil,
Recalling and hoping.

Baptist Softball League

Welcome to America,
To the red-clayed diamond
Of the Baptist softball league.

Feel the unforgiving leather
Of a new glove,
See the sun setting,
Hear the cheers of wives
And laughter of children
With popsicled chins.

Your safe here among your fellow patriots,
Driving trucks, loving guns, saying grace,
Holding fast to a false narrative.

So far from where you were born,
From the houses of your youth:
So far, so good
One imagines.

No one here knows
You are a refugee,
Born naked, famished, feral;
Just pretend you are normal.

Out in left field
As the sun gradually disappears,
Stand prepared to catch
Any ball hit to your space.

Ordinary
American, breadwinner, citizen, family man

Living the dream
In the Southern heartland.
Nobody knows how far away
I am.

Green Snake in the Spring Meadow

A shedding of skin is inevitable,
You cannot continue to be who you have been,
Nature requires progressive development.
Besides, you know it is time,
The past pulls tight,
Constricts your movement.
Time is palpable for sure.

So on a bright blue day
Brush stroked by the wind
Saunter through the meadow
To the pile of rocks by the pond,
Move upwards slowly,
Let your weight weigh heavy
On the edge of the highest rock,
And do what nature and time
Lovingly demand.

The Body

I.

Eternity starts
With the umbilicus,
Where the sacred, strange spark of life
is transferred.

From there, a world
All its own, is born;
An electric, rhythmic, dynamic
Micro-universe of being.

Tender trails
Of caresses,
Brush fires
In the night,

Tear trails
Under the chin,
Scar like a shooting star
Frozen in the darkness.

Who will wash my body,
As it was washed when I was born?
Who will look at my face, fallen still,
Recollecting love?

II.

A life spent unumbilicaled:
Flooding REM cycles,
Submerging disassociation,
Overwhelming neuronal cannonades
Of chaotic imagery.

Where is the dawn,
The light to reconnect my soul
To its original core
Before birth and war?

And who will see the naked, uniformless me?
Who will behold my unpunctual purity?
Can I relinquish my relationship with the enemy?
Can I find the narrative in my poetry?

Robert McCloy :

I am a strong advocate of a growth mindset, and as such I have attempted to pursue living as a journey. Writing poetry and reading biographies was my first positive coping mechanism, and has endured as such. I grew up in an adverse environment outside of Pittsburgh, and was fortunate to have a teacher, Mr. James H. Demcheck, who mentored and guided me with commitment and love starting in my high school years and lasting throughout my life.

After five years of military service, I settled in South Carolina. I am a grateful father of three--Lillie, Rawlins, & Price--and a happy husband--Christie Baker McCloy--of 15 years. I have had the privilege of being an educator, thus a student, for the last 19 years. I am now attaining my degree and as a Mental Health Counselor. In honor of my mentor and his profound influence on my wellbeing, I am working to publish my writing as well.

EMBODIED SOIL
by Sarah Conklin

You never loved me, I was just a body.

I come home to dead flowers hanging on the wall, parched but aesthetically pleasing
dry from humidity and a lack of love
The eucalyptus has lost its scent
the only odor stuck between parallel windows
smells of lust

The roses from the week before have lost their petals
for there are no kisses shared between drywall corridors leading to a bedroom
full of lavender and lilies turned gray
Because love doesn't live here anymore
And you can't grow in a place with a foundation of sex without love, nor intimacy being only physical.
When will you admit I was just a body, and this house is not our home.

Pretty sure I lost a good one.

And we talked over old fashions
stealing kisses over old memories
of forget me not's
a penny for your thoughts
and truth be told
with loud music in the background
our only distraction
in a room full of characters
accompanied by a double date.

After drinks
we went back to the apartment
full of a twin side bed for two
making space for lust and love too
four is a party,
for once told a story
of a time when kisses were hung in frames
and songs were heard through ears of lovers.

I've gone deaf, the music has stopped playing
and the bed is full of distance reaching to be loved by a body
that was once held by a love
tempted by lust and a lover
but no last lover at that.

But once a love that tasted of an old-fashion
who grew strong full of bitters
making this love story bittersweet.

About the Author:

Embodied Soil

Momma has a flower garden
filled with mixed vegetables
she calls it unique soil.

Secrets embodied
holding together situations with stems,
releasing poor nutrients in the ground
pesticides sprayed daily.

Daddy has a shed
full of tools
he helps Momma's garden grow.

A shovel to bury the bodies
and a rake to cover Mommas secrets
with a sheet
of basil
to cover the stench
of who Daddy can be.

Sarah Conklin is an undergraduate student working to get her PHD in child psychology, with a minor in creative writing.

MY YOUNG LIONS

by Lynne D. Soulagnet

MY YOUNG LIONS

Bondage

The intensity of your glare
could sear my flesh
burn a hole right through me.
I compress myself into the chair,
use a book as a shield.
I have done it again,
rubbed sandpaper on your wounds.
What did I say wrong this time?
Or was it the way I said it?
Maybe the inflection wasn't right
or the tone too strong.
Your stony silence stings
sharp as urchin spines.
This is how it always ends.
My texts will be ignored,
Emails not returned,
phone calls unanswered,
until I have served my time
for whatever crime
you deem I have committed
and you have exacted
your pound of flesh, my love.

prowl in ever decreasing circles,
isolate their prey.
Testing several times at first,
they take small nips on the run.
Skittish, they tear only
small pieces of flesh to taste,
carry them off to a safe place
where they remain watching, waiting
until they can attack again,
get their first taste
of real blood, raw meat.
With each assault they grow
bolder, more brazen
until they are ripping off
huge chunks of flesh
which they greedily devour.
Soon they reach the prize—

it is still beating. They begin
working in tandem until
it is torn apart. They lap up
the dusky-red, gelatinous pools,
then lick the marrow
and gnaw on my bones.

The Deer

In the east the elongated sun
begins its astral ascent.
Shades of apricot-pink, violet-blue,
fill the early horizon.

The pale moon almost a memory
fades in the western sky.
I travel alone down hilly lanes,
around winding paths.

Moving through the morning mist
a phantomlike figure emerges.
I notice his tawny beige flanks,
firm and muscular.

See his leathery black cloven hooves.
Upon his head a thorny crown,
ivory antlers sharp and pointy,
more tines than I can count.

He has appeared where ragged weeds
meet the road's edge.
Just beyond in a bed of grass
a doe lies bloodied and broken.

No silhouettes of fawns in sight.
Just these two images juxtaposed
and fixed in my mind.
At once I am awed and saddened.

Majestic beast of woods and fields.
Mighty as a towering oak he stands
rooted to the earth.
Wild and perfect.

I pray, no huntsman will fell him,
nor car without conscience intrude.
May he elude wires, snares--
man's many contrivances.

About the Author:

Lynne D. Soulagnet is a native New Yorker who grew up in Dix Hills on Long Island. She has been published in the Long Island Paumanok Review, Avocet Weekly, Creations Magazine, and others. She continues to live on Long Island where she spends her time writing and visiting her two children and grandson, Michael.

A LOVE STORY
by Gloria G. Murray

A LOVE STORY

we kissed in the dark hallways
of the Canarsie projects
backs pressed
against the concrete wall
lips sealed
with the grout of lust
your tongue swirling under mine
your ardent fingers curling
like a sculptor
around my nipples
under the summer silk

O love, you were my first...
and my last

in-between the years
of slaps, screams
splashes of hate like paint against
the peeling walls
of our suburban home
quelled only
by the bodies in remembrance
of that feral melding
almost five decades ago
that roller coaster ride
those bursting fireworks...

FEBRUARY MAN

you are my blizzard man
you come to me when storms
are brewing, rising
over the shores of my life

you come to me when winds rage
hail snaps against
the shutters of my heart

you soothe me
with marshmallow words
wit that dances
little elves at my feet

and when the door of the world
is shut with snow mounds
you open yours

where a fiery fire crackles
and glaciers break

FISHERMAN

alone in the queen size bed
I turn over, touch the empty space
your pillow holds

for a moment
half in sleep, floating
between this world and the next

I forget you are fishing
casting your rod
like a mysterious spell into the sea

or asleep, zipped in a bag
under the stars
on a beach with the wind beating

against your cap
the moon a spotlight on your face
the mosquitoes biting your ears

About the Author:

A member of Poets & Writer's Inc., **Gloria Murray's** poetry and prose has been published in various literary journals and anthologies such as Grabbing the Apple, The Paterson Review, Third Wednesday, The Pittsburgh Quarterly, Xanadu, Oberon, Long Island Quarterly, Ted Kooser's on-line American Life in Poetry and others. Gloria's one-act play What are Friends for? was performed off Broadway as well as presented in the Michigan Art of the One-act Anthology, 2007, New Issues Press. She the recipient of the Anna Davidson Rosenberg 2014 1st prize award in Poetica Magazine, as well as 3rd place 2017 Writer's Digest Poetry Award.

THE CROSS-TOWN
by Eileen Valentino Flaxman

The Cross-Town

makes its way in fits and starts, day
in and day out, from the east side to
the west and the doors hiss and the
brakes screech and people get on and
off, one corner after another, until
it's time to turn back around, and this

is where he queues up, same time
each day, only this day the wind's icy
intention threatens to steal his hat
and he feels a warm blast as he boards
but soon it suffocates, and off comes
his hat as he looks overhead and reads

the same ads he read yesterday and
thinks like every day that he should buy
a copy of the Times because no one talks
or makes eye contact as mass transit once
again picks up the masses to deliver them
right back where they started. But this day

he catches his reflection in the window
and no longer recognizes the man who
once stood out in a crowd and would
change the world, and it occurs to him
this day that he is just like everyone
else around him, because his life is not

turning out the way he had planned.

That Summer Night in Central Park

We wait in line for broiled chicken, stand
so close our shoulders touch, then make
our way to a spot on the grass near the
stage to spread our blanket. We can't
keep our hands to ourselves for love is
new, we are new, and today is all about us.

We devour our meal and lick each other's
fingers and drink chilled wine from plastic
cups. The sunlight dims on cue, floodlights
rise, and even Shakespeare seems new, his
comedy sharper, his love scenes our own
story told over and over.

Lust simmers but is patient, for the long
night stretches before us and belongs to us.
We see stories in one another's eyes and
we are hungry to hear those stories and
tell those stories and we will sit face
to face and there will be joy in the telling.

This promise of later sits like a mint on
the tongue to be slowly savored. We lean
back and settle into each other's arms,
content, as the backdrop of this evening
serenades us with music only
we can hear.

sometimes there is a day

sometimes there is a day
that goes unnoticed
slips through the fingers
for I have better things to do

than stop to catch the light
in my mother's hair, or
watch her housedress sway
as she works in the kitchen,
its rhythm a kind of silent music

sometimes there is a day
that claims a place all its own
and lodges permanently
in the mind, a keepsake

to take out and hold
in the hand, turn over
and examine from all sides
how you looked at me
that last time

then there are days
I look past the face
in the mirror and
don't meet the eyes

staring out of me
don't recognize
who I am or what I want
as the crush of days
swirls and rushes past

but sometimes there is a day
that rises brilliant and clear
and stands alone and
I stand at its center

and that is enough

Ode to the Rain and Lots of It

Rain pours all night long and throughout
the day and pummels the roof,
splatters the windows, puddles the
walkways and makes me very happy.

Don't I miss the sun, you ask? Not a whit.
Let it take a day off and well deserved.
Good excuse to stay inside and indulge.
Snacks and solitaire, novels or Netflix,

letters to answer or why not write one
to the editor and have my say. Raindrops
flicker on their way from the sky to
the striped awning, porch swing,

seedbed, sidewalk, doggie tongue, and
jet off car wheels that speed by with a
whoosh and a waterfall, or ricochet
off red rain coats and Kitty Cat umbrellas

that dot the landscape with the only
color in sight, like flowers that
uprooted themselves to take a
splishy-splashy walk in the rain.

Sunny skies are for extroverts. Soggy
days with overcast skies keep me safely
indoors, enjoying my own company,
which can be the best company there is.

About the Author:

Eileen Valentino Flaxman loves the written word – in all of its forms. She wrote her first letter, when she was 7 years old, to the President of Metro Goldwyn Meyer, asking for more kid-friendly movies (he wrote her back). She has since had hundreds of letters to the editor published in a number of newspapers. She donates her time to tutor high school seniors with their college admission essays and her memoir - - Pieces of Glass: Growing Up Catholic in the Fifties -- can be found on Amazon. Her first collection of poetry - I Have Something To Say About Love – was published in her youth and recently Eileen has written a poem for each of the 136 chapters of the classic novel, Moby-Dick.They can be seen on her website Call Me Ishmael's Apprentice. https://evflax.wixsite.com/ishmaelsapprentice.

RE-READING ULYSSES ...

by Louis Gallo

RE-READING ULYSSES IN MEDIAS RES
AFTER MANY DECADES WHILE STEERING
THE "SANTA MARIA" WESTWARD INTO THE DYING SUN

As Leopold savors his kidney with relish, his eye also cocked
on an advertisement for Plumtree's Potted Meat, and Molly
murmurs yes and Paddy Dignam returns to life, I scan
the flaming sky for traces of god and find god nowhere
and everywhere, the mechanic's monkey wrench aligning
strips of Victorian wallpaper, as Stephen converts the Paraclete
into a mythic aviator who defied Olympus, as, as . . . as
I fry a filet of catfish in Bertolli's extra virgin olive oil
with minced roasted garlic, a pinch of sea salt, sprigs
of parsley and chives, a sprinkling of capers, smoke
from the pan rising, smoging the kitchen, we two choking,
she switching on the exhaust fan because the fire burns
too bright, and Leopold's bar of lemon soap begins to speak
in Nighttown as Circe turns us all into swine
and I turn to embrace her thirty years earlier because
she has just walked into the room, outside a snow storm,
the cold reddening her cheeks, her eyes glittering
like warm ice, and I, chef wearing a splotched apron,
tug her forward, remove the peacoat, kiss her chapped lips,
and she, yes, we can eat later, burned fish, as Stephen
seeks succor from the Virgin, as Leopold grieves his Rudy,
Paddy's coffin sinks and . . . as everything exponentializes,
the heat heatifies, the universe expands and begins
to freeze, and Boltzmann unhangs himself from the rafters

and renounces his equations, and we consummate, yes,
nothing else matters, and Horace repeats dulce et decorum est
but scratches out pro patria mori, and information exceeds
its digital allotment, we become one and the fish is delicious
though the cat goes blind and a book drops to the floor
and Aeolus, that windbag, blows out our candle, and yes,
she says and I say yes and we know yes means no to time,
to clocks, to the centuries and eons, to Hades & Hell
and rigor mortis, deliquescence, entropy and grave wax
and Icarus falling.

OCCASIONED BY THE OKLAHOMA TORNADO
1.

I hear blasting from the television   in the next room
Wolf Blitzer's "devastating" on the Oklahoma tornado
            And of course recall the tsunami, Japan, Haiti, Kansas, Sandy,
                    Tuscaloosa, Katrina, Pompeii   all of it, ever and ever,
and much of it, as Isaiah verilies, as if upon an instant sudden

                an instant sudden
                                            whereas
            what instants are not sudden? Who not unscathed?

            And upon the next instant sudden
        a commercial for extra testosterone that women and babies
                must avoid
and men, well, podner, that hormonal charge
                        might just destroy the liver, jolt the heart awry,
                induce seizures, cause blackouts and–, and–, and–
stir up the lowest chakra, Abdomen, as its fumes rise
        intensify, whirl, concentrify, spew squid ink

            as the Oklahoma
                        in their minds
                                    explodes

Thing is, I can hardly bear such old news tomorrow much less today,

too much of it, Pater, too furiously paced,

                the slaughter of the usual innocents

misericordia   misericordia   misericordia

        I thought Katrina had done us in already

my family stranded in Hattiesburg, Mississippi, en route to here of all places

    that gas station vibrating with the big winds

      sold out of plastic wrapped sandwiches   out of Planter's

          out of gasoline, cars lined up for miles, stalled,

             the sky behind them a whorl of misery and evil

thinking they had lost everything save their lives, but everything else?

Remember, you're in good hands with Allstate. And Nationwide is on your side.

      Which side? Right or bent sinister? My hands are empty.

Heidegger asked, "Why is there something rather than nothing?"

      Does something include everything/or the reverse?

I am not seeking answers. There are none. I howl at the stolid walls of this house, baying, a wolf at the moon. Wolf now hugs a family of survivors. "Devastating," he repeats because there are no other words, not even that one. Sometimes we can only scream. Children buried under rubble; Sandy Hook; Boston; the Amish kids gunned down . . . ever and ever   as if upon an instant sudden.

2.

I have seen too much, and unlike Tiresias who saw more,

                learned nothing.

    The great diagnostician of the malaise, Walker Percy,

      declared that grandiose searches,

              which he deemed "vertical,"

    lead nowhere,

          that it is more profitable to stay horizontal

      and examine the scurrying of dung beetles

        in a trench in Korea: id est quod est

Thus I burn all of my books on the vast (the General Theory, black holes, the twenty-billion light years at the edge of the universe, the Heat Death, the gargantuan macrocosm . . .)

Burn all my books on the miniscule (the collapse of the wave function, the wave/particle nature of light, light itself—photons!–, Heisenberg's Uncertainty, atomic and sub-atomic shenanigans,

quarks, the microest microcosm . . .)

AND DO WHAT?

> how bout some nice white rice, some Woodchuck hard cider,
>
> some aged, smoky Merlot, a cathode-ray blitz not of Wolf (Blitz)er
>
> but Vanna White spinning her
>
> > > Wheel (Pat doesn't count)

Because . . . why? Because. Ragged claws? How 'bout

the serenity of a carrot burrowed in deep, ancestral, dark, wet, chothonian mud?

3.

> I have a feeling I've said all this before
>
> More a premonition but
>
> > can premonitions go backwards?
>
> I think I've thought all this before
>
> > but memory is a most unfastidious worm
> >
> > leading always us astray
>
> I know I've felt all this before
>
> > the heart does remember, the skin too
> >
> > > even the bones
>
> But I'd prefer not to, not to . . .

Krishnamurti: Time is Sorrow.

I have this dream . . . this vision . . . this–

> > mirabile dictu!

as I type a small white spider

descends from a filament onto

this computer screen . . . and, as we all know,

Spider is emblematic of Soul

so can we hope that all is not lost?

and pray when we can't pray, can we?

We Are Oklahoma

(but not that cheesy musical)

. . . we're buried too

4.

. . . underway too much history, my friend,

the rubble of which strains, a ziggurat, toward heaven

and by heaven I don't mean what you mean . . .

I mean the mind's aspiration, the gift to transcend

because the heaven of olde doesn't cut it,

doesn't rectify or compensate

for such woe

which may be finite

but so what?

one iota of such finiteness

does not, I swear, pay for

an eternity of bland harp music

from choirs of eunuch angels

5.

Footage of a metal interstate guardrail twisted and mangled, grotesque, a section about eight feet long, blown to a spot nowhere near the interstate, the reporter bending over to touch it: "You can imagine what a dangerous projectile this would make, slicing everything in its path. Enormous shrapnel."

But where is Wolf? Catching a wink. What a show! Like Boston! This is entertainment! Who can distinguish one program from the next? Like the child who asked decades ago, "When will the president be shot again?" Look, the Geico gecko! "Stop that, don't make me laugh." And Embrel . . . of course, don't use if you have tuberculosis or leprosy.

Oh, they've replaced Wolf with Anderson Cooper. Cooper, Cooper, he's our man, if he can't do it nobody can. Yeahhhhhhhhhh, Cooper!

Brought to you by Fred Thompson of AIG reverse mortgages.

THE ARROW OF TIME

I saw the straight arrow of time

streak before me, a blazing flame

with serrated forks or tongues

igniting the darkness, and I

saw that each fork demarcated

a moment then a day, month, year,

each of which signified a duty,

an imperative, a mission, and

to veer meant disgrace, ruin, failure,

these glowing notches of accomplishment

and triumph . . .but as if upon

an instant sudden I heard music,

sweet yet dolorous, enchanting

violins, harps, flutes, dulcimers,

a temptation I could not resist

even at the utmost peril, damnation,

and I so veered, stopped to listen,

broke my bones, lacerated my skin

on those barbed tongues

which screeched infamy, sedition

because I could not resist its lure
and I knew the tongues bore lies,
that they hated such delicious diversion
from the prescribed arrow, its abstract
fire and its gnarled, skeletal claws,
but I chose to listen and behind me now
the ashen, smoldering remnants
of rash irresponsibility, incomplete
tasks, wasted time, a deluge
of wasted time that had no power
to smother that arrow of fire . . .
because the music mesmerized me,
seduced me, tantalized me,
made me unwise.

IN THE WAITING ROOM AS MY CHILD
UNDERGOES SURGERY

A small flat screen mounted on the wall
across from where I sit digitally posts
the stages of surgical progression for each
patient. This is, I assume, meant to comfort
those of us here waiting. Below this glowing
bulletin board, a massive television screen—
Kelly Ripa chatting endlessly about nothing.
An aquarium to my right, home for two
bloated goldfish who with lidless eyes
that seem more like fashion buttons than eyes
gaze through the glass. Mostly they float
and so gaze but every so often the larger male
prods the female along her flank and the two
circle their cramped confines. Then they
gaze again beyond that glass impediment at us
and some of us return the gaze
though most of the waiters either nod off
or read magazines or work smart phones.
I had brought along a useful book to help
diminish the gulch of time these affairs
usually consume, but I could not concentrate.
The chosen magazines did not interest me
and Kelly Ripa . . . what is the point of Kelly Ripa?
So I commune with the goldfish, reddish
stationary verbs, either unaware of their captivity
or all too aware with no option but to float
and stare and every so often dart about
in frenzied circles.

And what if the glass shattered? Would they
plummet gladly to their deaths in a cascading wave
of liberation? Or prefer an eternal status quo?
I lift my heavily lidded eyes to the information
screen to learn that my child has now been put
under the knife, her flesh being now opened.
Now. As if at a moment sudden, I know
what the goldfish know.

About the Author:

Louis Gallo's work has appeared or will shortly appear in Wide Awake in the Pelican State (LSU anthology), Southern Literary Review, Fiction Fix, Glimmer Train, Hollins Critic,, Rattle, Southern Quarterly, Litro, New Orleans Review, Xavier Review, Glass: A Journal of Poetry, Missouri Review, Mississippi Review, Texas Review, Baltimore Review, Pennsylvania Literary Journal, The Ledge, storySouth, Houston Literary Review, Tampa Review, Raving Dove, The Journal (Ohio), Greensboro Review,and many others. Chapbooks include The Truth Change, The Abomination of Fascination, Status Updates and The Ten Most Important Questions. He is the founding editor of the now defunct journals, The Barataria Review and Books: A New Orleans Review. He teaches at Radford University in Radford, Virginia.

OF THIS HOUR
by Korkut Onaran

A NOCTURNAL SKETCH

The sliver moon
speaks to me of ancient lips
and I feel kissed.

I dwell
in my mind's flower
who receives me unconditionally

and the night deepens in my next hour
as I enter the innermost room
of the poem.

OF THE FRESHNESS

(or an ode to me sitting here
at this sidewalk table at this coffee house
and reporting this to you)

Three trees
    on the sidewalk
    dressed in white flowers
        that are bursting, as I watch,
        out of their buds
    in such determination
that

young legs and bare toes
    in delicate sandals, and exposed
    belly buttons
accompany the flowers
    in flooding this
    warm afternoon
        with sex.

About the Author:

Korkut Onaran's The Book of Colors has received the first prize in Cervena Barva Press 2007 Chapbook Contest. His poem House has received the second prize in 2006 Baltimore Review Poetry Competition. His first book of poetry The Trident Poems has been published by World Enough Writers in February 2018. His poetry has been published in journals such as Penumbra, Rhino, Colere, White Pelican Review, Crucible, City Works Literary Journal, Water –Stone, Review, Atlanta Review, Bayou, Common Ground Review, and Baltimore Review.

LAST NIGHT

there was a stream
of memories in the bedroom
and my dream was soaked in it

the distance between
today's faces and the faces of my past
has disappeared

and between here and there
there remained no time, just silence.
Within that deep silence

that I heard before
in an underwater cave,
I hear

heartbeats – I'm alive.
The heartbeats get louder
and I open my eyes – I'm awake

and cold
as if I have fewer;
I do have fewer – it must be

the shingles shot I had
in the morning!
I have -a headache too.

ANOTHER BAR JOKE

A deep sea creature
and a priest walk into a bar.
Where?

In a poem. In a high
mountain town at a landlocked state,
in a historic bar.

The priest drinks red wine
and talks about a crucifixion that happened
two thousand years ago.

The deep sea creature drinks a hurricane
and talks about the future
of beach towns.

Both love their solitude; they are
not in the habit of listening
to each other.

The bartender asks:
where is the narrator? Both the priest
and the deep sea creature turn

and look at me – but I am not there.
They are not satisfied. Look, I didn't
invite you, you just showed up in the poem.

Still, they are not satisfied.
You don't need a narrator to do what you do.
The deep sea creature replies:

Next thing you know
you'll talk about the avalanche
that is about to hit this bar.

He has a point.

MACHINE SHOPS
by Roger Singer

MACHINE SHOPS

It's a long whistle

putting the hand

on men and women

as the earth tilts

pulling them past

open wooden doors

into the maze

of machinery

where generations

stood and counted

hours and years

until the next

bodies of youth

replaced names

on lockers and

punch clock

numbers

as the work

produced exceeded

the quality of the

soul

About the Author:

Dr. Roger Singer has been in private practice for 38 years in upstate New York. He has four children, Abigail, Caleb, Andrew and Philip and seven grandchildren. Dr. Singer has served on multiple committees for the American Chiropractic Association, lecturing at colleges in the United States, Canada and Australia, and has authored over fifty articles for his profession and served as a medical technician during the Vietnam era. Dr. Singer has over 1,000 poems published on the internet, magazines and in books and is a Pushcart Award Nominee. Some of the magazines that have accepted his poems for publication are: Westward Quarterly, Jerry Jazz, SP Quill, Avocet, Underground Voices, Outlaw Poetry, Literary Fever, Dance of my Hands, Language & Culture, The Stray Branch, Toasted Cheese, Tipton Poetry Journal and Indigo Rising, Down in the Dirt, Fullosia Press, Orbis, Penwood Review, Subtle Tea, Ambassador Poetry Award Massachusetts State Poetry Society, Louisiana State Poetry Society Award, Mad Swirl Anthology 2018.

GREATER THAN ME

It was a blue
without end

an opening greater
than the sky
a place I touched

sand and rocks
I walked on

its where I could run
when running away

to hide in plain sight
while all other sounds
were blocked out
except the waves

I was a spot on the
shoreline
waiting to be pulled in
never to be disappointed
by its appearance
or it in mine

I'll never be the same
nor do I want to be

A GENTLE END

Leaves arrange for night,
the aroma of dark green
stays close to the branches

crickets capture a
cruel cadence

velvet breezes close
the roses and day lilies

reed tops lightly rustle
a sandpaper hymn

fireflies light a path
to the nearest screen door
flashing creative energy

everything is painted
with coolness,
a reverent covering

we are south of the river
where blackbirds settle
in at dusk

day ends
achieving its goal
without remorse

SPECTACLE

by John Grey

SPECTACLE

Dawn,
clouds break,
new light
nudges aside
leftover darkness.

Crowds already gather.
in the town square.
You trudge slowly
toward the waiting gibbet,
guards on either side.
A figure in a black mask awaits.

It's time to ride the horse
foaled by an acorn,
to ascend the nevergreen
that bears fruit all year round.

Knot is checked.
Trapdoor likewise.
Hempen fever is in the air.
Time for you
to waltz on nothing's dancefloor,
to loll your tongue for all to see.
The rabble is here for a show.
So die quick, die brave, be entertaining.

YOU WANT ME TO COME HOME

Sure I miss the snow.
That sunlight twinkle.
The purity. The fineness.

And this steamy heat
is like a python squeeze at times.
I laze about
Get nothing done.
It's weather for the uninspired.

But I remember all
that shoveling,
the effort it took
to dig myself out,
to live.
And the icy surfaces.
The paths here
may be overgrown from time to time
but they're always walkable.

Nothing quite like
sitting before the hearth
on a bitter day of course.
The local equivalent
is sitting out on the veranda
between the sun going down
and mosquito squadrons
taking off from swamps.

I've swapped cabin fever
for snakes,
numb fingers
for sweaty underarms,
blizzards for hurricanes,
and you
for the ones I've gotten
to know down here.

Isn't everything in life
a tradeoff?
Besides, I have to be somewhere.
Is it my fault
that everywhere else
won't hear of it?

DUCK EGGS

Oddities
cry out to our cameras,
as like all good tourists
we stop to admire the pyramids of duck eggs.
This, at home,
would be passed by in an instant
but, at this height,
with more mountains beyond us,
and the wild music of the land
piping into us from all directions,
cowbells and church bells
ringing in harmony,
and the flowers in full bloom
and under our noses,
and the men and women in native dress,
dancing and singing
when they're not selling,
and everything smelling of cedar
and cheese and cattle hides –
this is local color.
And local color is a stop sign.
It comes down from the houses on the hillsides
to greet us.
It's foreign,
It offers a view of something
other than ourselves,
with a goat thrown in for good measure,
plus cooking, alien to our nostrils,
but not to the quail
sizzling on the grill.
The air is thin.
The sun merely mimics the sun we know.
But we're surrounded by ceremonies,
can't stop pointing out another ritual
and snapping it prisoner
into our digital memories.
We need proof that we have been here.
Duck eggs and the cry of a vendor –
no way they don't come home with us.

About the Author:

John Grey is an Australian poet, US resident. Recently published in Fall/Lines, the Coe Review and Columbia Review with work upcoming in Cape Rock, Poetry East and Midwest Quarterly.

SPEAKING WITHOUT LANGUAGE
by Jan Little

Souls Stained Glass

When loving Death hovers over beds to call soul seeds,
They waft up from earthly husks to follow
His gentle breeze to leave this plane for another.
They bobble like lightening bugs just above tree tops,
Then dip respectfully inside doors of worship.
Sometimes people in pews feel light brushes
That somehow lighten loads of loss and woe
As souls take part of the heaviest griefs and pains
With them through stained glass portals.
Different hues have deepened from centuries
Of souls passing through panes to leave last taints
Of green's greed, orange's lust, yellow's arrogance,
To emerge clear to pass into the final home for all,
While worshippers on this earthly plane
Send prayers of need and thanks to One
Who waits beside them veiled in Spirit.

Could a Lover Love My Muse?

My muse mocks my left-brained world
With its trudging logical meeting

Daily objectives on chalkboards.

At moments between classes, she sneaks out,

Makes humorous analogies I share to amuse peers.

Connecting previous day's dots, she nightly roams

Between my two spheres and tidies up, even draws

Mandelas at times from kaleidoscopes of fractured images

My eyes recorded from conversations, walks, books.

Daily the alarm and coffee close her back up
Into her half-courtlike gym

Away from daily breadwinning left-brained chores.

--But still she peeks at odd moments through blinds to give me
Post-it note insights, word twists she has jotted at night
To slip to me when timing's right. She laughs through my eyes

When she's scored a strike or an ace with her witty repast,

Or scratches her head, returns to notepad when she fails to score.

Weekly trips to coffee houses, church services,
She speaks to me through ink in composition notebooks,

On church bulletins I spend summers sifting through
For gems hidden among chaff of random words and thoughts.

Never do I allude to her in conversations,

Especially with left brains, who might laugh

As we English majors did at stories of writers' odd antics

Of them as adults climbing trees along streets or

Misdelivering mail or composing on walls.

If only imagination could be like toothpaste

That writers could spread in controlled amounts.

Instead, I make multiple trips up and down stairs

Trying to remember errands and chores because

A plot twist in my novel has distracted me.

Or I look at a pair of scissors in one hand and wonder

What I was going to do with them because my muse

Interrupted with suggestions for another poem.

How could I explain such a creature as she to a lover?
Would he suggest analysis, sneak looks in my journals
To see her opinion of him?

Would he leave me time with her or feel threatened--
Or worse amused at me and her?

Or perhaps worse would be a right-brained lover
With more mature, published muse who then would slight mine--

Better a leftie lover then than right.

Since should she leave me now after years

Of becoming whole with her,

I would feel holed and halved--without her nightly
Knitting "up my ragged sleeves of care"
And these odd poems I never knew were in me.

About the Author:

Jan Little: A retired journalist/English instructor, I write poetry, short stories and a fantasy novel series. First published in Adelaide Literary Journal, I have also been honorably mentioned by First Millennium Writing and Beyond Borders, International, for poems. In addition, I am a finalist in Florida Writers' Association's Royal Palms Literary Awards for short stories. I live in Orlando, and my hobbies are Tai Chi, swimming, and movies with friends.

Speaking Without Language

Nurses, family friends and we all grapple
With an articulate mother suddenly unable
To speak to us now.

Charades and questions become new mode of talking:
Where the word "medicine" and hand's pointing to head
Means "shampoo," and we slowly adjust.

My now half-brained mother's world has shrunk
From Octobering in England's Cotswolds
To riding for an hour around her home in Kentucky.

The world dims when such Energizer bunnies wind down
And a stroke applies brakes slowly but one-sidedly to a life
Till my father joins her as he becomes my half-dad—
Right side also now frozen.

"You Are My Sunshine" signals last song together
As his speech also slowly strokes out.
But two aphasians need few words to say—
Looks, handholds suffice along with three phrases:
"I love you," "all right," and "home."

Two right brains can make a whole love until death
And their ashes commingle beneath Mary's statue.

A VIEW OF POLITICS
by Christopher Di-Filippo

Deciphering Politics

Refuge of a different voice
= (equals) an apology in motion.

Our policy has always been − (minus)
the previous government
= (equals) individual fascism.

Economic indifference2 (squared)
= (equals) households held hostage to
policy sinkhole.

Plagiarism of minority interests + (plus)
neglect of unfunded promises/ (divided by)
overburdened taxpayer − (minus)
fair go excise.
= (equals) trust fund for marginal seats.

Voters disillusionment (occurs when):
Two party preferred vote < (less than) independent grandstanding
OR
Watered down legislation > (greater than) Royal Commission logic
OR
Front page article >= (greater than or equal to) truly unbiased opinion.

Hold the Flag

Was there a voice before –
before they came, or was
the land always silent.
Don't move the flag,
it holds together this great nation,
providing shade for our labours,
and a place to plant tomorrow.
That's why they built the fence,
to grow a country;
it kept us together, and maybe
kept us apart, both from
our friends here and our
neighbours across the sea.
But their words still stood –
mateship, fair go, battler;
none were in law,
but they still meant something.
They knew the worth –
the worth of the land, which was
as much the worth of the people;
their hands knew the dirt,
and they built to a promise.
That's why they picked a voice,
one that mattered,
to be heard through the hardship,
when the days yearned for better,
to feel the sun's affection,
and know the drought in choice.
But did they hear all the voices –
the ones before; the voice of the land,
a country that saw different,
losing identity, as the soil was dug.

They are all part of the story,
and the long years remember –
but the flag is still standing,
it's been standing for a long time now;
and that's a good thing,
it shows there's meaning, and something more,
a nation,
which is worth the ache,
as long as we share the voice together.

Clarity of Opinion Program

The following twelve-step program will help you
deal with any unresolved political opinions:

Voting -
1. Acknowledge that voting is idealism sentenced to compromise
2. Choose the marginal agendas that won't benefit you
3. Stake your claim with the masses (say 'yes' to the topical issues of the day)

Democracy -
4. Recognise that equality is driven by minority interest
5. Buy into self-rule by consumerism
6. Align yourself to a commercial interest (one with preferential lobbying)

Politics -
7. Accept the censorship of reason
8. Consider how you can best avoid long-term perspectives
9. Make a list of undelivered promises

Elections -
10. Determine your goals for disseminating responsibility
11. Don't place judgement on media directed choice
12. Forgive impartial selection (by voter disinterest)

Enjoy your journey to a free and unbiased clarity of opinion.

About the Author:

Chris was born and raised in Sydney Australia. He completed university in Sydney and graduated with a degree in business studies. Chris has devoted his spare time to writing, with works published in Outposts of Beyond, Illumen, Neo-Opsis, Not One of Us, Abyss & Apex, Empty Silos (Inwood Indiana Book), Fantastical Savannahs and Jungles Anthology (Rogue Planet) and various works as part of Oz Poetic Society.

SAFETY

by Victoria Harris

Keep your distance from her. That's what has always kept you safe. Sane. Next time she tries to draw you into a conversation about yourself, steer it elsewhere. And don't have so many glasses of wine, especially when you have work in the morning. She has good intentions, but it doesn't matter. You'll hang around as you have for now, but if she's looking for a lifelong friend, she'd better look elsewhere.

*

There's no reason to withdraw just yet. Graduation is the perfect opportunity to let this friendship dissolve. That's the lovely thing about moving: you get to cut ties, and no one will question you for it. That's how high school was; that's how this will be. When she offers you her cactus-shaped pipe, take a hit, but just one. When she offers you her only umbrella, turn it down. You can handle the rain on your own. Isn't it enough that you're walking next to her when you value being alone more than anything else?

*

Focus on your classes. If you can keep from getting distracted, you'll leave this place with nearly a 4.0 GPA. Nearly. Isn't it something how you can never make up for one little mistake in the past. She'll ask you to come over, and you will say that you're busy with homework. She'll ask if you want to meet at the library and work side by side (in those armchairs with the poetic graffiti), and you will pretend you didn't see her text. There's nothing like the comfort of boundaries. Therapy taught you that, if not much else. Ignore the nagging feeling that maybe you should try therapy again, since it's been years. It's not like you have money to toss around. When you get sushi for dinner, don't let her pay. You know better than to get caught up owing her something.

*

When she asks if you want to go clubbing, say yes, because there's little chance of meaningful conversation and a decent chance of shaking away your stress for a moment. When you have a beer, don't let the scent remind you of your father. It should make you think of frat parties, not the nights your mom would have to pick your dad up from dive bars at 2am. When your mom asks if you've gone to church lately, resist the urge to say, "No, Mom, I'm going straight to hell." She means well, but when is that ever enough? If faith couldn't save her marriage or her brother from cancer, there's no way it could do anything for you.

*

She will ask if you want to go on a road trip up the coast with her and some friends over spring break. Tell her no, but be nice about it. After all, she didn't have to invite you. But the ocean looks the same no matter where you go, so you're not going to miss anything. Don't let her disappointment make you feel guilty. She'll get over it. Say, "maybe you and I could do a trip over the summer," knowing full well that will never happen. Don't feel bad about the way her eyes light up when you say that. You're just looking out for yourself; there's nothing wrong with that.

When she suggests you just crash on her couch, order an Uber and go home. So what if the cost comes out of your grocery budget? You're an adult. You can make your own choices and tolerate the consequences. Yeah, you had a fun time binge watching Kimmy Schmidt with her. But at the end of the night, it's best to be in your own company. To be able to wash your makeup off, unhook your bra, sleep in your underwear. To feel like you don't have to hold yourself together with your arms crossed. There's beauty in privacy.

*

When she asks about your post-graduation plans, don't tell her about New York. She doesn't need to know you're moving across the country. No need to put a damper on things. No need for her to know that soon, you won't see each other anymore. Because that adds pressure. And that would make things heat up and fall apart, friendship like pork that pulls right off the bone. Just tell her you don't know, and she'll say, "me either," and you'll both laugh and shrug. Wish that you knew what it was like for indecision to be anything but paralyzing.

*

Tell her you've changed your mind about the road trip. She will be excited, like she's just done a line of coke. Don't try to calm her down. Don't wonder why it matters so much to her that you're going. It's just a week of sitting in a car, cramped, tired, hungry. She will tell you about all the stops she has planned on the way from LA to Seattle. Allow yourself to look forward to seeing places you've never seen. Start budgeting now.

*

When her roommate locks her out after a spat, let her stay at your place. She can have your bed; you'll get by on the floor in a sleeping bag. Don't hug her when she cries because she is reminded of the time her own mother locked

her out. Offer her a drink, but don't drink anything. Don't make her breakfast in the morning; you've already gone out of your way for her. It's enough of a sacrifice to have someone in your personal space for a whole night. But let her know she can help herself to a bagel—poppyseed—even though there's only one left.

*

You will cancel your weekend plans with her because your younger sister is going to be in town. When she says, "bring her along!" tell her that you and your sister need some time by yourselves. Don't mention any of this to your sister. Walk along the Santa Monica Promenade and take selfies with the dinosaur sculptures. Try on that dress you love but can't afford. Buy your sister gelato, even though she pretends not to want it. When your she asks if there's anyone you'll really miss after college, tell her no. Which is the truth.

*

When she tells you, two days before the trip, that her friends have bailed, you will consider backing out too. You know it would be easier just to stay here. You could get ahead on your homework and study for the midterm that is cruelly scheduled for the day after break. But don't cancel on her. Say, "Well, they're going out miss out." You won't miss out. You owe it to yourself to have a little vacation. And it'll be more relaxing now that you won't have to socialize with her friends, who you didn't really know.

*

Pack everything the night before. Toothbrush, toothpaste, deodorant, sunscreen, shirts, jeans, sandals, underwear. Maybe even a few sundresses. Pack your bikini, because you don't have a swimsuit that is less revealing. Try on your bikini, because it's been a while. Don't have a breakdown about the way your love handles look. It's not like you care what she thinks. Sunglasses, shorts, makeup, Autobiography of Red (to read on the beach). Double check your list to make sure you aren't forgetting anything. Go to bed even though you're sure you've forgotten something—no way to know what it is.

*

Wait outside for her to arrive, backpack digging into your shoulders and bags in your hands. When she drives up to the curb and honks at you three times, give her the finger and laugh. Don't feel silly because it's unlike you. Let her help you put your stuff in the trunk. When you get on the highway, don't criticize her music choice (the Goo Goo Dolls). Just turn it up and sign along; you know the words.

*

When you get to the motel, exhausted from day one of the trip, don't freak out because the only vacant room has one queen instead of two. It will be like when you shared beds with your friends during middle school sleepovers. Don't argue that you should find somewhere else to stay; this is probably the only place for miles. Apologize in advance for all the tossing and turning you do in your sleep. Try not to be embarrassed. Anyone with nightmares like yours wouldn't be able to keep still all night. Let the sound of her breathing, even and slow, lull you to sleep—you need your rest. Let her "goodnight, sweet dreams," her smile, her gentle bump of her shoulder to your shoulder echo in your mind.

*

When she splashes you with seawater, splash her back. But don't let your hair get soaked. It's not worth how awful it will look for the rest of the day. Remember getting teased at that poo party when you were twelve. Don't stare at the tattoo on her left thigh, or the scars. When it's time to reapply sunscreen, don't ask for her help. Don't think about how her hands would feel on your skin. Walk along the tideline with her, picking up seashells. She likes all of them, even the broken ones.

*

When she shouts over the noise of the bar in San Francisco, "we're still going to hang out after we graduate, right?" say, "of course," because it's hard to imagine that you won't see her every weekend. You will move into a shitty apartment in Queens, and a year will pass, and then two, and she won't even think about you anymore. Time will eat this up, just like it does everything else.

*

This is too much, and you know it. You can take a plane back. You can't stand to be so close to her anymore. You have separate beds this time, but it feels like her body is inches away from yours, and you are burning, burning up inside. In the morning, just say that you're coming down with a cold, and your period just started, and you don't feel up to travelling. You can deal with the way her shoulders will sag. You can't deal with being around her any longer.

*

You wake up in the middle of the night and feel like you are dying. Don't move. How could you have let this happen? You were so careful. Fuck. No, you weren't. You thought you were in control. You thought you could have it all. Wrap your arms around your stomach. Hold it in. She's asleep, unaware that you are in agony and it is all your own fault. You have been driving along the edge of the cliff, foolishly certain that you'd never go over the edge. Cry, but be quiet.

*

Look at the alarm clock. It is 3am. Get up, go to the bathroom, close the door. Turn the light on. Splash cold water on your face. It won't make any difference. Look yourself in the eye. After all the people who have left you behind, is this who you have become? The one who runs away?

*

Sit on the edge of her bed. Run your hand along the cheap duvet; try to calm the thunder of your heart. Breathe in the fear. Hold it. Listen to the air rush in and out of her body. Be afraid. Be fucking terrified. You are breaking all of your rules, all the careful constructs that have held you together over the years. Whatever happens, you can finally release all that you've been holding in. You are going to boil over and it will be a mess and you have to do it. Put your hand on her sleeping shoulder. Say her name. Say it again. Relish the way it tastes on your tongue. Say it louder. She will wake, she will sit up, ask, "You okay?" Do not try to be okay. Find her hand in the darkness. Pause.

Notice the way her breath changes. Place your hand on her cheek, even though you are shaking, and kiss her. Kiss her like you're not afraid, like you don't care that you are a woman and she is a woman, like it doesn't matter that this will end someday and it will tear you apart, kiss her like you have always wanted to, kiss her because you are here and she is here and she deserves to be loved. Kiss her and open yourself up like heavy clouds offering a deluge to the parched earth. Kiss her.

*

You cannot turn back.

About the Author:

Victoria Harris works as an editorial assistant in Manhattan and lives in Brooklyn with her wife and their three houseplants. She earned an MFA in Writing from Sarah Lawrence College in 2018.